THE NEW SOVEREIGNS

MULTINATIONAL CORPORATIONS AS WORLD POWERS

edited by **ABDUL A. SAID**
and **LUIZ R. SIMMONS**

A SPECTRUM BOOK

PRENTICE-HALL, INC. *Englewood Cliffs, New Jersey*

Library of Congress Cataloging in Publication Data
SAID, ABDUL AZIZ.
    The new sovereigns.

    (A Spectrum Book)
    Includes bibliographical references.
    1. International business enterprises—Addresses,
essays, lectures. 2. World politics—1965-   —Ad-
dresses, essays, lectures. I. Simmons, Luiz R. S.,
joint author. II. Title.
HD69.I7S23   1975   338.8'8   74–11043
ISBN 0–13–615799–8
ISBN 0–13–615781–5 pbk.

ABDUL A. SAID and LUIZ R. SIMMONS are with the American University in Washington, D.C. Professor Said is the author of several books, including *America's World Role in the 70s* (Prentice-Hall, 1970) and *Protagonists of Change: Subcultures in Development and Revolution* (Prentice-Hall, 1971).

LUIZ SIMMONS is editor of and contributor to *The Politics of Addiction* and *Discrimination and the Addict.*

For Claire, loving wife, inspired teacher

10 9 8 7 6 5 4 3 2 1

PRENTICE-HALL INTERNATIONAL, INC. (*London*)
PRENTICE-HALL OF AUSTRALIA PTY. LTD. (*Sydney*)
PRENTICE-HALL OF CANADA, LTD. (*Toronto*)
PRENTICE-HALL OF INDIA PRIVATE LIMITED (*New Delhi*)
PRENTICE-HALL OF JAPAN, INC. (*Tokyo*)

Contents

Preface

It has become a cliché to say that we are entering a new era of international relations. But in the post–"Cold War" environment, basic questions of conflicting goals and perceptions of different international actors remain the organizing principles for analyzing relations among peoples, institutions, and nations. Despite some continuity, the operating environment—the stage setting—of international relations is undergoing a shift from its historic focus on nation-states as the predominant actors in a world environment organized around coalitions, blocs, and ideological groupings to a more complex, differentiated, even "metropolitan" order in which other kinds of actors wield significant influence.

This new system deemphasizes the importance of geopolitics and elevates issues like development, pollution, and economic growth to preeminence. New institutions such as multinational corporations (MNCs) have increasingly become the focus of interest of these emerging concerns. This change appears warranted, because several of the larger MNCs exert more collective influence than all but a handful of nation-states. The pattern of investment and activity of these corporations affect issues of war and peace, intervention and nonintervention, and may even determine the long-term prospects for world economic development.

Little is known about decision-making processes and their underlying rationale within and among these new (and not so new) corporate endeavors, considering their intrinsic importance. The tools of inquiry are alien to national intelligence efforts, because they focus on balance sheets, reports of board meetings, stock market quotations, and so on rather than official government white papers or biographies of statesmen. We are not accustomed to thinking of the foreign policy of Standard Oil or General Motors. But decision-making by these companies has as much or more impact on the emerging arenas of international conflict and cooperation as do the foreign policy decisions of nations that are receding in significance as actors (such as Brazil).

The nature of power is undergoing a truly radical transformation. It is increasingly defined in terms of the maldistribution of information. Inequality, long associated primarily with income, is coming to be associated with technological factors and the political and economic control over the international exchange of information. The advanced industrial nations have come to rely less and less on such markets as extractive industries and are bound together in fierce competition to secure new technologies to make good on domestic promises. It is of more than passing interest that the Institute for Politics and Planning notes that within the next decade the value of information exports from the United States to Europe will exceed the value of material exports.

The United States, despite Vietnam, the urban crisis, and ethnic unrest, remains the predominant protagonist in the emerging metropolitan system. But America's power is increasingly exercised by a pluralistic, diffuse, and differentiated elite, residing throughout the world but increasingly Americanized in style and outlook. The rise of a global system perhaps best characterized provisionally as "industrial feudalism," with power emanating from no single cohesive center, places the United States in a role analogous to Rome during the Middle Ages: a nominal center of power forced to exercise influence through indirect diffused means concentrating on long-term trends, in an international environment characterized by the proliferation of progressively smaller and more parochial local centers.

It is not improbable that by the first third of the twenty-first century foreign policy between the Great Powers and the medium-sized powers will be diminished to the point of exchanging ping-pong teams and ballet troupes. The traditional exercise and conduct of foreign policy, which developed in nineteenth-century Europe and which mainly concerned itself with such concepts as balance of power, the nation-state, national interest, geopolitics, and ideological competition and imperialism, will recede from the nomenclature of political discourse. Such a transformation will assure that foreign policy and the professional bureaucracy which attended its growth will never be quite the same.

This volume of essays focuses, often imperfectly, upon the role of the multinational corporation in the emerging international system. The approach is interdisciplinary and the contributors are both accomplished scholars and achieved practitioners.

The general model proposed for this study is three-dimensional—structural, functional, and developmental. The structural dimension includes a conceptual analysis of the phenomenon of the multinational corporation as an actor in the international system and a general overview of its historical evolution and present characteristics. The functional dimension focuses on the processes of multinational corporation–nation-state interaction, including the impact of multinational corporations on nation-states, the political, social, and economic consequences to nation-states, and the nature of influence and decision-making processes involved. Finally, the developmental dimension analyzes changing patterns over time and future consequences to the international system.

I

STRUCTURAL DIMENSIONS

c h a p t e r   o n e

The politics of transition

ABDUL A. SAID AND LUIZ R. SIMMONS

THE SYLLOGISM OF GEOPOLITICS

It is disconcerting to ask ourselves questions that touch the foundation of our beliefs. The prospects of obtaining candor in our inquiry become fitfully complicated when those beliefs have been rationalized into a functional ideology attended by an effusion of literature that seeks to legitimize it and opposed by popular interpretation that offers political and economic alternatives derived from the political economy of Britain in the nineteenth century. Perhaps it is fantasy to believe that any of us can relieve ourselves of these impostures, and yet as students of international relations that is what our theories and methodologies should be oriented to discover. Yet too often they become predicates to the study of international relations that evolve a separate identity and life of their own.

What do we mean by foreign policy? How do we measure it? Certainly our determination of these two variables will influence our decisions regarding who are the influential actors, what are the important issues in the international system and which ones to study. A reconsideration of the fundamental assumptions upon which international relations has flourished is very much needed. Yet it is no small endeavor. It is only marginally connected with counting the pieces of mail which pass between nations or professors between international universities. Yet even these measurements, associated with these kinds of transnational exchanges, reveal how different perceptions have shaped our thinking regarding the content of foreign policy in the past while challenging us to devise new measures to determine what the content of foreign policy should be in the future.

The growth of the multinational corporation with its diverse activities in marketing, research, manufacturing, and extraction compels us to understand the changing nature of foreign policy sooner rather than later.

The nation-state is an inchoate development in the political milieu. Its development encouraged a transformation of moral and political centers of authority, emasculating the political authority of the church and the family. It also inherited many of the primary functions which these social organizations provided, most importantly, the maintenance of security. Since the nineteenth century the foreign policy of nation-states has been preoccupied with this quest for security from external sources of disequilibrium. Political and cultural millennialism—what Edmund Burke once described in reference to the French Revolution as an "armed doctrine"—has been a persistent, unsettling feature of the international system. The apprehension of one nation by another has been the gravamen of international politics.

George Lichtheim is quite correct in delineating the symbiotic relationship that developed between nationalism and imperialism:

> Imperialism as a movement—or if one prefers, as an ideology—latched on to nationalism because no other popular base was available. But this statement can also be turned around: nationalism transformed itself into imperialism wherever the opportunity offered.[1]

The celebration of the nation-state was not the only impetus to political messianism, the idea of empire, both temporal and spiritual, being traceable to the first stirrings of history. But it did furnish focus and rationale and organization for the conflicting aspirations of men which earlier mass movements, such as the religious millennialism of Western Europe, had lacked.

The mercantile aspirations of the Portuguese and the Spanish, which could not be arbitrated by a Pope, the development of British capitalism and the British empire in India, a French empire in Africa, a Russian imperium in Central Asia, American imperial expansion beginning in the 1890s, Japanese and German militarism in the 1930s—all share a universal theme in world politics which the German academic Schmoller inadvertently captured by observing the phenomena in his own time and noting that

> the course of world history in the twentieth century will be determined by the competition between the Russian, English, American and perhaps Chinese world empires, and by their aspirations to reduce all the other, smaller states to dependence on them. . . .[2]

Lebensraum is not a concept peculiar to World War Two, and it places the conflict of nations on a historical continuum. *Misperception* of the

1. *Imperialism*, p. 81.
2. Cited by Fritz Fischer, *Germany's Aims in the First World War* (New York: Norton, 1967), p. 9.

expansionist tendencies of nations has been as important a factor in the international environment as the expansionist impetus itself.[3] The Revisionist historiography concerning American and Russian conflict after World War Two makes no attempt to grasp the point. Stalin was not a revolutionary, and the Americans were not maddened by some ideological commitment to sanitize the world. Yet as Adam Ulam has remarked while analyzing the causus belli of the Cold War,

> The struggle over Berlin was a struggle over phantoms which existed in the imaginations of both sides; in the West those phantoms were Soviet soldiers ready to sweep to the English Channel; in Stalin's mind they were millions of West German soldiers who were going to materialize in the near future.[4]

These phantoms have always informed the apprehension of nations. Foreign policy and international relations have been characterized by a compulsive preoccupation with the physical vulnerability of the state. If, as students of international relations, we were to seek out a common denominator that transcends the foreign policy formulations of both the strong and the weak, it would be the concern for *geopolitics*. External security was conceived as a function of geopolitics, and the foreign policy of nation-states has invariably been a function of the geopolitical context. It has been concerned with the exercise of a particular species of politics-geopolitics, a strong compelling emphasis on the control of strategic land masses and waterways and, of course, alliances. As one writer has reminded us;

> Alliances have traditionally been a major technique in the balance-of-power politics engaged in by states perceiving common threats. The obvious reason is that allies constitute an addition of the power of other nations to one's own.[5]

This proposition was first afforded its finest expression by the American geopoliticist Nicholas Spykman, who observed that

> In a world of international anarchy, foreign policy must aim above all at the improvement or at least the preservation of the relative power position of the state. Power is in the last instance the ability to wage successful war, and in geography lie the clues to the problems of military and political strategy. . . . Geography is the most fundamental factor in the foreign policy of states because it is the most permanent.[6]

3. Ralph K. White, *Nobody Wanted War* (Garden City, N.Y.: Doubleday, Anchor Books, 1970).
4. Adam B. Ulam, *The Rivals: America and Russia Since World War II* (New York: Viking Press, 1971), p. 151.
5. John Spanier, *Games Nations Play: Analyzing International Politics* (New York: Praeger, 1972), p. 191.
6. *America's Strategy in World Politics* (New York: Harcourt, Brace and Co., 1942), p. 41.

An environment that placed inordinate emphasis on the role of geo-politics also invested its analytical concepts and methodologies with this narrow historical experience. The study of international relations became the study of transactions between *territorial* states. The drama of inter-national relations became, in Palmerston's celebrated observation, the pursuit of permanent national interests, so defined in geopolitical terms. The content of international relations was merely a reflection of the content of foreign policy, threats, compromises, the creation of alliances and buffers, the cultivation of an elite foreign service, peregrinations by navies to show the flag, economic and cultural imperialism, ideological competition, and awakening nationalism—all of which have revolved, if only tenuously at times, around the quest for external security by the nation-state.

The indices that have been used to measure the velocity of specific foreign policies have been derived often from geopolitical bases of analysis, such as measuring conflicts and interventions between territorial states. The rationale behind giving foreign aid to less developed coun-tries, a preoccupation of recent years which originally was cast in terms of buying security and preventing the export to other states of worri-some political and economic models, still lingers on in subtle, yet un-controverted forms. Most importantly, the concept of capability in in-ternational politics, however illusive, was cast in terms of the military and economic power of nation-states.

> Military power is still a dominant reality in the relations between near equals . . . it is the keystone of that essential part of our foreign policy which is directed toward the containment of the Soviet Union.[7]

This statement of U.S. strategic policy is as influential today as it was in 1957, the year in which it was written.[8]

Thus the constants and variables which have dominated the discus-sion and analysis of international relations since the nineteenth cen-tury continue to enjoy currency. The theoretical foundations of such concepts as national interest, nation-state, our conception of power and balance of power, which are invoked to explain contemporary inter-national phenomena, are artifacts of a remote international environ-ment concerned with the rivalries between states.

The nomenclature of politics has changed remarkably little but the international environment from which the terminology derives its sig-nificance has experienced a major transformation, which can be ex-plained by the declining role of external security issues in the affairs of many nations.

---

7. *International Stability and Progress* (New York: The American Assembly, 1957), p. 32.
8. *United States Foreign Policy for the 1970's*. A Report by President Richard Nixon to the Congress, May 3, 1973.

Political messianism is no longer an important factor in international relations. Although the world has not moved beyond ideology, the possibilities of transnational geopolitical movements designed to subjugate one nation to another is a declining factor in the decision-making calculus of nations.

Since 1945 the two nation-states that have established capabilities to pursue their legitimate aspirations for security—as well as their fantasies—have been the United States and the Soviet Union. These two nations have dominated international relations because of their uncontested capability to influence and transform the political and economic transactions of other states. They have been the only actors in the international system able to furnish the guarantees and commitments to other states through their creation of and participation in vast security arrangements ("pactomania"). Only these two nations have been consistently able to satisfy the expectations and demands of client states in the Middle East, Europe, Asia, and Latin America in their quest for security. The fact that security fears were largely aroused by the ominous competition between the two super-powers themselves does not diminish the point, however comical it now seems. The stabilization of relations between the Soviet Union and the United States which occurred *prior* to the Cuban missile crisis has induced an international conciousness which apprehends the irony that the great powers possess nondisposable power. Nuclear weaponry does not lend itself to strategic uses, and tactical deployment is, despite a body of academic literature to the contrary, too speculative in conceptualization for policymakers who must actually make these decisions. Outside a very narrow transmission belt of influence in geographically contiguous regions, the Great Powers must develop other forms of disposable power in order to influence the affairs of other territorial actors in the system. But the credibility of overt or covert threats postulated against the identity of the state itself is but a bold and noncompelling probability; the expectation of the emergence of a twenty-first-century variation of the "armed doctrine" is a virtual impossibility. Whether or not the emergence of such a movement may defy the stability of a nuclear-guaranteed peace is something else again. As long as such an occurrence is not perceived to be probable, nation-states will refocus their efforts on a host of *nonsecurity* objectives.

The rise and fall of the technique of the national war of liberation, in reality more a religious dispute between Russia and China over doctrine than a serious political and military technique, was the last attempt by the Great Powers to make credible the fading canons of threatmanship against the identity of the state.

Coincident with the decline in the probability of an international messianic movement has been the declining threat of the physical subrogation of less developed countries by the medium and Great Powers.

Analysis of direct investment by world region reveals some significant trends. Historically, the less developed areas were considered attractive for investment, particularly in the extractive industries (50%) and manufacturing (25%) with all other fields accounting for the remaining 25%. But since 1945 the ex-colonial world has been of less and less importance to Western investors. The percentage of total overseas investment funneled into low-income countries fell from 36.4% in 1960 to 31.4% in 1964. One-fifth of 1968 exports of high-income nations went to less developed areas, contrasted to one-third in 1948. The drop in imports from low-income countries to high-income countries shows a similar disengagement. Even these statistics tend to overstate the importance of the Third World to the developed nations, for they consolidate petroleum with all other economic categories. If, for example, petroleum is not considered in the United States direct investment abroad, then U.S. investment in less developed countries constitutes only one-sixth of American overseas investment and provides only one-seventh of the income from these transactions.[9]

In 1968 exports comprised 4% of the Gross National Product of the U.S., 19% of Japan, 14% for Great Britain, and 12% for Germany. However, the percentages of U.S. exports to Japan, the United Kingdom, and Germany were 3.6, 6.3, and 5% respectively. The percentages of exports of these states to the U.S. was 3.2, 14, and 19%. Increasingly, it is the developed nations that are exporting to each other and engaging in reciprocal investment. Although their relationship to less developed countries is still dominant, it is not colonial.

Indeed, the divisions between the developed and less developed countries and the elimination of original sources of great and medium power confrontation over them has imperceptibly been declining.

The traditional foci of international relations, geopolitical subrogation, and economic colonialism, however indistinguishable they have occasionally become, are in decline as strategic variables that affect the decision-making process of states. One measure of this can be inferred from the decrease in the tempo of violence between states. Of the 164 outbreaks of significant violence within states between 1948 and 1966, only 15 were military conflicts involving two or more states.[10] External security issues have not become unimportant, but it would be myopic to concentrate on subsystems of objective conflict at the expense of an understanding of the new international environment. In such an environment, statistical violence between states should be expected to rise, however remaining well below a threshold which poses a threat of external disquilibrium to the identity of a state.

It is also likely that as we approach the twenty-first century and nuclear

9. Michael Harrington, *Toward a Democratic Left* (New York: Macmillan, 1968); also *Do the Rich Nations Need the Poor?* Center for International Studies, New York University, 1971.

10. Robert MacNamara, cited in Paul Seabury and Aaron Wildavsky, eds., *U.S. Foreign Policy: Perspectives and Proposals for the 1970's* (New York: McGraw-Hill, 1969), p. 5.

weapons begin to diffuse in the international environment so that international terrorist groups may yet acquire them, we face an unprecedented juncture in our historical understanding of the definition of power. Military power will not be pursued as much as simply taken for granted. As military power becomes increasingly nondisposable, our conception of the nature of power in the twenty-first century will be radically transformed.

In this regard it is interesting to note the possibilities that are developing for conceptualization of power in the international system as criteria other than geopolitics begin to creep into our discussion of power politics. Japan furnishes us with one example of how military power in the current system is increasingly unrelated to "power." According to a table compiled by the U.S. Arms Control and Disarmament Agency from 1970 GNP data, Japan at that time was thirteenth in military spending yet *third* in economic ranking.

By placing some historical distance between ourselves and the geographic theories of international relations, with their emphasis on the nation-state as the preeminent actor in politics between nations, the task of analyzing the significance of the multinational corporations becomes easier. The primary characteristic of this system is its emphasis on non-security issues, of which development is primary. The newspapers, speeches, and journals which emanate from both the less developed and developed areas echo this preoccupation with satisfying the rising expectations of national consumers. In the developed nations, including the Soviet Union, the emergence of international consumerism can hardly be ignored. Indeed, regimes seem more apt to fall over automobile production gaps than over missile gaps.

HISTORICAL EVOLUTION AND PRESENT CHARACTERISTICS OF THE MNC

Regrettably, the multinational corporation has become a popular subject for the mythologizers, some of whom see it as the insidious "el pulpo," others who would describe its putative achievements in verse. The multinational enterprise is not a recent phenomenon in international relations. In 1902 F. A. MacKensie's *The American Invaders* appeared in London, analyzing the impact of American direct investment abroad, and stimulated by many American companies, among them Otis Elevator, Singer Company, and General Electric. Before the coming of the Industrial Revolution, international financial institutions flourished in the fourteenth- and fifteenth-century cities of Venice, Barcelona, and Genoa. In 1689 the Bank of Amsterdam was established to finance the explorations of the Dutch East India Company. The Compagnie d'Occident was created in 1717 to foster trade with the Louisiana territories, and by the nineteenth century the center of banking activity in Europe had moved to Germany, which had established affiliates in South America, the Far East, and Eastern Europe.

Multinational banking saw its golden age in nineteenth-century England, where much of the economic development of the United States (particularly railroads) was subvented from capital originating in London. It was the failure of the British banking house of Baring Brothers that precipitated the first international financial crisis, a consequence of which was the massive depression in the United States of the 1890s.[11]

Another early form of multinational business was the seventeenth-century trading company, which obtained grants from the crowns of Europe to monopolize colonial trade. Such companies were chartered by the competing mercantile powers—England, Holland, Sweden, Denmark, and Spain—and were manipulated as appendages of the political and economic policies of the country that chartered them.

However, it has only been since the end of World War Two that the multinational corporation began to emerge as a pervasive force in international relations. Direct investment by an MNC in a nation-state, as distinguished from portfolio investment, has been a conspicuous feature of national development, generally yielding positive results. Since World War Two, direct investment in Australia has been the most important source of capital formation. In the 1960s American, British, and Japanese corporations assumed a major role in furnishing technology and capital to exploit the significant mineral discoveries made during these years. The role of direct investment in modernizing industries and stimulating domestic markets has been generally perceived to be beneficial in such diverse countries as Norway in the development of hydroelectric power, South Africa in mining and gold, Canada in oil, natural gas, and minerals, and also Argentina and the United States. In fact, until 1950 European direct investment in the United States exceeded U.S. direct investment in Europe, however slightly.

Direct investment in the less developed countries has been consistently associated with economic imperialism and colonialism. Although both historically and economically there is sufficient basis to draw such conclusions, often a passionate distaste for imperialism has clouded the separate issue of whether or not the colonized state has derived any benefits from the colonizer. The classic instance in this debate is India, where despite the undeniably inhibiting influences of the British presence, it still seems likely that though this country could have undergone modernization alone,

> examining the variables in the cost-benefit equation, it becomes apparent
> that Britain's presence in India, in the second half of the nineteenth century, does not follow a pattern of ruthless exploitation as has been suggested by many. . . .[12]

11. See Ralph W. Hidy, *The House of Baring in American Trade and Finance, English Merchant Bankers at Work* (Cambridge, Mass.: Harvard University Press, 1949).
12. Tapan Mukerjee, "Theory of Economic Drain: Impact of British Rule on the Indian Economy, 1840–1900," in Kenneth E. Boulding and Tapan Mukerjee, eds., *Economic Imperialism* (Ann Arbor, Mich.: The University of Michigan Press, 1972), p. 210.

There were indeed "substantial" improvements in the welfare of that colony. But it has only been since the end of World War Two that direct investment abroad leaped from $19 billion to $101.9 billion, while foreign private investment in the United States grew from $8.0 billion to $40.3 billion. The annual growth rate in investment has been approximately 10%.[13] The National Industrial Conference Board has projected that by 1975 the United States *and the rest of the world* would each have a GNP of approximately one trillion dollars per year and that 25% of the world's GNP would be generated from branches and subsidiaries of United States corporations; 20% of the Gross World Product would be "European or Japanese tinged."[14] The sales of "foreign-owned" production not only equals the volume of world exports but has been increasing more rapidly. Judd Polk has estimated that if the rate of growth is maintained, international production would be worth half the value of aggregate GNPs by the end of the century. It is estimated that between 5 and 10% of the total increase in aggregate GNP of the industrial nations was a result of direct investment.[15]

The world seems to be moving to a situation where a major portion of its industrial output will be dominated by several hundred large corporations.[16] The multinational corporation is in an excellent position to facilitate capital transfers between nations, stimulate capital formation, and serve as a conduit for the transfer of technology. The emergence of nonsecurity development-oriented issues has naturally focused on the activities of these economic entities, as a focal point of international relations becomes how nations can preserve their political, economic, and cultural identities while still sharing in the benefits of rapid industrial growth.

A working definition of the multinational enterprise is a "cluster of corporations of diverse nationality joined together by ties of common ownership and responsive to a common management strategy."[17] The majority of the world's multinational corporations are American-based; of the 500 largest corporations in the world, 306 are American and 74 are from EEC countries. Almost 250 of *Fortune*'s 500 largest corporations had overseas investments totaling $50 billion.[18] Not all large American corporations have extensive foreign holdings. General Motors has rela-

---

13. Devlin and Cutler, "The International Investment Position of the United States: Developments in 1968," *Survey of Current Business*, 49, no. 11 (October 1969), 23–36.

14. Rose, "The Rewarding Strategies of Multinationalism," *Fortune*, September 15, 1968, p. 100.

15. The Gross World Product is valued at $3 trillion, 15% of which is produced by multinational corporations.

16. See Stephen Hymer, "The Efficiency Contradictions of Multinational Corporations," *American Economic Review*, 60 (May 1970), 441–48.

17. Raymond Vernon, "Economic Sovereignty at Bay," *Foreign Affairs*, 47 (1968), 114.

18. See Raymond Vernon, "Multinational Enterprise and National Sovereignty," *Harvard Law Review*, 45 (March–April 1967), 156.

tively few foreign assets abroad compared to Ford, which is a network of 60 corporations of which 40 are abroad. Thirty-six % of Ford's $8 billion in assets is located in 27 foreign countries. In 1966 alone Ford spent $180 million expanding overseas operations. Other American corporations with significant foreign components include Standard Oil, Colgate-Palmolive, and Anaconda. Moreover, 187 U.S. multinationals account for one-third of the sales and one-half of the assets of U.S. enterprises (see Chart I). Sixty % of the sales of the Parker Pen Company,

Chart I

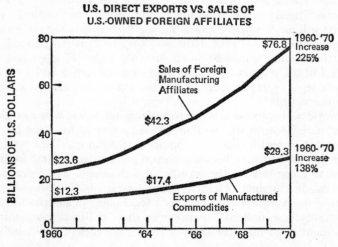

U.S. DIRECT EXPORTS VS. SALES OF U.S.-OWNED FOREIGN AFFILIATES

Source: The United States in the Changing World Economy, Volume 11: Background Material. U.S. Government Printing Office, 1971. Chart 57.

nearly $75 million, represents foreign business. Parker maintains 62,000 overseas dealers, uses 66 advertising agencies, and conducts business in 100 currencies; it operates in every noncommunist country and has plants in Canada, Britain, South Africa, Argentina, Brazil, Colombia, Mexico, Spain, Australia, Rhodesia, and West Germany.

But not all the large multinational enterprises are American; Phillips Lamp Works, headquartered in the Netherlands, employs 167,000 abroad and 85,000 in the Netherlands. Its affiliated companies operate in some 68 countries. Japanese-based multinational corporations have expanded rapidly so that today Japan is the second largest center of multinationals in the world. In 1965 this position was held by Britain (55 companies), but in 1970 the Japanese had 51 companies to Great Britain's 46.[19]

What, however, do these statistics suggest about the multinational enterprise as an actor in the contemporary international environment? Is

19. See George Modelski, "Multinational Business: A Global Perspective," *International Studies Quarterly,* 16, no. 4 (December 1972), 411, note 4.

it of political significance that the aggregate sales of General Motors are larger than many nation-states' GNP? Should we inquire how many divisions General Motors has, or does this merely beg the question? Is General Motors a sovereign actor in the international system, or are most multinational corporations merely appendages of nation-states' foreign policies? Is the multinational corporation an independent actor or a reflection? First, let us make an elementary observation. The multinational firm is an actor that possesses considerable influence but little power in the system. The little power it exercises exists in the ability to inadvertently trigger international financial crises. Multinational corporations control such vast quantities of money that they can precipitate international monetary crises by moving only a small proportion of their funds from one country to another. A study made at the request of the International Trade Subcommittee of the Senate Finance Committee estimates that some $268 billion of short-term liquid assets were held at the end of 1971 by "private institutions on the international financial scene" and that the "lion's share" of this money was controlled by *U.S.*-based multinational corporations and banks. The $268 billion was "more than twice the total of all international reserves held by all central banks and international monetary institutions in the world at the same date." [20] Because of the enormity of the multinationals' assets, only a fraction of money needs to move for a serious crisis to develop. That these largely American multinational corporations precipitated the devaluation of the *American* dollar in the monetary crisis of March 1973 as speculators unloaded dollars and purchased German marks and Japanese yen is beyond doubt.

Why, then, do some writers persist in seeing the American multinational corporation as a "tool" of American imperialism when it is evident that the American multinational corporation can pursue policies quite independent of the United States? Exponents of the New Left, for example, avoid acknowledging this because they attempt to explain foreign policy by merely counting a nation's capital assets abroad and by dwelling on those sensational episodes when the United States government has putatively intervened in the affairs of a sovereign nation on behalf of an American corporation.[21] Thus the multinational corporation is not viewed as an independent actor capable of pursuing objectives incompatible with the United States national interest but as a reflection of United States foreign policy. There are two problems with this analysis. First, it ignores the extremely tenuous relationship that exists between U.S. direct investment abroad and the U.S. GNP. Only in the wisdom

---

20. "Implications of Multinational Firms for World Trade and Investment and for U.S. Labor and Trade," Committee on Finance, United States Senate, February 1973, pp. 531–46.
21. Lewis Richardson, *Statistics of Deadly Quarrels* (Pittsburgh: Boxwood, 1960). This study of 83 significant conflicts between 1820 and 1929 discloses scant evidence for the proposition that American and European governments have actively pursued interventionist policies in behalf of international corporations.

of historical retrospect could so fragile a coefficient as the percentage of U.S. GNP invested abroad be seized upon as an index of national behavior.

Table 1.   U.S. DIRECT INVESTMENT ABROAD AS A PERCENTAGE OF GNP (in billions)*

	Total Direct Investment Abroad	Total GNP	Percentage
1929	7.528	104.4	.07
1936	6.691	82.7	.08
1940	7.000	100.6	.07
1950	11.788	284.6	.04
1951	13.089	329.0	.04
1952	14.819	347.0	.04
1953	16.286	365.4	.04
1954	17.626	363.1	.05
1955	19.313	397.5	.05
1956	22.177	419.2	.05
1957	25.252	440.3	.06

* Source: Bureau of the Census, *Historical Statistics of the United States, Colonial Times to 1957,* p. 566.

Robert Heilbroner has put the issue more starkly:

> Of our roughly $50 billion in overseas investment, some $10 billion are used in mining, oil, utility, and manufacturing facilities in Latin America, some $4 billion in Asia including the Near East, and about $2 billion in Africa. To lose these assets would deal a heavy blow to a number of large corporations, particularly in oil, and would cost the nation as a whole the loss of some $3 to $4 billion a year in earnings from those areas. A Marxist might conclude that the economic interests of a capitalist nation would find such a prospective loss insupportable, and that it would be "forced" to go to war. I do not think this is a warranted assumption, although it is undoubtedly a risk. Against a Gross National Product that is approaching 3/4 of a trillion dollars and with corporate assets over $1.3 trillion, the loss of even the whole $16 billion in the vulnerable areas should be manageable economically. Whether such a takeover could be resisted politically—that is, whether the red flag of Communism could be successfully waved by the corporate interests—is another question.[22]

The second problem is that such a position ignores to a significant degree the relationship American multinational corporations have had with the Soviet Union and the historical role the American business world assumed in assisting the Soviets with much needed technology.[23]

Although it is true that the U.S. government has occasionally intervened on behalf of multinational corporations, American business enterprise abroad was often a pretext for the United States to secure its na-

22. "Counter-Revolutionary America," in Irving Howe, ed., *A Dissenter's Guide to Foreign Policy* (New York: Praeger, 1968), pp. 254–55.

23. See Anthony C. Sutton, *Western Technology and Soviet Economic Development, 1917–1930,* and *Western Technology and Soviet Economic Development, 1930–1945* (Stanford, Cal.: Hoover Institution Press, Stanford University 1968, 1971).

tional interest objectives, wholly unrelated to the interests of the business enterprise.[24]

American foreign policy in the Middle East is another embarrassment to the theory of United States foreign policy following the flag of capital investment. As Michael Harrington has pointed out, the United States is pursuing an "anti-imperialist" foreign policy in the Middle East at the expense of large international American corporations.[25]

The friction-laden American attempts to enforce the Trading with the Enemy Act on U.S.-owned foreign subsidiaries is further evidence of the independence of U.S. multinationals from United States foreign policy. The Trading with the Enemy Act is often cited as an example of how the nation-state uses the multinational corporation to effect foreign policy objectives. In essence it permits the United States to deny to its own citizens the right to trade with certain countries such as mainland China. The Canadian Parliamentary Report on American direct investment observed that American prohibitions extend "to exports from Canada and other countries, affiliates or subsidiaries of American firms. Canadian law, however, permits trade with communist countries except for certain strategic goods. An obvious conflict of interest for Canadian-based subsidiaries and their directors and officers results when the American parent firm, under threat of legal action, seeks to impose these United States restrictions on the Canadian subsidiaries." [26]

However, the multinational enterprise should not be confused with a corporation like the British East India Co., created as a tool of a specific foreign policy idea. The very existence of the Trading with the Enemy Act and the possibilities surrounding its invocation is pregnant with this conflicting interest perceived to exist between the modus operandi of the business community and the nation-state. It is evident that the U.S. government has had to devise ways to control American business. The impositions are restrictive, not affirmative in nature, and after the celebrated Friehauf-France case the United States has relaxed its stand regarding the imposition of the Act's regulations on foreign-owned subsidiaries and licensees.[27]

GOALS OF THE MULTINATIONAL CORPORATION

The classic formulation of the motivations of nation-states is that they seek the accretion of power, and the disposal of that power in the service of its perception of security.

The classic formulation of corporate motivation is the profit-maximiz-

24. Eugene Staley, *War and the Private Investor* (Garden City, N.Y.: Doubleday, 1935).

25. Michael Harrington, "Imperialism in the Middle East," in Irving Howe and Carl Gershaum, eds., *Israel, the Arabs and the Middle East* (New York: Bantam, 1972), p. 350.

26. Standing Committee Report, 33:72.

27. A good description of the case can be found in William L. Craig, "Application of the Trading with the Enemy Act—Foreign Corporations Owned by Americans," *Harvard Law Review*, vol. 83 (1970), 579.

ing model. However, even this model does not furnish an objective norm for corporate behavior but rather establishes the permissible frontiers or limits of corporate behavior beyond which the corporation cannot go. These frontiers suggest that though the profit-maximizing model is by no means an infallible guide to predicting multinational enterprise behavior, it is closer to the mark than other analyses which persist in explaining the behavior of multinational corporations in terms of the political nomenclature associated with the behavioral phenomena of the nation-state. Baran and Sweezy argue that "all the major struggles going on in the world today can be traced to this hunger of the multinational corporations for maximum Lebensraum." [28] The assertion is quite fantastic. The multinational corporations tend to develop in stable regions of the world where the threat of economic nationalism and expropriation is not significant. The multinational corporation is not *power-maximizing*. Among the factors that inform the decisions of the multinational corporation to expand are the need to control resources, the saturation of home markets and access to foreign markets, scarcity of production factors at home, and preferential tax treatment in other countries.[29]

The American multinational corporations often seek access to foreign markets to move behind high tariff walls which would make the export of U.S. goods to these nations unprofitable. By having direct access to foreign markets, the multinational corporations are better able to guarantee a supply of products to their markets without the threat of incommeasurables such as dock strikes. Often less-developed countries insist that factories or refineries be constructed locally as a joint venture. If penetration of the market cannot be accomplished in any other way, then direct investment is the only logical alternative. Where relatively unskilled labor can be combined with sophisticated technologies, a prima facie case has been made for multinational enterprise expansion abroad.

A powerful motive for the move abroad is when a native corporation has surplus investment funds for which it sees only marginal opportunities in the U.S. The Senate Committee on Finance puts the issue succinctly:

> In all its product lines the typical large U.S. company reaches a market share plateau beyond which further market development may be too costly in relation to the returns anticipated. It may also fear government anti-trust action. If it does not diversify, it must generally be content to grow no faster than the economy in general. But the reward system of American business makes it imperative to grow faster than that. Some such growth can come via introduction of new products from research or from licensing others' research. Acquisition of other companies offers additional potential. Foreign investment is a third way to grow, a way which is often cheaper, possibly more profitable, and always glamorous.[30]

28. Paul A. Baran and Paul M. Sweezy, "Notes on the Theory of Imperialism," in Boulding and Mukerjee, *Economic Imperialism*, p. 170.
29. See *The Multinational Corporation: Studies on U.S. Foreign Investment*, U.S. Department of Commerce, 1 (March 1972), 14–16, for a brief analysis.
30. *Ibid.*, p. 120.

Japanese multinational concerns have also accelerated direct investment abroad in recent years. The Normura Research Institute has estimated that Japan's direct investment rose by $2.5 billion in the fiscal year ending March 31, 1972—three times the rise of the preceding year.[31] Among the reasons cited for the activity of Japanese multinationals are increased yen revaluation which has made Japanese exports prohibitively expensive, scarcity of land for industries such as aluminum and oil refining, the rise in Japan's labor wages, and the economic advantages of investing in countries with abundant natural resources. Sony, the Japanese electronics corporation, only recently has decided to go multinational by making direct investments in assembly plants in Brazil, Great Britain, and the U.S. A critical factor in Sony's decision was to circumvent fluctuations in the yen and to anticipate growing American protectionism. Japanese multinational corporations, fearing protectionism in the U.S., have begun to explore investment in Brazil in the hope that articles made with cheap Brazilian labor may still gain access to the United States market. Japanese investment in Brazil should bypass $1 billion by 1975. A Japanese business group predicts that by 1978 more than $2 billion more will be invested in the "economic miracle" of Latin America. Japanese investors have money in more than 100 types of business from supermarkets and ship-building to steel and banking.[32]

Professor Kindelberger observes that in a world of perfect competition "direct investment cannot exist." Nowhere is this more evident than in the differential rates of taxing multinational enterprise income that exist in different states as inducements to multinational firms.[33] Yugo-

31. "Japanese Concerns Lift Direct Overseas Investing," *The New York Times*, April 16, 1973, p. 59.

32. *The Wall Street Journal's Global Report* is an excellent source of information regarding the activities of Japanese MNCs. Salwa Spinning Company and Nissho-Inal Company plan to build a textile mill which will employ 1600. Sony intends to build in Sao Paulo to produce color television sets. Japanese-Brazil Pulp Resources Development Company, in a joint venture with a Brazilian firm, plans an $85 million pulp mill that will produce 750 tons daily by 1975.

33.

Global Tax Rate	
Singer	38%
Revlon, Inc.	39
Westinghouse Electric Corp.	42
Pfizer Inc.	42
General Electric Co.	43
Union Carbide Corp.	44
ITT	44
Johnson & Johnson	45
IBM	48
General Motors Co.	48
Eastman Kodak Co.	49
Ford Motor Co.	49
Avon Products Inc.	51

Source: *The Wall Street Journal*, March 12, 1973, p. 6.

slavia and Australia represent two distinct examples. On January 19, 1972, the U.S. signed an agreement with Yugoslavia to encourage capital investment in joint ventures. The agreement commits the Overseas Private Investment Corporation to provide insurance and financial aid to American investors. The Yugoslav government responded by eliminating requirements for reinvestment of 20% of profits and holding out an attractive tax rate of 35% on earnings. In the less developed republics of Montenegro and Macedonia the tax rate is maintained at 14% as an inducement to investors. *The New York Times* reports that "Yugoslavia has registered a total of 73 joint ventures so far. Only two foreign companies have chosen to withdraw. . . . The basic interest of the Yugoslavs is that the foreign partner introduces modern technology and that production be oriented toward the export market." [34]

Changes or fluctuations in a nation's posture toward the multinational corporations are factors to be weighed in predicting behavior. Often nation-states provide outright subsidies to multinational enterprises which can reach 40% of the investment, as in Great Britain.

Finally, it cannot be emphasized too strongly that multinational enterprises decide to invest in a specific nation, not necessarily in anticipation of a high rate of profit but for the contribution that plant will make to the multinational corporation's worldwide operation. Thus it may be that producing an item in country X will contribute to profits made in country Y where the item is combined with other technological resources and where item X could only be produced at a prohibitive price scale. This can lead to what is known as "transfer pricing," whereby the multinational enterprise adjusts its prices on intracompany sales to minimize losses and maximize profits. In this fashion multinational enterprises can seek to take their profits in nations with a lower tax rate or avoid the policies of states seeking to prevent the repatriation of profits that might upset their position in the foreign exchange. These by no means exhaust the rationales upon which multinational corporations have relied in their worldwide expansion.

Raymond Vernon reaches a particularly pertinent conclusion on this point:

> Because so many of the problems of large corporations are those entailed in adaption and change, other emphases tend to appear that are not consistent with the usual profit-maximising yield-on-investment model. Among other things, the management of the enterprise will generally regard its fixed assets as less unique and less difficult to reproduce than the people and practices and collective *memory* that comprise its organization: if there is an economic rent to be captured in the enterprises, therefore, it will be perceived as coming principally from the "investment" in the making of a functioning organization. On this assumption, the man-

34. "U.S. and Yugoslavia Sign Capitalist Ventures Pact," *The New York Times,* January 19, 1973, p. 217.

agement is concerned with maintaining loyalty, incentive, and initiative over the long run, and, if necessary, is usually prepared to modify the classic return on investment calculations to keep the principal members of the team in play.[35]

THE MULTINATIONAL CORPORATION AND THE NATION-STATE

The ranking of countries and corporations according to the size of the annual product raises the familiar argument that some multinational enterprises have evolved into powers more formidable than many nation-states (see Table 2). The economic dimensions of the multinational enterprise are indeed staggering, as the previous discussion of international production and direct investment have inferred. But how do these statistics lend themselves to the formulation that the sovereignty of the nation-state is being encroached upon, and its role as an actor in the international system obscured?

It is important to recall that the decline of the significance of the nation-state as the preeminent actor in the international system has more to do with the deemphasis of external security issues in international politics than the growth of the multinational corporation. Similarly, it is paramount that distinctions between such concepts as "power" and "influence" do not become blurred by the blizzard of statistics relating to international aggregate production. In the present international environment, Japan has little power but significant influence, as judged by the stability of the yen in international monetary affairs. Power is the ability, in a specific situation, to translate resources into capability to *compel* a settlement of an objective conflict on terms favorable to the actor. Israel has considerable power in the Middle East, none in Southeast Asia, but, however, surprising, *influence* among the African nations. The multinational enterprise possesses considerable influence in varying parts of the world. But influence is not power, and it is power that inspires the concept of sovereignty in international relations.

The nation-state retains a variety of means in its armamentarium to regulate the activities of the multinational enterprise. It should be axiomatic that the relationship between the multinational enterprise and the nation-state will be formed out of a relative advantage-disadvantage calculus which will vary with each specific situation. Canada, a recipient of an increasing portion of U.S. direct investment, has experienced remarkably little interference with its sovereignty. Professors Litvak and Maule have aptly observed that "in spite of all the research which has been undertaken, there is little concrete evidence of cases involving in-

35. *Sovereignty at Bay: The Multinational Spread of U.S. Enterprise* (New York: Basic Books, 1971), p. 117.

Table 2.   RANKING OF COUNTRIES AND CORPORATIONS ACCORDING TO SIZE OF ANNUAL PRODUCT* FOR 1970 (in $ billion)

Rank	Economic Entity	$	Rank	Economic Entity	$
1	United States	974.10	51	UAR	6.58
2	U.S.S.R.	504.70	52	Thailand	6.51
3	Japan	197.18	53	INT'L TEL. & TEL.	6.36
4	Germany, West	186.35	54	TEXACO	6.35
5	France	147.53	55	Portugal	6.22
6	United Kingdom	121.02	56	New Zealand	6.08
7	Italy	93.19	57	Peru	5.92
8	China, Mainland	82.50	58	WESTERN ELECTRIC	5.86
9	Canada	80.38	59	Nigeria	5.80
10	India	52.92	60	Taiwan	5.46
11	Poland	42.32	61	GULF OIL	5.40
12	Germany, East	37.61	62	U.S. STEEL	4.81
13	Australia	36.10	63	Cuba	4.80
14	Brazil	34.60	64	Israel	4.39
15	Mexico	33.18	65	VOLKSWAGENWERK	4.31
16	Sweden	32.58	66	WESTINGHOUSE ELECTRIC	4.31
17	Spain	32.26	67	STANDARD OIL (Calif.)	4.19
18	Netherlands	31.25	68	Algeria	4.18
19	Czechoslovakia	28.84	69	PHILIPS' GLOEILAMPENFABRIEKEN	4.16
20	Rumania	28.01	70	Ireland	4.10
21	Belgium	25.70	71	BRITISH PETROLEUM	4.06
22	Argentina	25.42	72	Malaysia	3.84
23	GENERAL MOTORS	24.30	73	LING-TEMCO-VOUGHT	3.77
24	Switzerland	20.48	74	STANDARD OIL (Ind.)	3.73
25	Pakistan	17.50	75	BOEING	3.68
26	South Africa	16.69	76	DUPONT (E.I.) de NEMOURS	3.62
27	STANDARD OIL (N.J.)	16.55	77	Hong Kong	3.62
28	Denmark	15.57	78	SHELL OIL	3.59
29	FORD MOTOR	14.98	79	IMPERIAL CHEM. INDUSTRIES	3.51
30	Austria	14.31	80	BRITISH STEEL	3.50
31	Yugoslavia	14.02	81	Korea, South	3.50
32	Indonesia	12.60	82	GEN. TEL. & ELECTRONICS	3.44
33	Bulgaria	11.82	83	NIPPON STEEL	3.40
34	Norway	11.39	84	Morocco	3.34
35	Hungary	11.33	85	HITACHI	3.33
36	ROYAL DUTCH/SHELL GROUP	10.80	86	RADIO CORP. OF AMERICA	3.30
37	Philippines	10.23	87	GOODYEAR TIRE & RUBBER	3.20
38	Finland	10.20	88	SIEMENS	3.20
39	Iran	10.18	89	Vietnam, South	3.20
40	Venezuela	9.58	90	Libya	3.14
41	Greece	9.54	91	Saudi Arabia	3.14
42	Turkey	9.04	92	SWIFT	3.08
43	GENERAL ELECTRIC	8.73	93	FARBWERKE HOECHST	3.03
44	Korea, South	8.21	94	UNION CARBIDE	3.03
45	IBM	7.50	95	DAIMLER-BENZ	3.02
46	Chile	7.39	96	PROCTOR & GAMBLE	2.98
47	MOBIL OIL	7.26	97	AUGUST THYSSEN-HUTTE	2.96
48	CHRYSLER	7.00	98	BETHLEHEM STEEL	2.94
49	UNILEVER	6.88	99	BASF	2.87
50	Colombia	6.61	100	MONTECATINI EDISON	2.84

Source: Lester R. Brown, *World Without Borders,* Table 1, pp. 214-15. Copyright © 1972 by Lester Brown. Reprinted by permission of Random House, Inc.

* The indicators used are gross national product for countries and gross annual sales for corporations. Though not strictly comparable (a value-added figure would have been more appropriate for industry), they are sufficiently close for illustrative purposes. Data for the centrally planned economies (excluding mainland China) and for the General Motors Corporation are for 1969.

fringement of Canadian sovereignty." [36] On January 24, 1973 the Canadian government proposed to Parliament a revised bill to control foreign investment in Canadian business. The regulations would apply to any takeover by foreigners of a business concern with assets of $250,000 or more or annual reserves of $3 million or more. The bill was designed to primarily cope with U.S. direct investment, which controls two-thirds of all Canadian industries. Gerald Regan, premier of Nova Scotia, has however articulated opposition to "any interference whatsoever" from Ottawa, citing his province's 10% unemployment rate.

Mexico has also proven itself quite capable of discouraging direct investment by U.S. concerns. An estimated 1000 American companies do business in Mexico. Foreign capital represents 8% of Mexico's private investment and 5% of total investment. As a result of a series of new laws governing foreign investment and technology, direct foreign investment in the country fell by 9% in 1972. José Campillo Sainz, undersecretary of industry, has framed the issue according: "We want foreign investment . . . but we want it in accordance with the purposes of our development." [37] Mexicanization will probably mean that many U.S. companies already operating in Mexico will have to assume a minority position in their concerns. Pragmatism will dictate its own exceptions. Mexico has also sought to attract German multinational enterprises to balance the role of U.S. capital within the economy.

In Australia, where direct foreign investment dominates the automobile, oil refining, and chemical industries, the Labor government has moved to see that direct investment conforms to the national interest. Treasury officials have commenced drawing up lists of strategic industries to be protected from foreign takeover.

The election of the Labor government on December 2, 1972 was attended by changes in Australia's foreign and economic policies. Australia has been for years an attractive country for direct investment; in 1973 almost $12 billion, one-third of which was American, largely because of the positive incentive program sponsored by previous governments. Australia's new federal treasurer suggested a reevaluation of these policies, stating that "we have almost gone begging and crawling for overseas capital. In some industries, foreign ownership or control has grown to heights that should never have occurred. There has been too much reliance on it." [38]

In Norway, multinational oil companies, led by Phillips, have been negotiating for rights to extract and export petroleum and gas reserves in

36. Isaiah A. Litvak and Christopher J. Maule, "Foreign Investment in Canada," in Isaiah A. Litvak and Christopher J. Maule, eds., *Foreign Investment: The Experience of the Host Countries* (New York: Praeger Special Studies in International Economics and Development, 1970), p. 99.

37. "Mexico Takes Hard Look at Foreign Plants, Discouraging Investment by U.S. Concern," *The Wall Street Journal*, March 21, 1973, p. 40.

38. See "Australia: The Picnic is Over for Foreign Business," *Business Week*, January 20, 1973, pp. 38–39.

the North Sea. Norway will acquire 50% ownership of the project while providing 5% of the capital and assuming 5% of the risk. The Norwegian government will have a substantial interest in the joint company that carries out the operations. One of the concessions made by Phillips in the negotiations is that the chairman of the joint company will be Norwegian.

In Southeast Asia, Japanese direct investment has become an object of national resentment on the part of host countries, renewing the old detestation of Japanese domination. Japan, which relies upon Indonesia for nickel, copper, timber, and low-pollution oil, has extended more low-interest long-term loans to Jakarta than to any other Asian nation. Indonesia has sought to balance Japanese investment with German, French, and British investment. Japan and Indonesia have split over Indonesian demands for Indonesian-based and controlled export industries. At Pomala, Mitsubishi agreed to finance a $25-million nickel smelter but only on condition that the state nickel company in Jakarta relinquish its controlling interest. The Indonesian government has threatened three Japanese companies which receive 900,000 tons of bauxite annually from Bintan with the loss of all or part of their concession unless the Japanese invest $415 million in an aluminum smelter and adjacent hydroelectric complex.[39]

In Thailand, Japanese companies have encountered demands for a greater degree of local control in the petrochemical projects and other pending joints ventures. Japanese direct and indirect holdings in Thailand probably reach $800 million. One-hundred-ten manufacturing and mining firms dependent on Japanese loans have nearly $600 million in net assets and 146 service and retail enterprises worth another $210 million. Eighty % of Japanese firms have a controlling interest of 70% or more in joint ventures, above the world average of 57%.[40]

Despite the considerable degree of emotional conflict between MNC and host countries, there is scant evidence that the MNC has emerged as arbiter of political affairs. Clearly the most celebrated example of an attempt by a multinational corporation to interfere in the political affairs of a nation-state is the Chile-ITT affair, which indicates that although a multinational enterprise may think political thoughts, it possesses pitifully little influence to effectuate them. Prior to the revelation by columnist Jack Anderson of the efforts of ITT to interfere in Chilean politics, Stephen F. Lau interviewed 57 persons in Santiago who had formerly been in the government and thus had knowledge of the question of direct investment in Chile.[41] Their responses indicated that a high percentage believed that foreign corporations possess limited or no *political* (emphasis

39. "Indonesia Prime Test for Japan," *The Washington Post*, March 2, 1973.

40. "Japan's 'Real' Investment Motives Questioned by Thais," *The Washington Post*, March 1, 1973, p. A17.

41. *The Chilean Response to Foreign Investment* (New York: Praeger Special Studies in International Economics and Development, 1972), p. 68.

added) influence, and much smaller percentages believed that some corporations exert influence and others do not or that foreign corporations are politically powerful. The respondents generally cited the absence of channels available to corporate personnel, the fact that corporate executives are aware of their tenuous position within the country, that industrial corporations "are small in comparison with the Chilean government," and that foreign firms have little to gain from political embroglios because they are economic entities.

The ITT affair, currently under investigation by both the United States Senate and the OPIC, will no doubt reveal the parameters of ITT's unconscionable scheme. However, it is plainly evident that the United States government as well as other U.S. multinational enterprises refused to participate in a plan to economically strangle the Allende regime, and in spite of the legal suits brought by Kennecott Copper against three important copper users in Rome, Milan, and Brescia as well as in Sweden, France, and West Germany, Chile was able to sell its 1973 copper output. The coup against the Allende government in 1973 by the Chilean armed forces was mainly a response to a complex internal political struggle.

The ITT affair should not obscure the fact that Latin American governments have moved freely to nationalize and expropriate American multinational corporations. Peru expropriated the International Petroleum Company and W. R. Grace Company. Bolivia expropriated the Gulf Oil Company, and in Chile the Ford Motor Company and Bethlehem Steel Corporation were forced to terminate their operations.

Bolivia, Chile, Colombia, Ecuador, and Peru have agreed upon the Andean Pact, which prescribes stringent norms for the regulation of foreign investment in the signatory nations. Brazil and Argentina have begun to articulate a commitment to similar principles. The wave of economic nationalism in Latin America is having a decided effect on new foreign investment. A survey conducted by the Council of the Americas reported that the Andean Pact would affect any investment decisions in signatory nations mildly or very negatively. The Andean Pact countries have indicated that they will insist upon "progressive nationalization" of foreign investments in important economic sectors.

But although it is clear that the MNC has rarely conceived of itself as a political actor, or that when it has, the limitations of its influence have been surprising, it is equally clear that its impact on the economic affairs of nation-states has grown steadily, creating a special interest in its transactions with the putatively less developed countries. Much of the thinking and analysis of the relationship between the multinational corporation and the less developed countries is characterized by sentimentalization of the respective parties. The relationship is, however, a complex one which defies summary injunctions.

The geographic trends in U.S. direct foreign investment tend to make Marxist and neo-Marxist explanations of imperialism something less than reliable in understanding the behavior of U.S. multinational corporations.

According to the U.S. Department of Commerce in 1970, U.S. direct investment in Europe and Canada was $47.3 billion compared to $14.7 billion for all of Latin America.[42] Direct investment in Latin America has declined by almost one-third of the 1950 total so that it constitutes 19% of the total U.S. direct investment.

Table 3.   PERCENTAGE OF TOTAL U.S. DIRECT INVESTMENT IN LESS DEVELOPED AREAS

	1929	1950	1960	1970
Latin America	3.5	4.4	8.4	14.7
Middle East	—	—	1.1	2.0
Other less developed areas	—	—	1.4	4.6

Nevertheless, the percent of profits from the less developed countries (LDCs) as compared to profits from investments in the developed countries is evidence that the true investments are by no means negligible.

An industry-by-industry analysis of the book value of U.S. direct investment abroad suggests part of the reason for the declining importance of the LDC to the multinational corporation:

Table 4.

	1929	1950	1960	1970
Manufacturing	1.8	3.8	11.1	32.2
Petroleum	1.1	3.4	10.8	21.8
Mining and smelting	1.2	1.1	3.0	6.1
Other	3.4	3.5	7.0	17.9

It is clear that direct investment in manufacturing is accelerating at a remarkable pace. Multinational enterprises are, generally speaking, *market*-oriented. These concerns make sophisticated consumer products to satisfy the demands of the international consumer class which has grown up in the industrialized nations. The role of cheap labor, usually associated with the LDCs, is no longer of primary importance to the multinational enterprise in the aggregate, however important a factor it remains with selected industries.

The assertiveness of local governments and the revolt against "dependencia" has also contributed to the shift in the direction of U.S. direct investment to regions perceived to be politically stable. The investment climate in the LDC is, as of this writing, considered to be alarming, especially after the notable expropriation of Anaconda and ITT holdings in Chile.

The basic question that must be asked, and to which there is appallingly little evidence from which to derive a satisfactory answer, is whether or not the LDCs have benefited from the presence of the multi-

42. *Survey of Current Business,* U.S. Department of Commerce, 1970.

national enterprise. Do the multinational corporations dominate the host countries? Who receives the lion's share of the profits? Has the multinational corporation adversely affected the LDCs' balance of payments?

As mentioned earlier, the bulk of U.S. direct investment in the LDCs is in petroleum. Therefore, it is of some interest to our study of the relationship of the multinational corporation to LDCs to pursue such considerations. And it is equally clear that host countries have managed to use the multinational enterprise for their own purposes, not in a zero-sum situation but rather as participants in the rewards of oligopoly. Since 1920 the oil-producing nations have raised their share of the profits on crude oil production from 10 to 15% to 80 to 85%. Bargaining positions of the LDCs vary with the international environment. Venezuela acquired favorable 50-50 profit accord during the oil shortages of World War Two. The oil-producing nations of the Middle East have steadily improved their market position with respect to the multinational enterprises until in 1971 these governments negotiated an agreement assuring them of 80% or more of the production cost of crude oil and the F.O.B. price of oil from the Middle East.[43]

A major factor in the change in the bargaining position of these nations has been the competition among the multinational corporations that have entered the market since 1950. The governments that form this world oil cartel will reap an estimated $70 billion in earnings by 1980. Recent events demonstrate that the oil-producing nations are quite capable of driving hard bargains with multinational corporations and resorting to nationalization of industries where the national interest is believed to be served. On June 1, 1972, Iraq and Syria nationalized the assets of the Iraq Petroleum Company in their territories. On February 28, 1973, President Ahmed Hassan al-Bakr of Iraq announced that foreign oil companies in Iraq had accepted nationalization of the Iraq Petroleum Company in return for compensation. Iraq is the fourth largest oil-producing country in the Middle East. In 1972 the nation's production amounted to 1.5 million barrels a day, almost 100% of the region's total production. Western oil companies have signed participation pacts with Saudi Arabia and Abu Dhabi which are likely to establish a pattern for petroleum operations around the world. The governments will acquire an initial 25% equity interest in the companies' Persian Gulf production. The governments' interest will rise by five percentage points a year (six points in 1982) so that the Persian Gulf states will acquire a 51% ownership of the properties by January 1982. It is estimated that the profits accruing to Abu Dhabi alone will reach $200 million by 1976. The Arab-Israeli war of 1973 has also added a new political element to the supply and demand for oil in the immediate future.

Turkey and Ecuador have also moved to strengthen the position of

43. Raymond Vernon, *Restrictive Business Practices: The Operations of Multinational United States Enterprises in Developing Countries,* United Nations Report, 1972, pp. 4–7.

local producers with foreign competitors. The Turkish National Assembly passed a petroleum bill that will give priority to the state-owned petroleum enterprises over local and private concerns, halve exploration, and quintuple rentals. In Ecuador Texaco, Inc. and Gulf Oil Corp., which jointly accounted for the only significant oil production in Ecuador, were ordered to return half of the acreage given them by negotiated agreements. The two companies retained some 1.2 million acres which had yielded 11 new field discoveries and 99 productive wells producing more than 220,000 barrels a day. The companies have sought compensation. Viewed both in terms of maintaining a rising share in profits and capital assets as well as enjoying an oligopolist position with respect to the rest of the world, the relationship of the oil-producing nations to the multinational enterprises has been more like client-agent than master-slave.

Harry Magdoff [44] has noted that between 1950 and 1965 the flow of direct investment from the U.S. to Latin America amounted to $3.8 billion, whereas income on capital transferred to the U.S. came to $11.3 billion, a surplus of $7.5 billion in favor of the U.S. In Europe, U.S. direct investment was $8.1 billion, with $5.5 billion in profits transferred back. Was Latin America thereby decapitalized? Not necessarily. Profit rates are in fact higher in Latin America and the Middle East because investments in the extractive industries such as petroleum are consistently higher than those in the service and manufacturing industries. George Lichtheim, a European socialist, has argued that these statistics "merely underscore the familiar fact that 'uneven development' is a source of surplus profit for the advanced countries including the USSR. It does not prove that no development takes place, merely that an extra price is paid for it during the critical transition period." [45]

Charles Kindleberger similarly raises objections to comparing interest and dividends remitted from a country with the inflow of new investment to a country. He argues that

> There is no need for foreign investors to re-invest their earnings, or for any single original investment to grow geometrically. The Latino comparison makes sense only where past investment has been used unproductively, or where the productivity has not been accompanied by the approximate reallocation of resources to produce the exports or economize on imports sufficiently to produce the foreign exchange needed for debt service.[46]

Professor Vernon furnishes a simple model to describe such a hypothesis.[47] If a U.S.-owned subsidiary receives $100 from the parent and, assuming

44. Harry Magdoff, *The Age of Imperialism* (New York: Monthly Review Press, 1969), p. 198.

45. *Imperialism* (New York: Praeger, 1971), p. 152, note 14.

46. Charles P. Kindleberger, *American Business Abroad* (New Haven: Yale University Press, 1969), p. 173.

47. Raymond Vernon, *Restrictive Business Practices*, p. 19.

an output-capital ratio of 1:3, a return on investment before taxes of 30%, and a local tax rate of 50%, and further assuming that half of the net profit is reinvested and half remitted to the parent, the record of capital inflow and profit outflow would be as follows:

Table 5.

Year	Capital Inflow	Capital Stock	International Production	Profit Outflow
1	$100.00	$100.00	$33.00	$7.50
2	—	$107.50	$35.83	$8.06
3	—	$115.56	$38.52	$8.67

Vernon observes that though after the first year the country would be regarded as undergoing decapitalization, "at the same time, however . . . the capital stock at work inside the countries grows each year as does the country's output."

These figures tell us little of the impact of the multinational corporation on the aggregate balance of payments of the developing nations. Professor Vernon poses two models of the balance of payments impact on LDCs. If it is assumed that investments were made for "import replacement purposes," then foreign investment will have had a beneficial impact on these nations if and only if there was a choice regarding whether to invest within the U.S. or go abroad. If the rationale for investment was for the purpose of not losing a valuable market to national producers, then the foreign investment would be detrimental to the balance of payments problems of the particular nations.

A crucial factor in determining the future relations between the MNC and the LDC is the question of technology transfer. A persistent theme in economic theory has praised large firms for their technological efficiency and rational allocation of resources. Professor Vernon's sample of 187 multinational firms revealed that they devoted 2.4% of their sales for research and development purposes, while the remainder of the *Fortune* list spent 1.85%. Much is still not known about how much of any technology transfer occurs, and in which kinds of industries.

The Report to the Committee on Finance of the United States, of which previous mention was made, furnished the most comprehensive data to date on the significance of technology transfer. Using income earned in royalties and fees as an index of technology exports, the exports exceed imports by a factor of 10. Ninety % of the $2.3 billion in income of royalties and fees were accounted for by U.S. multinational corporations. It is not unlikely that multinational corporations engage in a strategy of not exporting their first-line technology; however, this hypothesis may be of greater significance to developed rather than less developed countries, because in the developed countries there is substantial competition between multinational enterprises for international consumer markets, which may influence them to withhold certain patents and processes. It is thus interesting to note that it is the multinational enterprises in the high-technology class that continue to generate a favorable ratio of new exports to new imports rather than the multinational corporations in the medium- or low-technology classes, such as food products.[48]

But is it the nineteenth-century phantasmagoria of economic subjugation with which the MNCs threaten the sovereignty of the LDCs? Although it remains a factor that decision-makers must take into account, it is a diminishing one, and not the primary challenge to the viability of those nation-states. The future challenges to national sovereignty will be in the cultural, not in the political or economic, spheres of activity; and the threat of such challenges is likely to be mounted by the American and Japanese MNC. Nor is this a recent phenomenon.

European fears of American business were rooted in the nineteenth century. Cushing Strout notes that

> Transatlantic prophets of the "Americanization" of the world were heard as early as 1902, but during this decade European intellectuals began to see in America the dread face of the future: standardization, crowd culture and regimentation. . . . Just as Americans had created a symbolic Old World to represent the evils of the past in contrast to the hopeful promise of a New World emancipated from feudal darkness, so did the Europeans begin to create a symbolic image of America to represent the feared future of technology and mass society.[49]

A multinational corporation may clash with ethnic subcultures, as was the case in Canada where Premier Bourarra of Quebec intervened in a language dispute between General Motors and the United Auto Workers at an assembly unit outside Montreal. GM rejected demands that French be made the language of work for 2400 assembly-line workers.

The rationalization of other cultural styles, for which the rubric "Americanization" has been used as a kind of shorthand, is more diffuse than

48. An analytical framework to evaluate the transfers of "know-how" and "show-how" technology can be found in Robert B. Stobaugh, *The International Transfer of Technology in the Establishment of the Petrochemical Industry in Developing Countries* (New York: UNITAR Research Reports, No. 12, 1971). See also Terutomo Ozawa, *Transfer of Technology from Japan to Developing Counties,* UNITAR Research Reports, No. 7; Jack Baransom, *International Transfer of Automotive Technology to Developing Countries* (New York: UNITAR Research Reports, No. 8, 1971); Lawrence H. Wortzel, *Technology Transfer in the Pharmaceutical Industry* (New York: UNITAR Research Reports, No. 14, 1971); Walter A. Chudson, *The International Transfer of Commercial Technology for Developing Countries,* UNITAR Research Reports, No. 13; also Ciro E. Zoppo, *Toward a U.S. Policy on Nuclear Technology Transfer to Developing Countries,* Southern California Arms Control and Foreign Policy Seminar, University of California, Los Angeles, July 1971. At best, the literature on technology transfer is controversial.

49. *The American Image of the Old World* (New York: Harper and Row, 1963), p. 177.

the GM-Quebec controversy. It can be anticipated in the phenomenal growth of American fast-food enterprises, as well as service and culture industries. Heublein, Inc., maintains 400 Kentucky Fried Chicken outlets in thirty countries, and in 1973 anticipates adding 200 more, primarily in the United Kingdom, Japan, and Australia. McDonald Corporation maintains outlets in Japan (19), Australia (6), Holland (3), and Germany (4) and intends to double them by 1974. Dairy Queen International, Inc., and Pillsbury Co. are also active multinational corporations that receive scant attention. Dairy Queen has just signed a 50-50 joint venture with Marbeni Corp., of Japan and will construct 500 Dairy Queen Ice Cream stands within five years. Dairy Queen currently maintains 400 outlets in Canada, West Germany, Mexico, Australia, Iceland, Switzerland, and the Philippines. Pillsbury plans to actively expand its Burger King operations overseas after it resolves some marketing difficulties. Nestlé's Alimentara, a Swiss firm, is the twenty-ninth largest corporation in the world in terms of sales. The company had a total income of $4.2 billion in 1972, 53% from Europe, 33% from the Americas, 11% from Asia, and 3% from Africa. The Swiss firm maintains hundreds of subsidiaries which operate 300 factories and employ 110,000 people in sixty countries. Nestlé's products, such as Nescafé and Nesquick, are sold throughout the world. Has the candy bar become a transnational actor? Will the organizational imperatives surrounding the processing and distribution of Kentucky Fried Chicken create more social disequilibrium than the export of Marxist or Capitalist models of development, or are these only idle thoughts?

THE CRISIS OF DEVELOPMENT THEORY

The basic rationales that have been invoked to explain or encourage direct investment by nation-states and multinational corporations in less developed countries of the world have been overtaken by events. The national interest of the major nation-state actors in the international system lies increasingly in the economic interdependence of consumer markets and the limitation of the proliferation of nuclear weapons. Ideological competition for the Third World appears to have been an idea whose time has come and gone. The geographic investment patterns of the multinational corporations reflect similar realities. Even where multinational enterprises have made investments, they are usually in extractive industries which do little to encourage growth in agricultural or industrial markets within the nation. Throughout, the division between the rich and poor nations appears to widen (see Chart II).

Is there a utilitarian rationale for the development assistance? If not, which actor in the international environment is capable of acting upon other kinds of rationales? The Report of the Commission on International Development offers one alternative:

Chart II. The gap between rich and poor nations

GROSS NATIONAL PRODUCT PER CAPITA OF DEVELOPING AND SELECTED DEVELOPED COUNTRIES, 1960 and 1969

(IN 1969 U.S. dollars)

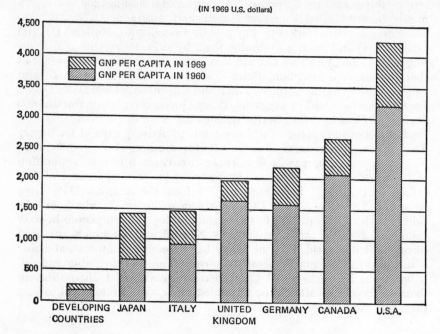

Source: *Trends in Developing Countries*, 4th Ed. (World Bank, 1971), Chart 3.3.

So we return to the question: Why should the rich countries seek to help other nations when even the richest of them are saddled with heavy social and economic problems within their own borders? The simplest answer to the question is the moral one: that it is only right for those who have to share with those who have not.[50]

This is a difficult rationale for assistance in a world largely bent on discovering an "enlightened self-interest" for assisting the poor. Regrettably, in the past, arguments stressing an illusory "national interest" associated with development have been made with relatively little impact, even during the height of the Cold War when such pronouncements were taken with more seriousness.

The multinational corporation is neither inherently evil nor beneficent. Its movements are governed by a narrow frontier of economic impetuses. Some writers suggest that the multinational enterprise is the best

50. *Partners in Development,* Report of the Commission on International Development (New York: Praeger, 1969), p. 8.

hope for the LDCs, but for the reasons we have already explored this does not seem very likely.

In the final analysis, it will have to be the nation-state acting through multilateral organizations, bilateral arrangements, perhaps through the multinational corporations themselves, if development assistance is to be made to the LDCs on the necessary scale. The multinational corporation is not a substitute for development theory. It can be an agent for growth but little else. Only people, acting through their governments, and governments acting upon their ideals, can furnish commitment and direction. Only the nation-state can base its motivations on a spectrum of concerns which include humanitarianism. Thus it is that while the territorial nation-state is slowly losing its function as a guarantor of security, it can acquire and reemphasize a different function if it so chooses. But it is a decision that only states or organizations of states can make. Multinational corporations provide possibly one means toward that end.

Development of the multinational corporation

HOWE MARTYN

INTRODUCTION

"Multinational" companies, corporations, enterprises or firms became a subject of academic, journalistic, public, and even governmental consideration with extraordinary rapidity during the single decade of the 1960s. They were recognized to be contributing substantially to the production and distribution of goods and services in many parts of the world, though quantities were difficult to measure. The distinctive features of the phenomena observed were (1) parallel operations within several national political jurisdictions, and (2) organizational structures differing from those occurring within single nation-states only. Awareness came with the labeling of firms under the term "multinational" as much as with their growth in numbers and size. Origins include, therefore, the introduction of the term. Origins may be traced, also, to circumstances external to the firm, some of which appear to be causes, such as national industrialization policies, while others are conditions, such as improved communications. Similarly, internal causes and conditions have influenced firms to become multinational. Some substantial effects of the formation of multinational firms are already discernible. Further effects depend principally on political conditions.

WHAT MAKES A CORPORATION, ENTERPRISE, OR FIRM "MULTINATIONAL"?

Some scholars have become concerned, like medieval Scholastics, that what is happening in the organization of production and distribution internationally is being discussed under a term that has not received a definition that they have devised and sanctioned. Some would still prefer other terms such as "transnational," "supranational," or even "global corporation." This last term disregards the complete exclusion of private businesses from more than half of the world and their existence elsewhere at the sufferance of the sovereignty of national governments.

The first and most important service performed by the new term, "multinational corporation," has been as a signpost, drawing attention to the substantial number of industrial and commercial organizations that are operating in new ways and forming large, new structures.

Although multinational corporations are indeed new, trade across the seas is, of course, as old as history, and trade from one national territory to others as old as the political organization of the nation-state. Such traditional trade involves production in one country for distribution in others, including further processing in the case of raw materials. Physical international trade continues and has even increased substantially in the recent period which has seen the emergence of multinational firms. Some of these firms participate in traditional trade.

What is new is that firms are duplicating their activities and essential parts of their organization in several national territories. Sears Roebuck has become multinational by establishing retailing businesses in Mexico and several South American countries, and also in Canada and Spain, complete with local buying offices as well as stores. General Motors manufactures automobiles, IBM manufactures business machines, and Pfizer compounds medicines, Unilever manufactures soap and processes foods, in Australia, Britain, Canada, France, Germany, the United States, and many other countries. They market as well as manufacture. The epitome of multinationalism is the Bata firm, founded in Czechoslovakia, transferred during World War Two to Canada, and by 1968 making shoes in 79 countries and selling them in 89 countries.[1]

Another service of the term "multinational corporations," is to make explicit the relationship of these companies to the patchwork of territorial nations that provide government for the peoples of the world. Acknowledgment must be made by the firm of the absolute sovereignty of a national government before production or distribution can be undertaken in its territory. Authorization from the governments of the areas must be obtained for all the activities of multinational firms within these areas. Included are activities that may have subsequently aroused criticism, such as making demands for foreign exchange to pay dividends. Not included are, however, possible activities that may fall between, or rise above, national jurisdictions, such as charging artificial prices between companies, or allocating production or export markets.

The duplication of the activities and structures of multinational corporations in several countries is not a separation, like cell division among amoebae. Umbilical connections are maintained. These provide not only the outflow and return of money but also the circulation of technology, which keeps firm from withering.

In practice, a multinational corporation pumps new products and processes into use much faster and more broadly than has been possible in any other way under existing political and economic conditions. It loosens the constrictions of patents and proprietary secrecy. It also overcomes ignorance of the possibilities of change that exists in the sluggish firms of static economies.

The continuous and active relationship among the duplicated national firms in a multinational group has most frequently occurred when there

---

1. Thomas J. Bata, "Shoemaker to the World," *President's Forum,* 1968.

has been ownership by one company of controlling shares in all the others—the parent-subsidiary relationship. This imparts flexibility to the collection of income from the use within a country of capital and/or technology that are the property of a company in another country. This also appears to supplement the spread of information about technology, with power to require its use. The power may be exerted through orders issued under the authority of the owners of the shares or by appointment under that authority of responsive executives, particularly the managing directors of the subsidiaries.

The continuous and active parent-subsidiary relations have been declared by many parent company officials to require complete ownership —100% of voting shares. Experience has shown, however, that effective control and attractive returns are obtainable with a bare majority ownership, or even a minority if it is a block and the majority is divided or acquiescent. Similarly, experience indicates that dissemination of information is a better coordinator than attempts to exert power by issuing orders and hiring and firing. It is not necessary for a multinational corporation to have total or majority legal and financial control of subsidiaries, or to have a hierarchical, authoritarian system of exercising control.

Duplication of operations in several countries on the basis of centralized ownership has been made possible by grants by sovereigns to foreigners of the same property-ownership privileges as citizens. Moreover, "persons" in law include companies or corporations. That this is an artificial position is indicated by the rejection of private ownership of subsoil resources—e.g., oil—in Spanish-law and Moslem countries, and of foreign ownership of land in a number of other countries, recently increasing. Thus multinational corporations have come into existence through acts of governments, though these have been acts of omission— failure to distinguish between real people and legal-fiction "persons," and between citizens or residents and foreigners.

AN ALTERNATIVE SYSTEM

Parent-subsidiaries are, thus, a special case. They are not the only possible pattern. A nascent alternative to parent-subsidiaries, the exchange of patents and know-how between companies in different countries that remained independent in ownership and management, was deliberately crushed by governments, led by the United States, in the 1930s. Cross-licensing had become significant, in the chemical and electrical industries in particular. This was attacked as restricting trade and therefore total wealth by reducing competition. Belief in the virtues of competition had become religious dogma in the United States. The investigation directed by United States Senator Gerald Nye into international "cartels" mixed heated emotions with xenophobia. Precedent-making convictions of Timken and duPont-Imperial Chemicals have had the effect that the only way in which American companies are able to extend their technology to other countries without risking conviction or the crippling expense of defense against an antitrust prosecution is by subsidiaries that are American-controlled to a sufficient degree to eliminate possible collusion with an independent foreign company.

The logic of the theory of competition has been brought into question, for instance by Professor Donald Dewey of Columbia University.[2] Dewey's recognition of the increase in production and decrease in price that a monopoly may give under modern imperfect competition may have significance that is larger and more urgent in smaller countries than in the United States. The only way they can apply it, however, in relations with American companies is, ironically, by creating nationalized companies. The Antitrust Division of the U.S. Department of Justice (and similar agencies some other governments have been influenced to form) is required to concede to State Department (or Foreign Ministry) the jurisdiction over agreements between American or other companies and foreign governments, including their national organizations for industry and trade. American companies are encouraged to make agreements with the Soviet Union and Communist China under the Nixon policy of 1972.

HOW AND WHEN DID THE TERM "MULTINATIONAL CORPORATION" BECOME CURRENT?

There was a considerable time lag between the appearance of what are now called multinational corporations and their identification by this term. They were not noticed in part because they did not have a name. There were other reasons, of course. One was the displacement of empiricism by algebra in economics. Another was that data with the assumed authority of government statistics included only financial transfers across national frontiers, nothing about what happened to the money afterward.

A few incidents connected with the appearance of the term in the English language in its present usage are known. The first occurrence the writer has discovered was in a speech by David Lilienthal in Philadelphia in 1958. This was included in a book edited by Melvin Anshen and George L. Bach in 1960.[3] Prior to finding this precedent, the writer had coined the term independently for the title of a pioneering course of study introduced at American University, Washington, D.C., in 1961. This was accepted with some reluctance, the dean concerned questioning the title on the grounds that "multinational" was unfamiliar and not easy to pronounce. The work in this course and the title were described to Dr. Howard Whidden, then foreign editor of *Business Week,* incidental to

2. *The Theory of Imperfect Competition* (New York: Columbia University Press, 1969).
3. *Business Management in the 1980s* (New York: McGraw-Hill, 1960).

his participation in a panel of which the writer was chairman at a conference in Washington on March 21, 1963. On April 20, 1963, a feature article appeared in his magazine with the title "Multinational Companies." [4] In 1964, the writer's book, *International Business*, was published with the dust-cover description "Organization, management, and social impact of the multinational corporation." [5] Quotations from the London edition provided much of the substance of a feature article on October 17, 1964, in the influential *Economist*.[6] In 1964, the suggestion was made to the Ford Foundation that this development in international business would be a subject of further research and publication worthy of Ford funding. In 1965, a very large grant for this purpose was made by Ford to the Harvard Business School. There followed a number of articles and books by Professor Raymond Vernon of Harvard and members of the team he recruited, most using the term "multinational" though with "enterprise" as the noun rather than "corporation." The acceptance of the term was so rapid and so general that by 1972, Christopher Tugendhat, a journalist and member of the British Parliament, was able to publish a book on the subject entitled simply *The Multinationals*.[7]

EXTERNAL CAUSES

National government policies of industrialization have been one cause of the appearance of multinational corporations. The causal relationship has been evident in Canada, which has been host to more subsidiaries of multinational firms than any other country, for a longer time —ever since the predecessor of American General Electric established a factory in Hamilton, Ontario, to get inside the tariff wall established by the Canadian "National Policy" of 1879.

The intention of the Canadian "National Policy" was to encourage domestic manufacturing industries, on the example of Germany and the United States. There was no intention to create opportunities for American and British companies to form subsidiaries, and in so doing to develop strategies that they would subsequently deploy in many other industrializing territories. British-owned subsidiary companies were allowed in Canada as an unquestioned survival of colonialism. That precedent opened the country to American subsidiaries also. The industrialization of Canada was under absentee ownership rather than domestic as intended. The National Policy had been subverted. This has gone largely unnoticed until the last decade. The National Policy was, indeed, discussed by Canadian economists and historians mostly as a tariff-protection aberration from the ideal/norm of free trade caused, in their opinion,

4. "Multinational Companies," *Business Week*, April 20, 1963.
5. Howe Martyn, *International Business* (New York: Free Press, 1964).
6. "Companies Outgrow Countries," *Economist of London*, October 17, 1964.
7. Published by Random House in New York, 1972.

by the self-interest of Canadian manufacturers. The connection of the Canadian National Policy of 1879 with the evolution of the multinational corporation was, however, mentioned specifically by this writer in *International Business.*[8]

Industrialization has become the objective of governments in many countries besides Canada that had been dependent for earning foreign currencies on "colonial produces"—i.e., commodity exports. This has been a phenomenon mainly of the second half of the twentieth century, although a slightly earlier manifestation was seen in Peronism in Argentina. Industrialization has been seen as a panacea for unemployment in the increasing world population for whom there are no prospects of even subsistence in agriculture, fishing, or forestry. The demand for industries to supplement or replace commodity production and exportation lent strength to the political independence movements which fragmented the free-trade areas of the British, Dutch, and French empires. It is significant to the spread of multinational corporations that one of the first actions of a newly independent nation is to impose tariffs on imports of manufactured goods.

Policies of industrialization at many new locations received approval and some assistance from the foreign aid programs of the United States, Britain, and the United Nations. The hope that was held in those countries for two decades after World War Two was that they would gradually be relieved of the burden of direct assistance and the danger of political turmoil by aiding internal economic development in less developed countries.

Results attributable to government-to-government financial and technical assistance have been disappointing.[9] Entrepreneurial management proved to be much more complicated than officials and their academic advisers, with only theoretical economics as preparation, were able to understand.

Even in the early stages of the postwar development effort, governments under pressure to create jobs through industrialization saw a shortcut. They may have recognized the contribution of foreign subsidiaries to the rise of Canadian living standards to the highest in the world before Canadians themselves did. In any case, the corollary to the policy of industrialization was the stimulation of the establishment of local industries by foreigners, who had knowledge of the equipment needed, where to get it, how to use it, and how to train local people to operate not only the mechanical equipment but the even more complex technology of marketing. Both penalties and promises were used by many countries during the 1950s and 1960s—penalties against failure to transfer production, promises of monopolies and tax exemption.

8. Howe Martyn, *International Business*, p. 28.
9. Lester B. Pearson et al., *Partners in Development* (New York: Praeger, 1969), p. 49.

INTERNAL CAUSES

Internal causes have also moved corporations to become multi-national. An important cause has been the awakening of companies to their dependence on markets and thus to the benefits of applying managerial energy and supporting resources to marketing—going after customers. This awakening has been general in American companies, and has contributed to their international preeminence. Foreigners have been seen to be potential customers, irrespective of nationality, race, religion, or location. More customers provide more sales, and if the price is right, an arithmetical increase in profits. Geometrical increases have been obtained by some firms from marketing abroad. Higher prices and profits per sale have been obtained for products which have been newer or of higher relative quality than the competition abroad.

The external cause, the national policy of many countries to promote domestic industrialization, already mentioned, has meant that tariffs, quotas, and government purchasing practices have made local production essential. There have also been internal causes for the decentralization of production to subsidiaries. One is that the economies of large, long-run factories apply, at best, only to staple, standardized products, and even there may run into labor reaction against the assembly line. Another is that production innovations such as digital-control machines have reduced costs of short runs.

Other internal causes have to do with marketing and with increased knowledge about marketing. People want products labeled in their own languages, in sizes and colors that suit their customs. By the time these adaptations are made, it costs no more to label and package locally, and for many products to be produced locally, especially when the costs of maintaining stocks and of transportation are offset against possible production economies. A crucial influence in the formation of subsidiaries has been the discovery of the value and the comparative costs of distribution. Efficient marketing involves keeping a product continuously available, and for much modern equipment, keeping replacement parts and service also available. Involved are not only the manufacturers themselves but also intermediaries such as local wholesalers and retailers. These can reduce costs and prices if they can increase turnover relative to stocks through having prompt and dependable sources of supply from local factories.

EXTERNAL CONDITIONS

The causes of the emergence of the multinational corporation might not have been sufficient to generate its present size and extent without a number of favorable conditions, some external, some internal.

Colgate and Heinz were multinational before World War Two; Otis Elevator, Massey-Ferguson,[10] and Unilever[11] were earlier still.

Two features of the legal environment were primary conditions for multinational operations. One was the allowing by national governments of the rights of domestic "legal persons"—corporations—to such corporations which were in fact foreign-controlled. This "absentee ownership" has already been mentioned in connection with the early emergence of foreign subsidiaries in Canada. It was, however, not so recognized or described. If it had been, the history of foreign subsidiaries might have been different—indeed, brief—in view of the violent resentment and resistance associated with absentee ownership of land in Ireland, from which many of the settlers of Canada had emigrated. Strangely, the right of corporations to dual, in fact multiple, citizenship has gone without serious question even to the time of writing of this paper.

Another legal condition favorable to the development of multinational firms has been reciprocity among nations in the protection of patents and trademarks. This was initiated by the International Convention for the Protection of Industrial Property, a multilateral treaty first negotiated in 1884, and revised and extended several times since. Acceding nations give citizens of other acceding nations the same patent and trademark privileges as they give to their own citizens. Patent rights depend on publications, and are restricted in time, limiting their importance. Trademark rights are, however, renewable without limit. This gives permanent ownership of the name Coca-Cola, for example, to the corporate heir of the American originator in all countries that are members of the Convention. Furthermore, foreign countries have accepted an obligation to maintain a monopoly in their jurisdictions of the use of names such as Coca-Cola as designation of the product or products of the company that has registered the trademark. This goes so far as preventing importation of products given those names by subsidiaries in other countries that have registered them there. A valuable indirect benefit for multinational firms is assistance from national governments in enforcing policies of allocating national markets to local subsidiaries, irrespective of comparative costs of domestic production *versus* imports.

Improvements in international communications and transportation have provided a favorable condition for multinational operations. It was very expensive in terms of executive manpower for the pioneers such as Otis and Unilever to maintain coordination among their overseas subsidiaries. High-ranking officers had to spend months in sea voyages. Air travel made a dramatic difference. Businessmen were passengers from the early days of the Fokker trimotor and the Sunderland flying-boat. They could also send by airmail detailed drawings and specifica-

10. E. P. Neufeld, *A Global Corporation* (Toronto: University of Toronto Press, 1969).
11. Charles H. Wilson, *History of Unilever* (London: Cassell, 1954).

tions for plant, machinery, and processes that could not be telegraphed, and receive detailed reports.

One more favorable external condition was the restoration of international currency convertibility, at generally stable rates, after the dislocations and restrictions of World War Two. Convertibility was allowed by most European countries including Britain commencing in December, 1958. This allowed foreign subsidiaries to make payments to their parents in the parents' currency. Exchange rates that remained fixed for months and even years gave accountants the illusion that they could calculate dollar values of foreign assets, capital appreciation, rate of return on investment, and the like, in addition to dividends, royalties, and other actual receipts.

External financial conditions took a sharp turn when official convertibility of the dollar was abandoned by U.S. Secretary of the Treasury Connally in August, 1971. This was that year's and that Secretary's "save-the-dollar" campaign that had recurred annually since 1961.[12] It did nothing to curtail the largest item in any realistic American payments deficit, which is military spending abroad. But international financial planning has been made more uncertain and further investments may be discouraged. This will not reduce the payments deficit, because in a dynamic analysis, U.S. foreign investments prove to bring back more than they take out.

American companies are, however, not blameless in the 1971 explosion. In fact, short-sighted finance managers in some of the multinational firms may have triggered it, though their part is revealed only by hints dropped in conversation, never for attribution, and cannot become a matter of record because of the anonymity of international financial transactions. These finance men, handling the large cash balances in various currencies that multinational companies maintain for paying bills, had received windfall profits on marks they held when the West German currency was valued upward in 1970. Intoxicated by becoming earners of profits rather than merely custodians, company treasurers speculated heavily in marks in the first half of 1971, converting any other currencies that came into their hot hands. After August they got more of those currencies, including dollars, in exchange for their marks. It was a Pyrrhic profit.

INTERNAL CONDITIONS

The leader of a delegation of senior officials of Japanese government and industry, touring the world in 1972 to study the multinational corporation, remarked at a private meeting with representatives of the U.S. Chamber of Commerce in Washington, D.C. on February 9, "we

12. Howe Martyn, "The 1965 'Save-the-Dollar' Campaign," *Sales/Marketing Today*, April 1965.

lack executives who can operate in multi-ethnic situations." Nevertheless companies springing from Britain, Canada, the Netherlands, Sweden, Switzerland, and above all the United States, have had people who are happy and congenial with other peoples, despite the canard about "the ugly American." They have been a condition of the success of multi-national companies.

Another condition is that shareholders, again most conspicuously in the United States, have looked favorably on expansion abroad. This can be seen reflected in the paragraphs headed at first "International" and more recently "Multinational" in company literature sent to shareholders and financial editors.

An aboslutely necessary internal condition has been the development of systems capable of handling the volume and variety of information involved in operations at a distance. Information has to be transmitted, and also it has to be filtered to avoid choking the recipients with details. Projective budgets are the core of the information and guidance system of many multinational companies. These give the revenue from sales and the expenditures on production, marketing, and administration to which each subsidiary commits itself for a year ahead, and in some companies for several years. Computers have proved helpful for sifting the data coming from many foreign operations at frequent intervals. The computer memory accepts results that are in accord with budgeted promises, but rejects variances, sending them to the company's trouble-shooters.

EFFECTS ON HOST COUNTRIES

There are still very few nation-states that have reached the stage of Canada, in which the manufacturing and the resources-exploitation sectors of the economy are "dominated," statistically, by multinational firms. More than half of the business in those sectors in Canada is done by companies that are under foreign ownership that is sufficient for voting control. But what difference does that make, if the Canadian standard of living continues to rise?

The alarm sounded by J.-J. Servan-Schreiber[13] has been that foreign penetration into national economies has been strongest in the most dynamic sectors, such as electronics. But what difference does that really make, except that nations gain technologically progressive industries?

The discussion of the effects of multinational companies has focused on the host countries. This has been speculative, however, because the data have not been collected for making a factual balance sheet of benefits and costs, even merely economic, much less political and cultural. One of the requirements would be a determination of the amount added to the Gross National Product by the companies entering an economy from abroad. A possible hypothesis is that multinational companies have made

13. J.-J. Servan-Schreiber, trans. Ronald Steel, *The American Challenge* (New York: Atheneum, 1968).

substantial contributions to GNP of host countries by adding know-how, enterprise, and some start-up capital to local resources.

Host countries have been looking, however, for industrial employment—something to occupy their people who are displaced from the land by efficient methods of food production. But modern manufacturing is little more labor-intensive than modern agriculture. In the more developed countries it is only the services sector that is expanding employment. Foreign subsidiaries give better jobs, paying more for higher skills, which they may be able and willing to provide by on-the-job training—but not *more* jobs. The experience with foreign development of natural resources has been particularly disappointing. There is employment in building railways to bring out iron ore and in laying pipelines for oil, but when they are completed, machines do almost everything. The boom towns full of construction workers become ghost towns. It is possible for a country like Canada to have rich natural resources and rapid industrialization, but high unemployment. Its planners, at their wits' end to make jobs and to win votes for the governments employing them, are driven to palliatives such as public housing construction.

Host governments obtain a benefit from foreign subsidiaries in manufacturing and natural resources that increases in importance with governments' social responsibilities. This is tax revenue. Governments have first claim on the incomes of subsidiary companies and of their employees. These have appeared to make additions to net national income in many cases. Furthermore, taxes on such incomes may be less difficult to collect than on some domestic sources. Mining, plantation agriculture, and forest industries also continue to earn foreign currencies, even while mechanization is reducing their attractiveness for employment. These financial reasons explain why host governments do more talking than acting on restricting foreign subsidiaries.

The issue that keeps up the talk about foreign penetration and domination by multinational firms in host countries is not economic or political, but cultural. It is likely to make a considerable difference to countries like Canada that the better jobs, the advertising expenditures, the lawyers' fees, the donations to charities and endowments to universities are largely the gifts of corporations that are foreign-controlled. It was the jeopardy of cultural self-determination that Norman MacKenzie, then president of the University of British Columbia and later a senator of Canada, drew attention to, in making one of the first major criticisms of foreign investment in his country. This is all the more serious when cultural distinctions are subtle, as between Australians or Canadians and Americans. Are multinational firms to be the instruments for homogenizing the varying cultures that had developed or were developing in different parts of the world? This possibility, based on the single-minded pursuit of material benefits by multinational firms, even though for the people of host countries as well as for themselves, arouses deep concern. This will be dispelled only by firms showing sensitivity to "cultural ecology."

EFFECTS ON PARENT COUNTRIES

Even the government of Britain, with a century of experience of the benefits of "invisible exports," has remained indifferent, when not hostile, to British companies operating subsidiaries overseas. The first reaction of the United States government, when it finally became aware in the early 1960s of the existence of American subsidiaries abroad on a large scale, was to blame their assumed "export of capital" for U.S. deficits in foreign payments. The arithmetic, which has been too simple to be believable to some government economists, is that by creating new wealth in foreign markets, subsidiaries are able to bring back more money than they send out, while at the same time adding to the income of host countries. The key is the creativity of the know-how that multinational firms possess and invest. They do this by sending out people who have skills and talents, often with little more cash than their traveling expenses. The subsidiaries of American companies have been highly profitable to the national economy of the United States, as well as to the shareholders of the companies and probably to the host country economies in many cases. A recent definitive answer to the criticism of U.S. balance of payments effects is the analysis by Susan Foster of the New York Federal Reserve Bank. She has calculated that "the net positive balance-of-payments flows cumulated to over $35 billion in the period 1961–1970." [14]

Objection to foreign subsidiaries as exporting jobs was adopted as official policy by the AFL-CIO in 1971. This took form in a proposal for legislation by Congress, known as the Burke-Hartke bill, that would effectively prohibit the establishment or continuation of foreign subsidiaries by American companies. The two basic arguments are (1) that subsidiaries exploit cheaper foreign labor, and (2) they use abroad know-how that should be retained and used exclusively in factories within the United States because the know-how was developed within the American economic, political, and educational system, in considerable part financed by American taxation. Authority could be found by the AFL-CIO economists, if they cared to look, in the writings of Maynard Keynes, no less, who had no high regard for foreign investment, claiming that it deprived Britain, in the period between the two world wars, of investment that was needed at home.[15] The debate on foreign subsidiaries has just begun in the United States. The fears being aroused by emotive terms like "export of jobs" and "runaway plants" will be hard for companies and governments to allay. The American public will

14. *New York Federal Reserve Bank Monthly Review*, July 1972, p. 172.
15. Quoted in R. F. Harrod, *The Life of Maynard Keynes* (London: Macmillan, 1951), p. 347.

have to face the unpalatable truth that it does not have a monopoly of technology, and that other peoples are as determined to industrialize as the Russians and Chinese have proved to be, and may turn to Germany and Japan if the United States prohibits cooperation by its companies.

When the U.S. State Department became aware of the extent, size, and vigor of the network of foreign subsidiaries under the financial control of U.S. companies, it may have been tempted to use parent government power over parent companies to make the subsidiaries instruments of American political policy. Only in a negative way was this ever done publicly, through imposition of the restrictions of the Trading with the Enemy Act. That contributed to estrangement in Canada and France, among others, that has weakened American influence. There has also been suspicion but little evidence that pressure has been brought by the State Department on American companies to establish subsidiaries for the political advantage to the United States. There was the instance of a pharmaceutical firm building an antibiotics plant in India, encouraged by the U.S. government, in an effort to forestall the Russians. But there were also the contrary instances of failure to build a synthetic rubber plant for the government of Rumania and a motor truck plant for Russia, despite State Department approval.

Multinational companies of American origin undoubtedly maintain informational liaison with the State Department, as do British companies with the Foreign Office and French with the Quai d'Orsay. But those who did not realize it already learned, from the Jack Anderson exposure in 1972 of apparent collusion between ITT and American political representatives in Chile, that business must be kept clearly separate from foreign policy.

There remains, however, a long-term, indirect, unplanned political benefit to parent countries from multinational firms. This should receive respect from policy-makers. It is that subsidiaries making visible contributions to host economies win friends, particularly among customers, suppliers, and the people for whom they provide jobs.

EFFECTS ON COMPANIES

The concept of power, even market power, and much more so political power, is foreign to the ideology of modern business management. A strong share of market is pursued, including the market abroad, but the objects are growth of sales and expected accompanying growth of profits. The nearest goal to political power is the side benefit of company prestige. Multinational companies have not seen themselves as creating a new world economic order. They have not set out to convert people to materialism and to subvert other values, or to undermine political nationalism. As for combining to form a bloc of economic power to apply on political issues, they have not even been able to present a united front in the United States against the threat to their existence being made by the AFL-CIO. If they are barbarians who destroy the political nation-state civilization, it is by accident.

An early and essential lesson for managers in multinational companies is that the value systems of many societies embrace more than acquisition of material goods. This is a lesson that can also be helpful in understanding changes and extensions that are appearing in the values of Americans at home. A restriction on values that multinational firms and their managers are being led to question is chauvinistic nationalism. But they are not about to overthrow the nation-state system. Indeed they are partners in it through the subsidiaries they have organized and the trademark protection and other privileges they receive from national governments. There may, however, be effects from the emergence of numerous rich corporations and influential executives with interests in and loyalties to not merely one, but a number of different countries. These may be long-term effects but their tendency will surely be to support peaceful and friendly international relations.

II

FUNCTIONAL DIMENSIONS

c h a p t e r   t h r e e

The multinational corporation
and the American political process

F. PATRICK BUTLER

HR-62

IN THE HOUSE OF REPRESENTATIVES

January 3, 1973

Mr. Burke of Massachusetts introduced the following bill, which was referred to the Committee on Ways and Means:

A BILL

To amend the tariff and trade laws of the United States to promote full employment and restore a diversified production base; to amend the Internal Revenue Code of 1954 to stem the outflow of United States capital, jobs, technology, and production and for other purposes.

Be it enacted by the Senate and House of Representatives of the United States of America in Congress assembled.

That this Act may be cited as the "Foreign Trade and Investment Act of 1973."

In order to try to understand the relationship of political interactions to the MNC and vice versa, one must determine the main actors in the scenario. There are four major actors: (1) the multinational corporation, (2) organized labor, (3) Congress, and (4) the Administration, each interacting as a consequence of its interest, authority, ability, and power. In respect to the interactions of these four actors, the environmental characteristics depicting the domestic and international economic situation must be added as the catalyst which has brought this subject to the headlines.[1]

For the purpose of this essay, HR-62 was chosen, because of its rele-

---

1. One resource that is particularly enlightening in this respect is Peter G. Peterson's *The United States in a Changing World Economy*, Vols. I & II (Washington, D.C.: Council on International Economic Policy, 1971).

vance and publicity, as the sample that best portrays the countervailing forces pressuring to enact or defeat bills of such an international character authored in the name of the "general welfare of the United States." HR-62 is not the only piece of legislation recently being considered on Capitol Hill in respect to the changes in foreign trade and investment,[2] nor is the U.S. government the only organization[3] deeply concerned with the investigation of this subject. It should also be understood that of the many bills recently before the Congress, relatively few have such a distinctive relation to the multinational corporate character.

THE MULTINATIONAL CORPORATION

> This [Burke-Hartke] is a legislative attempt to turn back the clock of history and is the old protectionist threat in a new form. . . . The motivation [of MNCs] is not to find low-cost labor in the advanced countries. Rather it has been a quest for market participation in areas which would otherwise be closed to exports. (*MNC Executive.*)

The current status of the MNC seems to be one of considerable wealth and power creating the outlines of a genuine global economy. By 1975 nearly 35% of the Western world's non-U.S. production will be accounted for by American subsidiaries or American-associated firms. (Since the end of World War II, American firms have established over 8000 directly owned subsidiaries abroad.)[4] In terms of individual size, the 1971 sales of General Motors, more than $28 billion, exceeded the Gross National Product in 130 countries.[5]

Before discussing the MNC in terms of its impact on legislation, a short summary of the international investment environment, the status

2. For example, the Dent Bill (HR-7130), submitted in the 92nd Congress. Not as well-publized as Burke-Hartke, the Dent Bill would increase minimum wage and its Title III would bar U.S. government contracts to foreign corporations which pay less than the U.S. minimum. Also Senate hearings, under the chairmanship of Senator Church, delving into the ITT-Chilean affair, were underway in March 1973; and Senator Ribicoff's Finance Committee survey of multinationals portrayed in the Tariff Commission Report.

3. A number of international organizations are conducting studies in this area, a current example being the International Labor Orgaization's working paper on "The Relationship Between Multinational Corporations and Social Policy," prepared for the ILO Meeting in Geneva 26 October to 4 November 1972. The Canadian government is also looking for ways to regulate foreign investment. Alistair Gillespie, Minister of Trade, Industry and Commerce, introduced a bill in Parliament that would require screening of new investment by foreigners as well as foreign bids to take over existing Canadian companies.

"Foreign interests, 80% of which are American, own or control 58% of Canada's manufacturing, 65% of its mining, and 74% of its petroleum industry," "Canada May Control U.S. Investment," *The Washington Post*, January 26, 1973, p. A21.

4. Charles Levinson, *Capital, Inflation and the Multinationals* (London: George Allen and Unwin Ltd., 1971), p. 71.

5. Ralph C. Deans, "Multinational Companies," *Editorial Research Reports*, II. No. 1 (July 5, 1972), 501.

of U.S. activities in that environment, and the motivations for international investment will be delineated. The summaries are not intended to be exhaustive—they should only establish an unbiased frame of reference.

ENVIRONMENT

What are the environmental factors that directly affect the motives for U.S. international investment and function as the dynamic nature of the international investment scene? Domestically, such considerations as corporate taxation, antitrust measures, security and exchange regulations, recent and soon-to-become-law pollution abatement measures, labor costs, interest, transportation, demography, and a variety of other factors make up the scenario in which decisions for investment are determined. Internationally, not only the market structure must be defined but also understanding of political alliances such as the European Common Market and the Andean Common Market is necessary. The existence of exchange rate disequilibria, foreign investment incentives, the international capital market, trade barriers, rapid growth of new markets, and the internationalization of technology must also be taken into consideration.

STATUS

In order to portray, statistically, the relative position of American-based MNCs, the following data in summary form, taken from the Department of Commerce's "The Multinational Corporation," Volume I, March 1972, is cited below:

> In 1969, total U.S. international investments *and assets* stood at $167 billion compared to $54 billion in 1950. [Italics added]
>
> In 1970, in terms of location, about ⅓ ($23 billion) of U.S. long-term investment was in Canada, ⅓ ($25 billion) in Europe, ¼ ($20 billion) in Latin America, the Middle East and Africa and under ⅙ ($11 billion) in the rest of the world.
>
> Classified by industry, 41% of U.S. direct investments in 1970 were in manufacturing ($32 billion), 28% ($22 billion) in petroleum, 8% ($6 billion) in mining and smelting, and 23% ($18 billion) in trade, services and other categories.
>
> The yield on U.S. direct investment has declined steadily since 1950, from a high of 19% in 1951 to 12% in 1970.
>
> Foreign investments in the U.S. in 1970 were $97.5 billion, growing at about the rate of 9% a year between 1950 and 1970.
>
> The net investment position of the United States rose from $36.7 billion in 1950 to $69.1 billion in 1970, the largest single factor accounting for this dramatic increase being direct investments which are explained to a large extent by the foreign operations of multinational corporations.

MOTIVATIONS

According to the Department of Commerce study, if one were to inquire into the motives for international investment by MNCs, the following list might be typical:

- A need to get behind tariff walls to safeguard a company's export markets.
- Greater efficiency and responsiveness by producing in the local market as compared with exporting to it.
- The possibility to lower production costs, which makes it cheaper to produce components abroad.
- The fear that competitors going abroad may capture a lucrative foreign market or may, by acquiring foreign sources of supply, threaten the domestic market position of the company.
- A need to diversify product lines to avoid fluctuations in earnings.
- A desire to assist licensees abroad who may need capital to expand operations.
- A desire to avoid home country regulations, e.g., antitrust laws in the United States.
- Fundamentally the motivation is one of a quest for profits and a fear of domestic or foreign markets lost to competition.

(*Note:* a somewhat more aggressive presentation of these or similar motives is given in the National Association of Manufacturers (NAM) publication, *U.S. Stake in World Trade and Investment: The Role of the Multinational Corporation,* which was developed as the antagonist position to the proposed Foreign Trade and Investment Act of 1972.)

The MNCs in the U.S. outweigh organized labor when it comes to protecting their own programs in Washington. Despite the fact that the labor movement can fall in behind the AFL-CIO as the central rallying point for promoting its special interests, for which management has no counterpart, it cannot muster the money, pressure, and finesse that comes naturally to the large corporations which (in fact) are certainly not talking to the members of the labor class when they are talking to Congress.[6]

The MNC's cause has been taken up by the National Chamber of Commerce and the NAM as part of each's constituency, but a specific organization, the Emergency Committee for American Trade (ECAT), has recently been initiated solely for the purpose of defeating the Burke-Hartke bill. The ECAT is chaired by Don Kendall, a long-time friend of President Nixon. According to the Government Research Corporation, ECAT, whose membership consists of 55 of the largest U.S. multi-

---

6. The average American is not the average congressman. Representation is not equitable for blacks, other ethnic groups, women, or blue-collar workers. Most congressmen come from the professions that serve business organizations or from business itself.

national corporations, along with NAM and the Chamber of Commerce, have all made their positions known on Capitol Hill. "Having concentrated their initial efforts on Congress and the administration, industry spokesmen are now working hard to educate their employees, stockholders and consumers to the dangers of Burke-Hartke." [7]

It does not seem possible at this particular point to determine the sole stand of the MNCs in reference to the Burke-Hartke bill but the NAM study cited above believes the implications of the bill would be to politicize international investment decisions of the private sector, to reduce remittances of foreign earnings to the U.S., to increase the price of domestic programs, to increase rather than reduce unemployment, and to further the process of socializing U.S. business and industry by inserting government controls over private investment.

LABOR

Organized labor represents a constituency (approximately 20 percent of the labor class) who sees its interests jeopardized by the "runaway corporations," which, according to George Meany, President of the AFL-CIO, live outside the reach of U.S. law or the laws of any single nation. Fundamentally the labor position on international trade and investment is that the economic problems of the United States, particularly in the realm of unemployment and a declining trade balance, can be solved only by what some would consider to be protectionist trade policies.

A member of the AFL-CIO Research Department, in a personal interview, voiced the opinion that the Burke-Hartke bill was not constructed as a bludgeon to beat the MNC to death (submission would be more like it), but rather to bring attention to all the trade and investment policies that had been initiated as part of the post–World War Two reconstruction which have now outlived their purpose.[8] In other words, our priorities must change from those held just a decade ago when a strong economy in Europe and Japan meant stability in the world status quo. The fear now centers less on the Soviet SS-9 than in Japanese

7. Kendall was quoted in a July 1972 committee newsletter account of its study of MNCs, in *Congressional Quarterly*, Vol. XXX, No. 48 (November 25, 1972). "We have firmly established the attack on the multinational is a case of mistaken identity. These companies don't export jobs. . . . The public must realize that the earnings of overseas operations would be severely diminished—even lost—if measures like the Burke-Hartke bill were enacted and that nothing would take the place of those earnings."

8. According to a Chamber of Commerce Report, *United States Multinational Enterprise 1960–1970* ("This Report is a response to attacks being made against U.S. international investment and its main agent, the multinational enterprise"), there are three main charges that form the centerpiece of organized labor's attack against the U.S. multinational corporation: (1) foreign direct investments result in the "export of jobs"; (2) American plants abroad generate increased U.S. imports while discouraging exports; (3) corporate rationale for operating abroad is to take advantage of cheap foreign labor and to ship the related production back to the U.S.-based parent company.

television, German automobiles, and Swiss chocolate. The items themselves, of course, are no threat; how and who produces them is.

According to the AFL-CIO Executive Council Report, Resolution No. 126, there is a critical need for the United States to adopt new international trade and investment policies to meet today's international realities. "To assure these goals, new U.S. legislative, administrative and negotiating policies should be established to prevent further displacement of U.S. production, market disruption, the export of American jobs and erosion of the tax-base of the federal government, the states and local communities." And finally, "The AFL-CIO urges recognition that multinational firms juggle their production, employment, bookkeeping, prices and taxes, from one country to another, to meet corporate needs," implying that this juggling supports only corporate interests and works to the ultimate disadvantage of the United States.

In 1971, the AFL-CIO Executive Council adopted those considerations cited above into a nine-point slate which ultimately served as the progenitor of the Burke-Hartke bill. HR-62 is therefore the embodiment of organized labor's position.

What does the bill provide? [9]

> *Title I* revises the Internal Revenue Code in a number of ways, each designed to discourage American companies from establishing subsidiary corporations abroad. American firms would no longer receive tax credit for payment of foreign income taxes. Income earned by the foreign facilities of U.S. firms would no longer escape capital gains taxes. Income derived from the transfer of patents and licenses would be taxed. The special tax exemption that now benefits U.S. employees who spend 17 out of 18 months abroad would be repealed.
>
> *Title II* establishes the United States Foreign Trade and Investment Commission. There would be three commissioners: one representing labor, one industry, and one the public. Supplanting the present six-member Tariff Commission, the new commission would administer import quotas, the Anti-Dumping Act, the countervailing duty statute, and the adjustment assistance program.
>
> *Title III* provides for quotas on virtually all imports. Section 301 provides that 1972 quota levels for each category shall not exceed the 1965 to 1969 average. For subsequent years a permissible amount would be the 1972 level, increased or decreased by the amount the commission estimates is necessary for imports to maintain the same market share as they had in 1972.
>
> *Title IV* gives the new Foreign Trade Commission the authority to decide whether an excess of goods is being sold ("dumped") in this country at unfair value, causing injury to domestic industries. Workers, as well as firms, could file complaints with the commission on behalf of a domestic industry. At present, the Tariff Commission decides whether or not a domestic in-

9. "The Politics of Foreign Trade, Tax and Investment Policy," *The Government Research Company*, June 1972, pp. 2–3.

dustry is suffering unfair competition from imported goods, and then the Treasury Department determines whether or not the articles are being sold at less than fair value.

Title V stipulates that petitions for relief from an influx of imported goods ("escape clause relief") be presented to the new Trade Commission; if the increased imports "contribute substantially" to reducing domestic sales, unemployment, or underemployment, the petitioner would have a legitimate claim to relief. To also provide for trade adjustment assistance.

Title VI gives the president the authority to prevent a direct or indirect transfer of capital to any foreign country "when . . . the transfer would result in a net decrease in employment in the United States." The president could also prohibit the use of licensing of any U.S. patent abroad.

Title VII requires that all goods sold here be labeled to disclose their country of origin; small component parts must be labeled (as) also (well). American materials or components that are assembled or processed abroad would be taxed at full value (not simply on the value added abroad).

With the introduction of the Burke-Hartke bill, the stage was set for a debate of considerable significance among influential pressure groups in deciding the future of a new phase of U.S. trade and investment policies and subsequent repercussions in global economics.[10]

CONGRESS

Although no hearings were held in 1972, the 93rd Congress has at least three forums for addressing problems posed by multinational corporations: HR-62 and S-151 (the Hartke version companion bill), plus a Foreign Relations Committee investigation called to investigate the ITT-Chilean affair and a Senate Finance Committee investigation chaired by Senator Ribicoff.

Despite considerable attention to the multinational corporation and the Burke-Hartke bill, as of this writing there are still no hearings scheduled on HR-62 in the Ways and Means Committee.[11] Oftentimes,

10. "Backed by task force teams in 25 city and industrial areas, 'wide-spread grass roots support,' the 'declared intent of fellow congressmen and senators, to join with us' and in an effort to 'reverse next year the record whopping' $6 billion 1972 U.S. foreign trade deficit, the Foreign Trade and Investment Act of 1973 was introduced in both houses of the 93rd Congress by Senator Vance Hartke (D-Ind.), and Congressman James A. Burke (D-Mass.)." Vance Hartke, USS, news release, "Hartke-Burke Foreign Trade Bills," January 5, 1973, Washington, D.C.

11. Wilbur Mills has been Chairman of the House Ways and Means Committee since 1958, when he abolished all subcommittees, thereby concentrating power in his own hands, controlling information and appointments of junior committeemen on all legislation. Mills, a congressman for the last thirty-three years, holds the key to special tax breaks and import restrictions of considerable importance to businessmen.

According to Mark J. Green et al., *Who Runs Congress?* p. 72, "Loopholes in the tax laws which Mills' committee administers, for example, permitted . . . Gulf Oil . . . only 1.2 percent tax on its $990 million. . . . In 1971, Mills' committee quietly buried numerous tax reform proposals and instead had measures passed to re-distribute income *to* corporations: the Revenue Act of 1971, which cut federal income taxes by

however, separate pieces of the bill can be worked on individually and incorporated in another bill or redrafted as a "new" bill under committee sponsorship. This may be done in terms of the chairman's legislative priorities (as Mills' aides suggest) because of time constraints, need, or simply lobbying pressure. At the same time, the Administration can be expected to be developing its own trade bill reflecting administration priorities.

These considerations have been accounted for by the sponsors of the bill, and in the case of Hartke's sponsorship the bill was divided up and separately introduced under eight different legislative packages incorporating all of the proposals included under the original seven titles.

Recent action by Ways and Means on tax reform has in fact included consideration of HR-62's Title I specifically relating to foreign taxation.[12] However, at this time Title I, perhaps the most important element of the bill vis-à-vis the MNCs, is the only section of the Trade and Investment Act of 1973 presently under consideration by Congress.

The Burke-Hartke bill has polarized some members of Congress into labor or business factions, but statements of design are ambiguous and steadfast positions to be taken by any member of Congress cannot easily be found.[13] The nature of this ambiguity is partially based on the desire not to offend various constituencies, but also on inconclusive data, which is probably best exemplified by the conflicting claims put forth by determined interest groups on, for example, the "export of jobs."

THE ADMINISTRATION

The Administration's attitude toward the Burke-Hartke bill is inextricably bound up with its own legislative attempts to meet the

$9 billion annually, with over $75 billion of that cut going to corporations, a $70 million tax cut for banks, sponsored by Chairman Mills himself, and numerous other, similarly inclined bills."

12. "Compilation of Press Releases Announcing Panel Discussions and Public Hearing and Releasing Names of Panelists to Appear before the Committee on Ways and Means on Tax Reform Beginning on February 5, 1973," *Committee Print, Committee on Ways and Means*, 93rd Congress, 1st Session, GPO, Washington, D.C. 1973, p. 4. This announcement states that panel discussions utilizing expert witnesses would cover such items as taxation of foreign income. "XIII. Taxation of Foreign Income—This includes but is not limited to consideration of foreign tax credit, the deferral of income of controlled foreign subsidiaries, the tax treatment of Western Hemisphere Trade Corporations, whether the present exclusion of 'gross-up' on dividends of less developed country corporations should be continued, tax exemptions of ships under foreign flags, DISC corporations, the exclusion of income earned in U.S. possessions and the exemption for income earned abroad by U.S. citizens."

13. Even Senator Hartke is seeking ways to ameliorate the total impact of the bill. "Well, flat out . . . I think Hartke-Burke in certain features may very well be better served without confrontation." From "Away from Confrontation, the Road to Hartke-Burke," speech by Vance Hartke, USS, before the Board of Governors, Phoenix, Arizona, January 26, 1973.

overall problem of an unquantifiable economy that, like a rudderless ship, seems at times to drift incomprehensibly between recession and inflation, the modern-day Scylla and Charybdis. This particular problem has haunted the few Republican administrations of this century and most particularly President Nixon.[14] The Administration must react to the legislative positions of the Burke-Hartke bill in terms of the overall U.S. economy.

The AFL-CIO's assertion that the policies of U.S.-based firms and banks are designed solely to profit the corporations and are made with disregard for the needs of the United States, its economy, and its people is met with the Administration's admonition that the presumption (of proposals such as the Burke-Hartke bill) is that these corporations are adversely affecting our export position when, in fact, the data gathered by government sources suggests that some of those fears are certainly exaggerated; also, that it is quite possible that they have stimulated exports rather than reduced them.[15]

In what might be best described as a preliminary position, the Administration looks at the MNCs as posing both new challenges and new opportunities. New policies are needed to insure that "the full potential inherent in this phenomena for improving the utilization of the world's and our nation's resources is realized, and that problems that can arise in international investment are dealt with fairly and effectively. These policies will be concerned with, among other things, investment controls, taxation, extraterritoriality, expropriation and treatment of investors, effects on employment, and the promotion of foreign investment in the United States." [16]

CONCLUSION

The evolution of the multinational corporation portends a change in our society which could be, within decades, radical (and at this point in time, unpredictable).

The multinational corporation bears no resemblance to the proprietor-owned and managed organization of over a century ago at the

14. "Attempting a reduction in the rate of inflation from 1953 through 1960, President Eisenhower's economic policy induced three recessions, with disastrous consequences for the Republican Party: (1) the Democratic landslide in 1958 establishing huge Democratic majorities (persisting to this day), (2) the election of a Democratic President, (3) reinforcement in the voter's mind of the Republican image—formed in the days of Hoover—as the 'party of bad times.' Now, eight years later, blessed with not a fraction of Eisenhower's unlimited popularity, Nixon would have to take far more unpopular actions to fight a worse inflation." R. Evans and R. Novak, *Nixon in the White House* (New York: Random House, Inc., 1971), p. 178.

15. Secretary Peter G. Peterson, in a 1971 press briefing by the President's Council on International Economic Policy (Peterson was then assistant to the president for international economic affairs; he has since been replaced by Peter Flanigan).

16. Peter G. Peterson, *The United States in the Changing World Economy,* Vol. 1: *A Foreign Economic Perspective,* December 27, 1971, Washington, D.C.

time of the Industrial Revolution. The rapid growth of the corporation has developed an institutional mutation in the form of the multinational corporation, which differs in structure, function, and management from its progenitor. Its structure presupposes a centrally coordinated global network of financial specialists, research laboratories, manufacturing plants (or service industries), marketing and sales divisions— all contributing to the appropriate division of labor, despite their nationality. Functionally, the multinational corporation employs an international allocation of global resources which operate in respect to profit maximization and efficiency despite national bias, and objections. The personnel of the multinational corporation are maturing into an international management elite which serves the organization not only in terms of personal identification with corporate objectives (and commensurate pecuniary interest) but also with an expanded Schumanesque approach to world unity through economic cooperation and integration. None of these conditions exist under the definition of a purely national corporation today.

Through the multinational corporation the economic imperative has sublimated the political imperative in subtle fashion by fostering an increase in the standard of living, not by nationalism but by consumerism. In its intrinsic urge to grow and profit while extrinsically serving the public need, a great share of which it helped to create, the multinational corporation has sometimes sought to involve, usurp, constrain, or subvert the political process to its own imagined greater ends. The U.S. government as the biggest customer has become deeply involved in this metamorphosis.

The role of the multinational corporation, as an institution of comparatively recent origin, is becoming so heavily integrated into the political system as to blur the boundaries between public and private organizations, particularly in the extent to which MNCs serve and are responsible to the public.

The MNC in the United States has become a global inhabitant which has supported its objectives with business ethics that sanctify international consciousness, continuous growth, the maximization of profits, and the creation of the "organization man" as a modus operandi which is sometimes confused and taken to be commensurate with the "general welfare of the United States." This type of philosophy has perhaps contributed significantly to the loss of public confidence in both business and government—for the faults of one are often closely allied to the foibles of the other, undermining the institutions, both public and private, traditionally endowed with public trust.

The MNCs have unquestionably opened new vistas of international integration and cooperation yet to be explored; however, the principles within which the capitalistic venture has been so successful now stand drained of meaning as the rape of earth's resources explodes on the world, with its pollution, social alienation through corporate monopolies, and technical destruction by instruments of war or automated waste. In order to further corporate goals of growth and international expansion, a liaison was long ago established with the government which, despite its necessity, has often corrupted both participants and process of the constitutional system. Public representatives are tempted (too often successfully) with paid vacations, credits, contributions, investments, and other largesse to enable a corporation to make a special presentation or to buy a biased vote for special legislation. Administration posts of considerable bureaucratic power are open to successful businessmen with excellent management and appropriate campaign credentials (the Dulles brothers, for example—one was Secretary of State and the other the director of the CIA; both were stockowners and top management personnel, Allen being president of the United Fruit Company). Major corporations are represented on government policy advisory boards such as the National Industrial Pollution Control Council, the National Export Expansion Council, or the Business-Government Relations Council, in order to officially present private business recommendations to government officials. Unfortunately, this occurs without representation by any other sectors of society.

The MNC contributes to both the cause and effect of the accelerated growth and changes within the USA and the world community. Certainly, the expansion of trade and investment of the MNCs adds significantly to a greater understanding and commonality among nations through communication and cultural awareness, but as so often seen before, means do not justify ends. The principles of corporate and managerial imperatives must be subsumed to those of constitutional democracy and human dignity. MNCs influence legislation by pressuring those individuals whose responsibility it is to seek and maintain laws that through Congress reflect and serve the general interest of the people of the USA, as defined by the Constitution. The maxim of business self-interest will not serve as the basis for distorting the constitutional process. Each indiscretion on the part of an MNC in favor of corporate growth adds, like individual grains of sand, to a heavy burden of weight on the public confidence. The MNCs may have the potential for helping to establish peace in the world, but they cannot do so by distorting the political process that allows them to exist.

The multinational corporation and the exercise of power: Latin America

RONALD MÜLLER

Five years of investigating the role of multinational corporations in less developed countries has led me to conclude that the MNC is one of the most powerful impediments to Third World development that was operating in the international economic arena during the period 1950–1970. To evaluate this, I have accepted the following normative meaning of justice; that no one may enrich himself at the expense of another. I base my assertion on the responsibility that can be attributed to the MNCs in bringing about two basic and familiar facts: the first is that on a global basis 60% or more of the world's total population is becoming relatively, if not absolutely, poorer compared to 30% or less of the world's population, which is becoming relatively richer; the second is that inside the individual nations of the Third World, particularly those in Latin America, we again find that 60% or more of these populations are becoming relatively poorer compared to the small strata of rich in each of these countries. More specifically, in nations such as Mexico and Brazil where multinationals have invested heaviest, there is compelling evidence that anywhere up to 40% of the population have actually experienced a *decrease* in their absolute level of consumption in the past ten to twenty years.

This paper is divided into two interrelated parts. First, it will entail a discussion of the basis of power which MNCs have been able to establish in Latin American societies, specifically relative to the institutions of government, organized labor, and the domestic business sector of these nations; second, an explication will be made of how the MNC uses this power in terms of its economic behavior and its impacts on these countries.

MULTINATIONAL CORPORATIONS: FACES OF POWER IN LATIN AMERICA

The basic goal of the managerial policies that direct MNC behavior is to maximize *worldwide* profits. This may mean operating individual subsidiaries at an "officially reported" loss or a subsidiary in such a way that officially reported profits are minimized. In such cases the operations of the subsidiary need not increase the welfare of the nation in which it is located. To accomplish the worldwide maximization of profits, MNCs utilize an international market strategy, the basic thrust of which is to maintain or increase their share of the market (vis-à-vis local and foreign competitors) in each of the countries where they operate. The means by which this strategy is implemented are relatively simple to understand and can be easily gleaned from the business and economic literature on MNCs. The first method is to control the technology in the industries in which they operate, and the second is to control the financial capital by which investment and thus expansion in the industry takes place. It is thus the control of technology and financing that must be analysed if we are to understand the basis of the power which MNCs hold in Latin American economies.

UNDERDEVELOPMENT: THE INSTITUTIONAL SETTING

Third World countries are called "less developed" for some very specific reasons. In an institutional context, "less developed" means a lack of adequately trained governmental civil servants to examine and investigate whether or not commercial and business laws are being enforced. It also means that these very laws are antiquated, designed for times past and for too long remaining unrevised to take cognizance of the major changes in the origins of economic power. (For example, laws governing patents and taxes are frequently found to be outdated in LDC.) Finally, in most LDCs where organized labor is either weak or largely absent, "less developed" may mean the absence of an important countervailing force or check to the power of corporations.

Thus, a basic part of the meaning of underdevelopment is a set of institutions which are either lacking or misfunctioning relative to similar institutions in industrialized societies. For those of us accustomed to life in the "developed" world, we cannot emphasize enough the need for a fundamental understanding of this basic aspect of underdevelopment when analyzing the impact of MNCs on Third World economies. Whether we look at legal institutions, those of organized labor, or those of financing, we shall find that the "bargaining power" of the MNC to maximize profits is far greater than in rich countries because of this absence or weakness of institutional mechanisms to control the behavior of subsidiaries in poor countries. Stated in Galbraithian terms, Third World countries are characterized by an absence of the "countervailing" power of government and of organized labor (and, as we shall see, of domestic business as well), for setting limits on the power of the modern international corporation.

UNDERDEVELOPMENT: THE STRUCTURE OF TECHNOLOGY

Fortunately or unfortunately, most Third World countries have already set in motion a process of industrialization highly similar to that found in the advanced capitalist nations of the West. This industrialization is similar not only in terms of the output of industry (capital goods and private consumption goods) but also in terms of the mechanical technology and human technical skills needed for its implementation. In other words, the voluntary or involuntary institutionalization of Western consumption values as the goal of economic growth has, in turn, brought about the need for a technology that can satisfy this pattern of consumption.

Given this need, what are the sources of this technology? LDCs are virtually entirely dependent upon foreign sources for their technology—more specifically, upon the advanced nations of North America, Western Europe, and Japan.

But foreign versus local control of technology does not indicate the actual concentration of control in the hands of a very small number of large corporations. For example, in the U.S., of the 500 largest industrial corporations, the top 30 own 40.7% of the patents in their respective industries.[1] The mirror image of this concentration of technology control in the advanced nations is found to even a greater extent in the underdeveloped areas. Thus in Colombia, for instance, in the pharmaceutical, synthetic fiber, and chemical industries 10% of all patent-holders own 60% of all patents, and these 10% are all foreign MNCs.[2]

The impact of such concentrated control of technology can be found in any standard introductory economics textbook. Concentrated control of technology is one of the most effective means to establish oligopoly power over the marketplace, restricting the development of local competition and permitting an astounding rate of profits, the greater majority of which leaves the country. What must be emphasized here is that once such a process is underway, it becomes cumulative and self-perpetuating. In almost all LDCs studied to date MNCs, through their patent-holdings, control about 99% of in-place industrial technology. (See the work by Müller cited in Footnote 2.)

UNDERDEVELOPMENT: THE STRUCTURE OF FINANCE

There is a twofold dilemma in the financial structure of LDCs. On the one hand, there is a growing gap between the supply of *available* local savings and the demand for investment funds to alleviate the growing poverty. On the other hand, the particular technology which the industrialization process necessitates is not only expensive, but must be paid for in foreign, not local, exchange.

1. Scherer in John M. Blair, *Economic Concentration: Structure, Behavior and Public Policy* (New York: Harcourt Brace Jovanovich, Inc., 1972).

2. Constantine V. Vaitsos, *Patents Revised: Their Function in Developing Countries* to be published in *The Journal of Development Studies*, 1973. A complete statistical review of MNCs technology control is found in Ronald Müller, "The Multinational Corporation and the Underdevelopment of the Third World," in C. K. Wilber, ed., *The Political Economy of Development and Underdevelopment* (New York: Random House, Inc., 1973).

The result of this dilemma, from the viewpoint of domestic enterprises, is a perverse form of noncompetitive financing patterns in most LDCs. Contrary to accepted notions about multinational companies in poor countries, these firms do not bring their own finance capital from abroad —the overwhelming majority is derived from local, host country sources. What is important for the present discussion is the impact on domestic enterprises. Namely, the subsidiaries of MNCs in LDCs borrow from local financial institutions with the credit rating and financial resource back-up of the entire global network of the parent MNC of which they are a part. This is in contrast to the credit rating and financial resource back-up of the very small typical local business enterprise when it attempts to obtain finance capital. The vicious circle begins to close. The local financial institution, faced with limited loan capital relative to its demand, and like any other business interested in risk-minimization, will inevitably show a lending pattern biased toward the subsidiaries of MNCs.

This conclusion is even more obvious when the local financial institution is, in fact, a branch or subsidiary of a so-called private multinational bank such as Bank of America, First National City Bank of New York, etc. These banks are playing a powerful role in the financial structures of the Third World where in many instances they control close to 50% of the private deposits of a country.[3] The LDC operation of a multinational bank will prefer lending to the subsidiaries of MNCs for the same reasons as locally controlled financial institutions. But in addition and more essential is that in such a lending operation there is more at stake than just the particular profitability of one or a series of loans in a single country.

There is first the well-established fact that the worldwide parent networks of, respectively, banks and corporations are not two distinct entities, separated by a competitive market in which one is a seller and the other a buyer. Instead there are interlocking interests of common ownership, management, and technical personnel in the groups that control banks and corporations.[4] Furthermore, whatever the consequences of these interlocking interests may be, there is a second well-established fact of a near-perfect correlation between the worldwide expansion of MNCs and the commensurate expansion by multinational banks. Whether the banks or the corporations led in this expansion is not the point. The point is a mutual process of interdependent expansion charactertized by common familiarity, experience, and objectives.

The relatively greater bargaining power of MNCs in finance has, over

3. Miguel Wionczek, Novena Reunion de Technicos de los Bancos Centrales del Continente Americano (La Banca Extranjera en America Latina: Lima, 17–22 de Noviembre de 1969); Aldo Ferrer, "El Capital Extranjero en la Economica Argentina," *Trimestre, Economico,* No. 150, Abril–Junio, 1971; Aldo Ferrer, "Empresa Extranjera: Observaciones sobre la Experiencia Argentina," Seminar on *Politica de Inversiones Extranjeras y Transferencia de Technologia en America Latina,* organized by ILDIS/Flacso, Santiago, 1971.

4. Blair, op. cit. pp. 75 ff.

time, the same consequences as it does in technology. It becomes the equivalent, as noted above, of what the economist calls oligopoly power, meaning the power to erect "barriers to entry" against potential new competition or, on the other side of the same coin, to eliminate existing competition, usually by absorbing or buying into local firms.[5]

STRUCTURAL IMPACTS OF MNCS: CONCENTRATION AND POWER

Our analysis of the economic structure of LDCs, with reference to technology and finance, has shown why MNCs have a high and ever-growing degree of oligopoly power in contrast to national firms in LDCs. Just how great this power is can be determined from the empirical reality of societies in underdevelopment. A focus on pre-1970 Chile will reflect this reality for almost all LDCs in which MNCs operate.[6] In the industrial sector between 1967 and 1969, foreign participation (in terms of assets owned) increased from 16.6 to 20.3%, while domestic participation diminished from 76.1 to 63.0%, the difference between the two being made up of state-owned firms. Of the 100 largest industrial firms (on the basis of asset size) in the country, 40 were effectively controlled by MNCs; when the sample was expanded to the largest 160 firms, over 51% were under the control of MNCs. Even these figures do not accurately convey the degree of power involved. When we look at control by industry, we see that in 7 of the more important industries in Chile, 1 to 3 foreign firms controlled not less than 51% of production in each industry. In a behavioral analysis of 22 of the largest MNC operations in the country, 5 of the MNC subsidiaries were monopolists in their respective industrial markets, 6 were duopolists, and 8 were oligopolists, with each of these 8 being the largest supplier in its market. For 18 of these subsidiaries for which rate of growth in sales data were available, 16 showed a growth rate much higher than the average for the industrial sector as a whole. These figures reflect not only the reality of Chile prior to 1970, but are representative of most LDCs where MNCs are currently operating. Taken together, these concentration indicators demonstrate the degree of oligopoly power of MNCs in the Third World as well as their ability to increase that power over time.

5. This is further explained in Müller, "The Multinational Corporation and the Underdevelopment of the Third World."

6. The figures for Chile are taken from Luis Pacheco, "La Inversion Extranjera y las Corporaciones Internacionales en el Desarrollo Industrial Chileno," in *Proceso a la Industrialization Chilena* (Santiago: Ediciones Nueva Universidad, Universidad Catolica de Chile, 1972) and from Corporacion de Fomento de la Produccion (CORFO), *Las Inversiones Extranjeras en la Industria Chilena Periodo 1960–69*, Publicacion 57 a/71, Febrero, 1971.

For an analysis of Mexico see Ricardo Cinta, "Burguesia Nacional y Desarrollo," in *El Perfil en 1980*, III (Mexico: Siglo Veintiuno, 1972) pp. 165–209.

For an analysis of Argentina cf. Ferrer, op. cit. 1971. For Brazil and other LDCs, see Barnet and Müller, *Global Reach*, chaps. 6 and 7.

If the nonbusiness institutions of government and organized labor cannot act as a sufficient check on the power of the MNC in a Third World country, there still remains the check of other business institutions, namely domestic competition. But the nature of the economic structure of underdevelopment, exemplified in the technological and financial spheres, makes it highly unlikely that domestic business institutions will be able to perform this function. Given this industrialization process and the nature of the technological and financial needs to implement it, the result is a diminution in the power of domestic enterprises to compete and a further augmentation in the oligopoly power of MNCs.

Having presented a rationale and evidence for the manner in which MNCs achieve their powerful positions in the economies of LDCs, what follows is an analysis of how that power reflects itself in their day-to-day operations and of the resulting impacts upon the people of these countries.

HOW MNCs USE THEIR POWER

THE IMPACT ON THE PEOPLE OF THIRD WORLD NATIONS

The Council of Americas is a lobbying organization sponsored by the largest U.S.-based multinational corporations that have operations in Latin America. In the literature produced by the Council of Americas, which is quite representative of other sources of pro-MNC studies, a number of claims are made as to the contributions which MNCs bring to Latin America. These claimed contributions include:

The financial contribution and the creation of new production facilities. MNCs bring much-needed scarce financing capital with which they create additional facilities for the host country.

The balance of payments contribution. Through the finance capital they bring plus their production of items that were formerly imported, plus their increased exports relative to local firms (which are acknowledged as less efficient than MNCs), they alleviate the balance of payment deficits of their host countries.

The contribution of new technology and increase in employment. The MNCs transfer to Third World nations more efficient technology, including the managerial skills that go with its operation, and by creating new productive facilities bring about an increase in employment.

The last of these three major areas of contributions claimed for the MNC by pro-business literature will be dealt with first. There can be no doubt that MNC technology is efficient in the sense that a dollar's worth of investment in MNC technology relative to local technology does in fact better increase the total output resulting from an investment. However, the other face of this "contribution" is that as total output increases, less and less labor is required to produce that output. A recent study in

Colombia in the industries in which MNCs have been investing most heavily during the period from 1965 to 1973 showed that the dollar investment required to employ one unit of labor almost tripled during this period.[7] Another way to see this impact is to study the manufacturing sector as a whole for all of Latin America. Thus, in 1925, manufacturing accounted for only 11% of the total output of the region, but in 1970, it accounted for 25%. In contrast, during the same period the percentage of total employment absorbed by the manufacturing sector actually decreased from roughly 14½ to 14% during the same period. And in Mexico, which has received the largest amount of U.S. multinational investment in the manufacturing sector, the rate of increase in total production during the 1960s was double that of the rate of increase of new jobs. It must also be remembered that MNC technology is utilized not only through its direct investment operations but also through the vast amount of licensing of that technology to domestic enterprises. And as we have seen, this technology accounts for more than 99% of the total operating technology now in the manufacturing sector of Latin America.

This then is the dilemma of the technology brought to Latin America by MNCs. Although output can most assuredly be increased, it is accompanied by a relative decrease in the expansion of employment. Is there an alternative to this? It would appear not, given the social organization of production in Latin America, namely that of interfirm competition and maximization of private profits. Other countries, however, have found alternatives. For instance, the Soviet Union has long shown the capacity to purchase technology from MNCs and then modify that technology so as to increase its labor usage time. The most famous example of this is the Ford Motor Company's River Rouge Plant, which was in all details reconstructed in the Soviet Union based on a purchase from that company. However, the Soviets were able to modify the basic engineering of the design of the plant in order to utilize labor-intensive techniques side by side with capital-intensive methods. Similar experiences can be found in the recent industrial history of Yugoslavia, Tanzania, and China. On the whole, however, it would be illusory to expect Latin American enterprises to modify their technology, given the fact that the MNCs with which they currently must compete are not motivated by labor-absorption criteria but instead by total output at minimum cost, more specifically at minimum labor requirements.

Technology is a key variable in explaining unequal income distribution in countries undergoing industrialization. In countries where the overall key legal institutions governing economic relations is the private ownership of productive resources (the labor and technology embodied in capital), it follows that the larger the proportion of total output due to capital-technology resources, the greater will be the amount of income going to the owners of these resources. In addition, where there is a rela-

7. Dario Abad, in Albrecht Gleich, ed., *Las Inversiones Extranjeras Privadas en America Latina* (Hamburg: Instituto de Estudios Iberoamericanos, 1971).

tively rapid change in technology biased toward *labor-saving* techniques, and where capitalist legal institutions are not modified via, for example, more progressive tax rates to keep pace with this change, then, again by definition, income distribution will become even more unequal over time. Just how unequal is this distribution of national income becoming in less developed countries?

The results from a recent World Bank-sponsored study, performed by Irma Adelman and Cynthia Taft Morris, show that in LDCs, from subsistence levels throughout the industrial "takeoff" until an average per capita income level of ca. $800, there is a profound change in income distribution.[8] During this takeoff, the richest 5% of LDC populations experience a "striking" increase in income while often the bottom 40% experience an absolute decline in their level of income. That is, their intake of food, clothing, and shelter actually declines throughout the takeoff period. The case is even more dramatic in those two countries where MNCs have been the most active—Mexico and Brazil. Thus from 1950 to 1965 in Mexico, the ratio of the income of the richest 20% to the percent of the poorest 20% went from 10:1 to 17:1. In the Mexico City area, it is even more disheartening; the richest 20% received 62.5% of the area's income while the poorest 20% attempted to survive on 1.3% of the income.[9] In Brazil from 1963 to 1973, the share of income of the richest 5% went from roughly 28 to 37%, while the share of some 40 million other Brazilian people (the poorest 40%) dropped from 10.6 to 8.1% of the nation's total output.[10]

This then is the second aspect of the contribution of the modern technology being transferred to the Third World by the MNCs. It is a contribution to the richest 5, 10, or 20% of these populations, but an absolute disservice to the human condition of the greater majority of the populations of these countries.

The impact of this *employment-displacing technology* of the MNCs would not be as severe if in fact their new investments all resulted in the creation of new production facilities side by side with existing productive assets. This unfortunately is not the case; from 1958 through 1967, 46% of the subsidiaries in Latin America established by U.S. MNCs were made by taking over existing Latin American domestic enterprises. Even more notably, the percentage of total foreign investment devoted to such acquisitions of domestic firms has been increasing consistently since 1929. It has also been found that in industries where the percentage of

8. Cynthia Taft Morris, and Irma Adelman, "An Anatomy of Income Distribution Patterns in Developing Nations: A Summary of Findings," *Economic Staff Paper No. 116*, IBRD, September, 1971.

9. James P. Grant, *Multinational Corporations and the Developing Countries: The Emerging Job Crisis and Its Implications* (Washington, D.C.: Overseas Development Council, 1972), p. 6.

10. ECLA, *Economic Survey for Latin America* (New York: United Nations, 1969). For similar estimates see, an unpublished study by H. P. Miller, U.S. Bureau of the Census, Washington, D.C. 1971. The Latin American UN estimate is from ECLA op. cit.

foreign investments going to acquisitions had decreased, the decline was, as quoted from *Business Latin America,* issue of January 15, 1970, "probably attributable in part to the scarcity of local firms remaining in these industries." [11]

The implications of this analysis for Latin American nations are clear, particularly if the data on domestic takeovers is combined with the source of the financing of MNCs' investment in the region. Taken together, these two types of information provide a means for evaluating the so-called financial contribution of MNCs to Third World countries; i.e., the contribution of financial capital to capital-scarce nations. There is insufficient space to give the complete analysis of this information, so only the basic conclusions derived from this data are presented here.

In the manufacturing sector, currently most crucial to the future development of Latin America, 78% of MNCs' foreign investments are actually financed from local savings. Of this finance capital, an estimated 46% is used to buy out existing locally controlled firms, whose profits would otherwise have been retained domestically and thus would have contributed to either local consumption and/or savings. But from the date of the acquisition and henceforth, some 52% of those profits will leave the country, resulting in a net decrease in the LDCs' savings which would have been otherwise available, *and* a net increase in their already acute shortage of foreign exchange. Given these results, it is impossible to see how the MNCs' financial impacts on Third World countries could possibly assist in the alleviation of their underdevelopment.[12]

Having explicated briefly the financial impact of MNCs on Latin American nations, it is clear that this financial situation also has implications on the balance of payments of these countries. What are the claims made by MNCs as to their balance of payments contributions? In the pro-MNC literature it is often held that these corporations are making a positive impact on the balance of payments of LDCs. Often quoted is the statistic that roughly 50% of Latin America's exports, particularly manufactured exports, are now being sold by multinational corporations. At the same time equal emphasis is placed on the fact that multinational corporations come to Latin America and produce products that in the past had been imported. These arguments derive the simple conclusion that because exports are increased and imports are reduced, the MNCs are therefore making a positive contribution to the balance of payments situation of Third World countries.

But here, as everywhere, simple statistics and simple arguments are very deceptive. Examining the exports side of this argument, it is known that the majority of the exports of MNC subsidiaries from Latin America are sold to other units of the same parent MNCs of which they are a part. These sales are called "intracompany transactions." The accounting term

11. The absorption of local firms and the statistical data are found in Ronald Müller, "Poverty is the Product," *Foreign Policy,* Fall/Winter, 1973–74.
12. Data and details are in Müller, ibid.

utilized to designate the price of an intracompany transaction is called a "transfer price." From the point of view of the host country, the key question is whether or not the transfer price is equivalent to the true market value of the good being exported. A second question to be asked is whether or not the transfer price represents the true market value of the good being exported to a member of the parent MNC—if not, then what is the motivation that would lead the parent company headquarters to take such an action?

Until the past few years, we knew very little of the so-called transfer pricing policies that parents dictated on to their MNC subsidiaries in LDCs. Now, however, there is a well-documented body of information, the results of which have dramatic ramifications on the future development of Third World countries. Recently, from a paper presented at the 1972 American Economic Association Meeting, a colleague and I were able to document and verify that on the average, MNC subsidiaries in Latin America *underprice* their exports by an estimated 40% to 50%. The meaning of this is clear. An export article that is sold, for example, by a 100%-owned Argentinian firm to an independent foreign buyer at a price of $100 is on the average sold by MNC subsidiaries to other parent units for $50. The result is a direct loss of $50 worth of Argentinian resources and more directly, a loss of badly needed tax revenues for the concerned government.[13]

There is involved here a phenomenon that has come to be known in the literature as a "triangular trade." Exports are sold to a subsidiary in a low or non-tax area—i.e., tax havens such as Panama or the Bahamas— at a price less than the true market price. From the tax haven area they are then re-exported at their true market value to their final destination. This same triangular trade is at work in the transfer pricing policies of MNC parents on their intersubsidiary imports coming into Latin America. Only in this case, instead of underpricing, there is substantial *overpricing* relative to the market value of the imported good.

Thus, for instance, a subsidiary located in a Latin American nation can import an item that has an independent market value of, say, $100. But instead of paying $100, the subsidiary pays $400, thereby succeeding in transferring $300 of locally generated income (resources) out of the country, escaping both the local tax authorities, and even more importantly, depriving that nation of that much more income! Just how large these losses are to developing countries has been amply documented by a whole host of studies conducted by various international agencies in different parts of the Third World. It should also be mentioned here that these extralegal transfers by multinational corporations have also been the subject of numerous investigations by U.S. tax courts.

There are other ways in which MNCs are detrimental to the balance

13. Ronald Müller and Richard Morgenstern, "Multinational Corporations and Balance of Payments Impacts in LDCs: An Econometric Analysis of Export Pricing Behavior, "KYKLOS, April, 1974.

of payments situations of the Third World countries; such things as the fact that some 79% of all MNC subsidiaries are prohibited from exporting at all by dictate of their parent headquarters. Even more profound is the fact that 92% of the nationally owned firms utilizing MNC technology under licenses are also prohibited from exporting. This occurs at a time when the political leaders of advanced nations are encouraging Third World countries to export more and to become more self-sufficient but are failing to note that the MNCs of their own countries are making it hard for LDCs to enter the one export market viable in the long run, manufactures.

Earlier in this article the technology of the MNC and its impact on employment and income distribution in Latin America was discussed. One other aspect of the so-called technology transfers must be mentioned here; namely, the price that is paid for that technology. When MNCs invest in a subsidiary in Latin America, part of the total value of that investment is accounted for by the placement of technology from the parent to the subsidiary's location. The key question then is the valuation placed on that technology, inasmuch as it makes up a part of the final net worth of the subsidiary. Here the information is still rather scant; but in all of the cases thus far investigated and where information was available, it was found that the valuation on this technology is overpriced by anywhere from 30 to 50%. Some of these cases also show that used technology was being transferred, but it was being declared as new to government officials in the host countries. Finally, in research being conducted (by Richard Barnet and myself for the forthcoming book, *Global Reach*), interviews with managers of subsidiaries in many cases confirmed the fact that the overvaluing of technology is a common practice.

In the Appendix will be found the effective annual rate of return on net worth of investment of fifteen wholly owned MNC drug subsidiaries in a Latin American nation. These figures range from a low of 44.2% to a high of 962.1%, with the majority of firms earning in excess of 100% on their investment per year. The average of their effective returns was 136.3%, while the average of the declared returns to the host country tax authorities was 6.7%. These figures show that some 82% of actual profits earned by the MNCs is due to the overpricing of imports alone. But even these figures *understate* the real return that these corporations are realizing, for they do not take into consideration the possibility of the underpricing of exports nor the overvaluation of the declared investment value of these subsidiaries. These facts and arguments have now been confirmed across the many industries and LDCs where MNC, have been operating during the period 1950–1970. Thus, a recent Rand Corporation study, in reviewing the *actual vs. reported* profit rates of MNCs in Latin America, has concluded "how totally unreliable these U.S. Commerce Department (reported profit) figures are." [14] It is from these actual profit rates that we

14. Rand Corporation, *Latin America in the 1970's*, prepared for the U.S. State Department, #R-1067-DOS, Dec., 1972. Detailed figures for other industries and countries are given in Barnet and Müller, op. cit., chap. 7.

get the true impact of the economic power of MNCs in less developed countries compared to their more limited power in advanced countries where there are well-developed government organs for controlling foreign investors and well-developed modern domestic competition to provide a further check on the excessive use of power by the MNCs.

SUMMARY AND CONCLUSIONS

There can be little doubt as to my overall conclusions concerning the impact of MNCs on Latin American nations. In summary, there exists more myth than reality in the claims made about the three most important contributions of MNCs. Our analysis of the technology contribution revealed instead a basic cause of further unemployment and a further concentration of already extremely unequal income distribution, while noting the excessive prices being charged by the MNCs in transferring this technology. Upon examination, the financial contribution turns out to be a financial drain, thereby decreasing both current consumption and available local savings and thus future consumption for the vast majority of Latin American inhabitants. The third area of analysis, the balance of payments contribution, led to similar conclusions. In contrast to a contribution, the empirical information showed no superior export performance by MNCs relative to local firms unless it was accompanied by export underpricing. Concomitantly, exports were further limited via restrictions placed on their technology by the MNCs. Although potential inflows were minimized, the balance of payments outflows were accentuated through import overpricing and inflated royalty payments.

There can be little doubt that such an impact can only contribute to the further impoverishment of the poorest 60% of Third World population. Summing up the specific consequences thus far analyzed leads to an overall consequence. In the Third World, the MNCs are involved in a *structuring process* which cannot be ignored. The fact that this process permits an ever-tightening control over the technology and finances of the majority of LDCs results in what Celso Furtado, among others, has shown to be an ever-growing external dependency of the poor nations on the few rich nations of the world. Besides the transfer in of inappropriate technology and the transfer out of financial resources, this process includes one further destabilizing force.

The MNCs are also involved in the transfer of a consumption ideology, the goals of which only 30% at best and, more realistically, 20% of LDC populations can hope to achieve in the foreseeable future. Just as the MNCs are involved in the restructuring of the production sector, so too are they a major force in restructuring the consumption sectors. This is a glaring contradiction, for the new structure of consumption is in serious imbalance with the inadequate consumption capacity generated by the very production structure which MNCs have pivotally helped to create, and therefore negates any possibility of attaining the new consumption goals by all except a small minority. Here is a major cause for the deep and growing frustration that is so easily sensed in so many underdeveloped nations. When many share the same basic and intense frustration, then the problem goes beyond the realm of economics and becomes truly a social, and therefore a political one.

Latin America, which has suffered this frustration relatively longer than other Third World areas, has already witnessed several patterns of political response to it. The political decision of Brazil and Mexico has been to continue the present reliance on the MNCs via the expedient of growing political oppression. Cuba is attempting to detach itself from industrialization via the MNCs by establishing socialist institutions as did Chile under the late president Allende. And the Peruvian military appears to be in the midst of deciding to what extent it desires, let alone is able, to minimize and/or modify the role of MNCs to pursue a new form of national development.[15] What the long-run viability of any of these responses will be cannot be dealt with here. There is, however, a clear message. The continued and unaltered expansion of the MNCs into Latin America will increase the instability of the societies there and bring about significant political change.

15. More recently, however, even such LDCs as Brazil and Mexico and those of the Andean common market are beginning to develop techniques of "bargaining power" to mitigate the negative impacts of MNCs. For an appraisal of these techniques during the 1970's and beyond, see Ronald Müller, "The Underdeveloped and the Developed: Power and the Potential for Change," in *Papers and Proceedings of the International Sociological Association's World Conference of Sociology–1974*, forthcoming. The details of bargaining power strategy by LDCs are presented in Ronald Müller, *The Political Economy of Direct Foreign Investment: An Appraisal for Latin American Policy Making*, prepared for the Prebisch Group; published in Washington, D.C. by Inter-American Development Bank, Special Studies Division, July, 1970.

The multinational corporation and the response of host countries: Western Europe

WARRICK E. ELROD, JR.

Europe is a natural area for studying the growth of the multinational corporation and the relationship of such a corporation to a nation-state as well as to an association of states, the European Economic Community.

These relationships are of immense importance to the United States. Although the United States has been in the process of establishing closer contacts with the Soviet Union, the People's Republic of China, and Japan, Europe remains the area of paramount importance to the United States. It is here that the U.S. (1) finds the one major market in which it still manages to sell more than it buys; (2) has the largest stake in overseas investment; (3) remains most committed to military defense; and (4) probably faces increasing economic and political difficulties. The United States must be prepared to renegotiate with its European allies new long-term working relationships based on the new realities of reduced American power. With an end to America's overwhelming military and economic superiority, American corporations operating abroad will try to find other and more subtle foundations on which to base their own expansion abroad.

It is in Europe that the American-dominated multinational corporations have had their greatest impact and enjoy their major markets. In 1973, total sales by U.S. firms in foreign markets are expected to amount to roughly $240 billion, of which approximately $55 billion will represent exports from American shores and approximately $185 billion will represent sales in foreign countries by foreign affiliates of American corporations, many of them characterized as multinational. Of this, approximately $75 billion will be sales in Europe by such affiliates. From 1950 to 1972, direct investments by U.S. firms in Europe rose from a little over $3 billion to over $30 billion.

By similarity of cultural and social backgrounds as well as by economic and financial connections, Europeans and Americans may find themselves as the first co-managers of the multinational corporations, working in increasingly closer association as their corporations do become multinational, mutually advising with respect to the foundations for corporate relationships to their respective nation-states.

It is in Europe that the main locus of the emerging multinational corporation is to be found, and it was a voice raised in Europe, that of Servan-Schreiber, that first called attention to the implications of the increasing role of American firms, operating multinationally, in Europe. What Servan-Schreiber called the American Challenge might better have been called the American Response because it was the formation of the European Economic Community in 1958, creating what American businessmen saw as conditions that might drastically reduce their role and their markets in Europe, that stimulated American investment, particularly direct investment in plants and equipment, in the Common Market countries. So in part, the growth of the multinational corporation was a natural reaction to what was seen as the challenge of a potentially closed European market.

In a somewhat belated response to Servan-Schreiber's warning, the European countries today are the most vigorous in their criticism of the multinational corporation and its role vis-à-vis the power of the nation or the power of their community of nations. But they are not alone in questioning the role of the multinational corporation. Canada has introduced legislation to control foreign investment, particularly corporate investment, as a possible challenge to state power. Australia has introduced legislation of a similarly inhibiting character, most specifically with respect to "takeovers" by foreign corporations of Australian firms. New Zealand is also concerned with the threat of outside control of developing New Zealand industry. And, of course, restrictive controls on foreign investment in Japan are designed to preserve for the Japanese the dominant management of their own corporate activity.

It is the argument of this essay that the multinational corporations, as such, will not pose a dangerous threat to the sovereignty of any nation; that they will, overall, be economically beneficial to the nations in which they operate and to their citizens. Ideally, in some distant day, the multinational corporation may even become an agent for improved political and social relationships among people.

In my opinion, a multinational corporation is a corporation, wherever its headquarters might be, that thinks multinationally and not just internationally. The ownership and management will likely have no predominant nationality. Ownership will in time become so dispersed that no exclusively national interest can be exerted through ownership control and management will become thoroughly international. Our approach to emerging multinational corporate activity does not envision a need for specific national police actions to control large corporations engaged in international operations. The power all modern governments exercise over corporate enterprises in general, together with the power of nationalization of foreign-owned assets (also claimed by the United States in the Trading with the Enemy Act of 1916) should be quite sufficient. Moreover, cooperation of the corporation with the nation in which it operates should be mutually beneficial—in most cases the operations of such corporations have actually generated higher profits, raised world production and income, and improved human welfare. Increased international trade, which tends to raise per capita real incomes in the trading countries, is almost invariably beneficial.

Thus, several conclusions seem tentatively acceptable: (1) international corporations will expand and many of them will evolve into multinational corporations; (2) such corporations increase real incomes in the countries in which they establish their operating enterprises; (3) the net effect on world employment and output is positive; (4) in the case of U.S. corporations abroad, although the net effect on the U.S. balance of payments is originally obviously harmful, this effect tends at least in part to be counteracted later on by the repatriation of earnings in the form of dividends, royalties, and fees.[1]

Obviously, the European nations see these developments from their points of view. European concern over the multinational corporation touches about all areas of activity of the corporation. Although basically, Europe sees the multinational corporation as having had an undeniably beneficial effect on the economy of the members of the European Economic Community (thus agreeing with points 2 and 3 above) and though acute observers of the European business scene note that the image of the multinational firm has been steadily improving, the multinational corporations have given rise to definite fears associated with the increase of foreign control over employment, research, and the sources of supply of both raw materials and manufactured goods. There is also the fear that such corporations pose a threat to the regional programs (of the EEC), to monetary policies, and particularly to the balance among labor, industry, and government.

We will look first at the last fear, the upsetting of the balance. Since the end of World War Two, the European nations have sought to establish an appropriate balance among labor, industry, and government both from the point of view of achieving maximum output and employment and of social equity. Such a balance, in the European view, will assure optimum allocation of resources and contribute to the battle against inflation. Thus, as examples of attempts to achieve such a balance, there have been the incomes policies of the Netherlands, Belgium, and the United Kingdom, the "indicative planning" of France, and the "co-determination" of industrial policy by management and labor in West Germany. All such programs rest upon a fundamental cooperation among

---

1. U.S. labor sees U.S. investment abroad as "exporting" U.S. jobs (i.e,, extinguishing some jobs in the U.S. when new ones are created abroad by US. foreign investment). However, insofar as U.S. investment abroad is associated with the shipment of U.S. equipment, and at a later date, insofar as it raises foreign incomes, the effect on U.S. exports, though difficult to measure precisely, raises employment in the U.S. export sector and thus counteracts the initial job loss, at least in part. However, the investment usually creates more jobs and output abroad than it would have created in the United States: hence, the net effect on world employment and output is usually positive.

labor, business, and the government. The European countries see, quite rightly and obviously, that the balance must be maintained in an atmosphere of change that will be both necessary and rapid, particularly in view of the swift strides of scientific research and technology. Maintenance of the balance, in European eyes, thus requires control of their own research and development.

The European view is a sophisticated view of the future. There is the realization that industrial progress will take place in a social environment of greater and greater complexity, an environment in which the workers and their unions ("organizations syndicales") must of necessity play an increasingly more important role in regard to not only the level of employment and salaries but also the conditions under which labor works and to the influence that labor will exercise in determining the economic choices of a corporation. There is a fear that a national labor group will be at a disadvantage in its negotiations with an industrial giant transcending national boundaries and may accept conditions not in harmony with the national goals, thus upsetting the balance. There have been suggestions that, to meet this possibility, European labor organize in order to carry on their negotiations with the corporations at the international level.

Establishing and maintaining balance among the participants in an economy obviously requires this noted cooperation of labor, business, and government, and the European nations consider it essential that multinational corporations not distort, as some believe they already have, the balance by the growth of their power and influence. The expansion of industry, through the multinationals, beyond national boundaries makes maintenance of the balance on a national level all the more difficult; thus the concern of the European nations. And, to the extent that the balance in the individual members of the Common Market may be upset, the day of harmonization of economic policies and legislation, upon which ultimate European economic and monetary union rests, is delayed.

Beyond the upsetting of this balance, what Europe seems principally to fear from the multinationals is (1) competition, (2) technological dominance, and (3) the effects of their possession of overwhelming financial assets. Increasingly the European firms have come to live with foreign competition. Many have recognized its benefits. Although all nations think to some extent along de Gaulle lines—i.e., that a nation must have its own technology or lose its national power—most are coming to recognize that technology is becoming more and more international and that although each nation will reserve to itself certain areas of production (e.g., defense), no nation can long maintain a monopoly of a technological process.

The financial power of the emerging multinational corporation constitutes the real threat, not to national sovereignty, but to national financial policy. The U.S. Tariff Commission has placed the assets of American multinational corporations at $268 billion. It is a stupendous sum. Only a small portion of the assets can be liquid, but even a small part of $268 billion in liquid form can, as recent foreign exchange crises have shown, be highly destabilizing. Large capital inflows to a country fighting inflation can be damaging and make monetary policy far more difficult for the authorities. The French see the financial power of the corporations as permitting them to escape the capital controls France has used to police its national economic plans. And the Germans are increasingly pressed to devise new monetary policies to offset corporate capital flows which make the battle against inflation extremely difficult. No one knows just how much of the $82-billion Euro-dollar holdings belongs to the multinational corporations, but it is certainly sufficiently large and volatile to justify the concern of French and German authorities, even though they have various powers to counteract such flows. (For example, a new firm has to obtain permission from French authorities in order to undertake operations in France; certainly here the authorities can ascertain what a foreign firm intends to do.)

On a microeconomic level, what Europe basically fears is the capability of the giant international corporations to raise large amounts of capital, amounts beyond the power of national corporations of intermediate or even fairly large size, and to use these funds either to take over European industrial firms or establish firms in a multinational complex that will harm the competitive position of the national firm. Although there is as yet no concerted European effort in regard to the problem, there is in many of the European countries a desire for a closer regulation of the Euro-dollar market, particularly as a source of funds in "takeover" operations. And though, in the financial area, the Euro-dollar market is the principal concern, the European nations also would welcome the abolition of the U.S. Interest Equalization Tax (which raises the cost of industrial borrowing in U.S. capital markets) as an incentive for firms, particularly American, to shift financing to the New York capital market and relieve the burden of demand on the relatively thin and nationally limited European capital markets. It is here that European nations see the foreign firms as absorbing funds that might otherwise finance to a greater extent the growth of European firms, thus perhaps reducing foreign takeover of European industry. A far more restrictive policy, directly limiting foreign investment in Europe, would seem to be needed if such investment is to be curtailed to any significant degree. But such a restrictive policy, if it could be agreed upon by the European nations, would seem to go against the European desire for a truly European capital market. Capital markets do not grow within the constraints that such a policy would require.

Several European countries have used the financial resources of their respective national institutions (the *Kreditanstalt fuer Weiederaufbau* in Germany, *le Crédit National* in France, the *Banque d'Investissement néerlandaise* in the Netherlands, the *Instito Mobliere Italiano* in Italy, etc.) to aid their industries, particularly where advanced technology is involved, to grow and to strengthen their competitive position against the multinational firms. It has been suggested in more than one European forum that these institutions should increase their collaboration and pool resources to finance the rationalization of certain sectors of European industry in order to make them more competitive and to provide, in conjunction with the private capital markets and other appropriate national financial institutions, the risk capital to innovative firms which face the severe competition for funds from better-financed firms, among them the multinational corporations. Although equality of competitive strength is a sporting and desirable goal, the European nations must guard against any form of subsidized financing that would prove an obstacle to the optimum allocation of resources, which is one of the announced major goals of the European Economic Community.

In almost every European country there exists enough concern and ability to prevent the development of an excess of foreign or "multinational" dominance. For more than a decade there has been a continual debate in France for and against foreign ownership of French industry. As early as 1964, the French government stated that foreign ownership had progressed beyond a safe point. In contrast, proponents argued throughout the late 1960s that the nation should import foreign capital because (1) the country could not domestically generate enough capital to modernize French industry to make it competitive with industry in other Common Market countries, and (2) other Common Market countries were allowing foreign investment and thus by financing their industrial modernization through foreign funds were gaining an even greater competitive advantage over France. Throughout the late 1960s, France actually received about a quarter of American investment in the Common Market area.

In Germany there have been both proponents and opponents of foreign investment. Increasingly, however, the German view is turning against foreign investment, particularly American. Perhaps this is predominantly a German bankers' view because the argument is made that such investment not only provokes nationalistic reactions but is also harmful to the U.S. payments balance and thus to the international monetary system.

The movement of funds into Germany has largely represented conversion of borrowed Euro-dollars into German marks for portfolio or direct investment, or to take advantage of interest rate differentials, or for speculative gains based on the expectation of currency appreciation. Large movements of this kind force preventive action on the German monetary authorities seeking to control the inflationary pressures that have plagued Germany throughout most of the 1960s. A massive conversion of U.S. dollars into marks also tends to disturb exchange markets throughout Europe, thereby making the task of national monetary authorities more difficult. Unless the German monetary authorities allow the mark to float freely, they must absorb the inflow of dollars. Such action not only encourages further inflows as long as the conditions favoring speculative action continue but also increases the domestic money supply in Germany and thereby aggravates inflation.

In the spring of 1971, massive flows of dollars into Germany occurred to such an extent that the German authorities closed the exchanges on the morning of May 5. On May 4 and the morning of May 5, an estimated $3 billion moved into Germany, most of it conversions by the large international corporations of Euro-dollar balances into German marks. But the actions of these firms, although while forcing the hands of the German authorities, were not a challenge to the right of Germany to control its economic life.[2]

Basically, the inflow of such huge sums into Germany was not caused by the existence of "multinational" corporations but rather by the massive availability of dollars in the Euro-dollar market (estimated in 1972 at $82 billion), which permitted any market participant—whether or not it was a multinational corporation—to engage in speculative or merely defensive exchange operations. Even more basically, it is the huge amount of international liquidity—in dollars and other currencies—that makes possible destabilizing international flows of funds.[3]

In the 1960s, the Netherlands and Belgium encouraged foreign investment. Belgium has viewed foreign investment as beneficial to the extent that it leads to introduction of new industries not previously developed by the Belgians (automobiles, petrochemicals, machinery, electronics and electrical goods, etc). In the early sixties Belgium welcomed many foreign industries which had first sought to locate in France. To date the Belgians have considered the benefits of foreign investment (foreign introduction of new processes, increased competition) to outweigh all disadvantages. The Netherlands has more reservations about foreign investment and has always protected itself against excessive foreign investment by limiting foreign access to its capital market and giving first priority to Dutch firms seeking capital. Belgium has used strong monetary measures, including

2. The author had numerous conversations in May and June of 1971 with the American businessmen whose firms had moved funds into Germany. Although they conceded that no international financial manager could continue to hold large sums of dollars when the mark might be revalued by 10 percent or more, they maintained that fear that Germany adopt exchange controls to halt the massive inflow of dollars prompted the rush to convert dollars to marks.

3. See, for a discussion of the Euro-dollar market, Paul Einzig, *The Euro-Dollar System* (London: Macmillan, 1972). In the author's view, there have been no attempts to control the Euro-dollar market because national authorities and international financial experts do not know whether the market is beneficial or harmful. If the former, it would be unwise to impose restrictions. And, of course, its harmful effects could be greatly mitigated if governments had the political courage to reduce excessive balance of payments surpluses and deficits and in their efforts to control domestic inflation to use responsible fiscal policy in conjunction with, or in place of, monetary policy.

a two-tier exchange system, to prevent the inflow of funds from disrupting the national economy and hampering Belgian stabilization policies.

The same determination to protect the domestic economy against actions of foreign firms is to be found in Switzerland. Many firms sought to establish themselves in Switzerland, but as the number of foreigners in the country increased, immigration was restricted, work permits became harder to get, and employers were forced to reduce the number of foreign workers in their Swiss operations. Though these measures applied equally to domestic and foreign firms, it was the latter that suffered the greater inconvenience. The Swiss have also always responded promptly to the threat of inflation from inflows of capital by placing limits on its import. Like other European nations, Switzerland will introduce measures to control foreign nationals and foreign capital whenever the flow of either becomes too large.[4]

In the United Kingdom, foreign investment is heavy and over recent years has increased more rapidly than in any other European country. But there are strict controls. By law the British Treasury must grant permission for the import of foreign capital into the country, and rather clearly defined conditions are usually attached to foreign takeovers. The British are concerned about the absorption of many British companies by American firms, and have conducted a thorough debate about the effect of foreign takeovers on British national policies. The British carefully weigh the advantages of such takeovers—the inflow of needed capital, increased exports of goods, improved management performance, greater technical knowledge, reduced dependence on traditional occupations in the area where a foreign firm locates—against the disadvantages. And they seem to have concluded that advantages outweigh disadvantages.

Italy remains generally favorable to foreign investment. This is not surprising in view of the relative scarcity in Italy of domestic capital. In addition, Italian authorities have expressed the need for Italy to gain from the technology foreign investment usually brings.

Thus, the European countries look carefully at the effects of foreign investment and although on balance they are not against multinational corporations, all seem ready to act to halt undesirable operations of any foreign corporation.

One final comment should be offered. As size, especially economic size, becomes an increasing concern of citizens of all nations, the nation-state will likely assume a more sympathetic role as defender of the citizen against mammoth corporations. The new awareness on the part of citizens of the destructive potential of unregulated industrialization is putting

---

4. Although free movement of nationals of the Common Market members through all the member states is provided for in the Treaty of Rome, employment opportunities effectively limit the interchange. The Germans combat unemployment in periods of recession by discharging workers from Italy, Spain, Yugoslavia, Greece, and other nations, who then return to the home countries.

additional power into the hands of the state. Britain and France have created Departments of the Environment to exercise control over all industrial plants, domestic or foreign, further evidence that a state will act to reflect the will of its people and provide protection against industrial giants.

The multinational corporation and the diffusion of technology

HAMID MOWLANA

A MODEL FOR THE DIFFUSION OF TECHNOLOGY

In order to examine the international diffusion of technology it is useful to take into account the alternative channels through which it is available.

Within a given entity or state (for example, a given country, as shown in Figure 1), a certain level of technology exists. This level includes the products (the technological innovations) and the "environment" that leads to the invention of the product (the scientific research, the ideas and concepts it generates). When we speak of diffusion of "technology," we are speaking not only of the diffusion of a specific product but also of the diffusion of the ideas and concepts behind that product.

Considering the MNC as the channel of diffusion of technology, the flow of information or goods can go in either direction, as shown in the model. However, it tends to be unidirectional from the country having the more advanced technological state to the country having the less developed state of technology. The frequency of such communications and the degree of clustering of communications over various areas (industries) are aspects not to be ignored.

Technological innovation may spread from one country to another either through transfer by imitation of production functions or new goods, or transfer by companies and corporations that establish the innovation operation as a subsidiary, or in joint-venture terms with the recipient country. Imitation is a process demanding national willingness. Japan actually capitalized on the United States' innovation of the transistorized radio. Industrial skills and management sophistication are also necessary prerequisites. Lags in technological change can be lessened where the transfer of innovation takes place in a truly multinational organization.

I wish to acknowledge the research assistance of Tom Gregg, Patricia A Harris, and Chaim Even-Zohar.

In development of the model discussed in this chapter, I have been stimulated by analysis of the new environment of international relations provided in Harold and Margaret Sprout, *Foundations of International Politics* (Princeton, N.J.: D. Van Nostrand, 1962); and by Bryant Wedge, "Communication Analysis and Comprehensive Diplomacy," in Arthur S. Hoffman, ed., *International Communication and the New Diplomacy* (Bloomington, Ind.: Indiana University Press, 1968).

Figure 1. Channels of international diffusion of technology

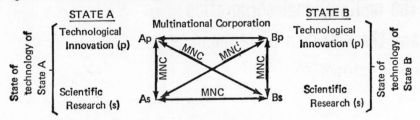

Holding the direction of flow constant from A to B, the following transactions are possible. Note that the primary transactions are the bases for secondary and tertiary transactions.

PRIMARY FLOWS: Ap to Bp = Import of product for market sale
Ap to. Bs = Import of product as model to stimulate research, to build a similar model or product
As to Bp = Import/sale of patents/ideas/information to the foreign country facilitating production of product for market sale
As to Bs = Import/sale of patents/ideas/information to the foreign country to stimulate research in the foreign laboratories

SECONDARY FLOWS: Ap to Bs to Bp = Actual production of product (or similar product) from transaction Ap to Bs
Ap to Bp to Bs = Scientific research stimulated by transaction Ap to Bp
As to Bs to Bp = Actual product produced as result of transaction As to Bs

TERTIARY FLOWS: As to Ap to Bp to Bs = Scientific research in A leads to production of a product in A which is imported to B, where further research is generated.
Ap to As to Bs to Bp = Product produced in A leads to further research in A, the ideas of this research being sent to researchers in B which produce a new product

THE MNC AND THE CURRENT TRENDS IN DIFFUSION

The foregoing raises a number of questions, among them: What is meant by diffusion of technology? How is it practiced by the multinational corporation? To what extent is the diffusion of technology possible? What are its limits and constraints? To what extent is it currently practiced? To what use is it put? And, what are the basic assumptions?

Technology is the application of knowledge in a systematic fashion with a view of achieving control over nature and human processes. Thus, a new seed strain is as much a mark of technology as is the supersonic transport. In short, technology consists of ideas about how to make goods rather than the goods themselves or their production facilities.

The source of these ideas for new technology is scientific research and corporate or individual invention. For example, American corporations have increasingly accepted the idea of technological innovation as the key to their expansion and growth. Planned innovation is an essential concept of this acceptance. Today, in many societies information technology is the most powerful resource. Unlike other resources, it is heterogeneous and is not consumed in the process of use. In fact, it is a prerequisite to the organization and allocation of other resources. It is suggested that the new social wealth generated by information/communication technologies will eventually be less dependent on the older forms of ownership such as land and other material property. Before the Industrial Revolution, land constituted the primary resource for generating new wealth. Later, land gave its place to investment capital. Now technological know-how and information is the major source for generating the required capacity, efficiency, and wealth to meet the needs of human societies.

Diffusion is a type of communication process by which innovation (in the form of new messages) is transferred to members of a social system. The careful analysis of the process of diffusion of innovation has become imperative in the study of social change. The course to mapping diffusion is the one through which innovation, be it technological or cultural, is transferred. Most often, the view of this course is that innovation (particularly technological) moves out from one or more strategic points to permeate a "market," and in some way affects culturally defined identity and behavior. In this approach, systems of diffusion are critical to understanding the learning capacity of the society or organization.

Those who have tried to promote new systems for diffusion have relied upon what can be termed a center-periphery model.[1] This rests on three basic assumptions; (1) an innovation exists fully realized prior to its diffusion; (2) the diffusion path is traceable from central initiator to ultimate adopters; and (3) diffusion is a directed and centrally managed process for training and dissemination. The effectiveness of the center-periphery model depends, it seems, on several functions characteristic of a communication system of control and maintenance. First, it is dependent on its level of internal resources and control, then on the points at the periphery that support the direction given by the central initiator. This function of direction and support is dependent on the relations of linkage between the center and periphery points. The diffusion capability of an agricultural extension agent, for instance, depends upon his particular skills and motivations, the number and location of the farmers he serves,

1. Franklin R. Root, "The Role of International Business in the Diffusion of Technological Innovation," *Business and Economic Bulletin*, No. 24 (Summer 1968), pp. 19–27.

and the time and effort he must devote to each. Infrastructure organization can also play its part. In the film *Phantom of India,* we learn how public health officials spread new methods of birth control into isolated villages, traveling by elephant. This use of traditional transport not only reflects a solution to the needed transportation, but serves as an ingenious means of public relations. Effectiveness of regulating and directing the diffusion process depends on the movement of information from center to periphery. In the center-periphery model all regulation or modification can be initially presumed to originate from the center.

The center-periphery model, with its elaboration in the extended form of the proliferation of centers, is not only of historical importance for understanding the multinational corporation but has also become the dominant normative model for analyzing and applying the diffusion of particular innovations. When the introduction of an innovation requires significant disruption of the social, cultural, and technical components of the system, the situation becomes quite different. In such transformation over time, the diffusion looks less like the dissemination of information and more like a sequence of related disruptions of complex systems central to the society. Here the unit of diffusion is no longer the traditional product but the whole technological system and know-how with new processes, purposes, and industrial alignments. Nevertheless, as the multinational corporation seeks expansion and growth, the innovation and diffusion process is carried along. Research and development laboratories are being taken to research workers in other countries, and multinationals are cutting research expense by using small and medium-sized production facilities of subsidiaries for trial runs and new products.[2]

It is now clear that the highly industrialized countries of the world may have to increasingly export technology instead of goods—a trend accelerating toward the end of this century. For example, as might be expected, the United States has the largest technological balance of payment surplus. Receipts from the sales of technology abroad increased from $362 million in 1956 to an estimated $2.2 billion in 1970. The United States' exports of technology now exceed the total imports of countries such as Colombia, Nigeria, or Egypt.

The 1964 data on international technology transactions showed five countries—the United States, Britain, West Germany, France, and Japan —each accounting for just over one-tenth of world imports of technology, a total of 61% and leaving only 39% for all other countries.[3] This indicates the growing diffusion of technology and the exchange of know-how among the big industrialized countries of the world. Although no comprehensive data on the worldwide diffusion of technology is available, it is estimated that United States exports of technology now ac-

2. Howe Martyn, "Manfacturing Abroad: Opportunities and Problems," *Michigan Business Review* 20, No. 3 (May 3, 1968), p. 12.

3. Lester R. Brown, *World Without Borders* (New York: Random House, 1972). See also his article in the *Washington Post,* November 12, 1972.

counts for about one-half of the world total. In 1972, a report of the Committee on Invisible Exports in London, called "Overseas Earnings of the British Professions," put the earnings of the nine leading British professions at $280 million a year. According to the report, the earnings of solicitors, accountants, and management consultants have increased rapidly in the last few years in overseas markets.[5]

In regard to the importation of technology by the less developed countries, it is assumed that the supply and demand conditions differ according to major types of industry. One important area is the field of mineral development, which involves a great deal of sophisticated technology. The most striking feature has been the increase in the degree of oligopolistic competition among major international companies representing an increasing range of nationalities; in the case of petroleum and to some extent, copper, a measure of collective bargaining by the host or supplier countries has evolved. In consequence, host countries are now exacting from international firms terms more favorable to themselves.

Another important area of industry is the field of manufacturing proper. It includes (1) franchising, (2) "conventional technology," and (3) "high technology." In franchising industry, the supplier has a special standard product or service which may be protected by a trademark. (Coca Cola, Hilton Hotels, or Holiday Inns are examples of such franchising.) Marketing is the main motivation of the supplier of technology. In "conventional technology" the manufacturing firm is involved with a considerable high level of know-how and technology both in the product design and production system. Marketing is still a dominant feature of this class of technology. Bata Shoe Co., Ltd., of Toronto and a substantial number of Japanese-controlled enterprises spread all over the Middle East and Asia are examples of conventional technology. Here the technology is standardized, centrally controlled, and relatively capital-intensive. The "high technology" type is characterized by a highly sophisticated level of technology accompanied by large research and development expenditure. Automotive industry, transportation equipment, heavy electronic devices, and certain areas of the chemical industry are examples of this type of technology. Here the bargaining position is such that the host country is in a rather weak position because the supplier of technology has almost a monopoly over the know-how and is in a very strong position. The conflict between the multinational corporation and the nation-state is more evident here.[5]

4. The *Christian Science Monitor,* November 25, 1972.
5. Walter A. Chudson, *The International Transfer of Commercial Technology to Developing Countries* (New York: UNITAR, Report No. 12, 1971). See also Jack Baranson, *International Transfer of Automotive Technology to Developing Countries* (New York: UNITAR, Report No. 8, 1971); Lawrence H. Wortzel, *Technology Transfer in the Pharmaceutical Industry* (New York: UNITAR, Report No. 14, 1971); and Robert B. Stobaugh, *The International Transfer of Technology in the Establishment of the Petrochemical Industry in Developing Countries* (New York: UNITAR, Report No. 12, 1971).

Finally, among the most important aspects of the diffusion of technology by the MNC is the training and personnel policy process. Although training may be provided through all the types of contractual agreements, the bulk of training activities is usually associated with direct investment. Nevertheless, the MNC, if committed to a policy of training, will spend considerable effort in various forms of training at both academic and industrial levels. The transfer of "show-how" rather than "know-how" has been a description of much of the activities of the firms dealing with "low" and "high" technologies.

NATIONAL POLICIES FOR THE DIFFUSION OF TECHNOLOGY

In a recent marked swing toward nationalism, country after country has begun imposing restriction on foreign investment. Arrangements that allow greater domestic participation and control, such as joint ventures, are being legislated or considered. In some cases, new laws and regulations are being enacted by the less-industrialized countries to rationalize the purchase of foreign technology and the activities of the multinational corporations. Conversely, the industrialized nations are initiating legislative measures to prevent the know-how drain. Yet in most cases the technology of the multinational corporations is still welcomed, and indeed sought. Technology is equated with industrial modernity and progress and power in the international arena. The steps taken by Iran and Mexico are two cases illustrating the perceptions of both the diffusion and transfer of technology as well as the activities of the multinational corporations.

In 1971 Iran paid $250 million in foreign exchange for technological know-how, an import which is expected to rise to $500 million or even more per annum by the end of this decade.[6] To some extent the increase in invisible imports is a measure of the success of the Iranian economy, which has been growing at a rate of 13% for the past five years. Two decades ago Iran's total imports—including both goods and services—hardly amounted to 50% of what the country now pays for imports of invisibles. Ten years ago total imports by the private sector was less than $250 million. Interestingly, about one-fifth ($50 million) of the foreign exchange bill for invisible imports accounts for the cost of keeping Iranian trainees, technicians, and students abroad. The rest of the invisible imports include payment for patent rights, licensing arrangements, and simply provisions of know-how and technology.

The diffusion of technological know-how and its availability in the international market has cut into the competition of major international firms in search of concessions. In 1971 when the Iranian concession-hold-

6. *Kayhan* (International Weekly Edition), Teheran, June 17, 1972 and September 27, 1972.

ers and their foreign partners announced their failure to arrive at financing the resources needed for exploitation of the vast copper resources in Iran, the Shah ordered that a fully Iranian concern with no foreign participation should take over the exploitation of copper. In September of 1972, Iran entered the first vital stage in exploitation of the huge Sar Cheshmeh copper deposits in the southern province of Kerman when the government-owned copper mining company signed an agreement with the American firm Anaconda to provide technological know-how. The development of these deposits, which the government hopes will enable Iran to enter the international copper market directly as a major supplier, represents a unique agreement. It provides for Anaconda to furnish training and technical services on a fee basis during the planning and construction period and then for a period of ten years afterward. This will include all necessary know-how and technological data for copper mining, processing, and blister making. The cost of exploitation and processing of Sar Cheshmeh copper mines has been estimated at $400 million, all of which will be raised by the Iranian government.

Iran's future concerns will not be with export promotion and intensification of industrial drive—but rather it will be to close the technological gap that currently exists between this country and the community of scientific and technologically advanced countries. Obviously, technological change can improve the productive capacity of a country only if it is accompanied by a parallel improvement in the skill of the labor force and industrial management, and by far-reaching social, economic, and administrative reforms. For example, experience has shown that educational reform is closely linked to administrative reform, while both of them are directly influenced by politics. In other words, skills of varying levels and dimensions are needed to man a new machinery which will have to establish a technological base. Aware of the difficulties that lie ahead, the current industrial and technological agreements between Iran and international firms stress the technological transfer and know-how by emphasizing the manpower training.

Yet the disappointing aspect of the present state of diffusion of technology is that it has already led to a wider gap between countries. The technological gap between advanced and developing countries is still growing. Ninety-eight % of the scientific and technological research at present is being undertaken in the advanced industrial countries—drawn on their own experiences. Only 1% of the research is directed at the special problems of less developed countries.[7] Therefore, a simple transfer of technology by the big industrial nations to the Third World will not suffice to reverse the trend unless it is controlled and modified by some legal and organizational machinery. Much of this technology is capital-intensive, and thus labor-saving, and will not in the long run meet the

---

7. Wilfred Jenks, "Technology for Freedom," International Labor Organization Meeting, Geneva, Switzerland, 1972.

needs of the recipient countries which have an abundance of labor and shortage of capital. At the third United Nations Conference on Trade and Development, President Echeverria of Mexico expressed a concern often heard in the Third World: the need to "increase our country's capacity for creating, assimilating and adopting the technology that today is largely concentrated in the industrial nations. From them should flow aid to finance the research programs and specialized technical centers we need in order to cope with our specific productivity and employment problems." [8] To rectify this imbalance, in November of 1972, he introduced legislation regarding Registration of the Transfer of Technology and the Use of Exploitation of Patents and Trademarks. The bill will, according to Mexico's president, provide a means to rationalize the purchase of foreign technology, make use of that available in the country, and foster the development of local technology.

The conditions under which Mexico up to now has been exposed to technology from abroad are, principally, the following:

> The machinery and equipment used by foreign subsidiary companies are frequently obsolete. This produces poor-quality and high-cost articles, reducing possibilities to compete in foreign markets and harming consumers.
>
> Technology is often too sophisticated for the needs of Mexico's industrial plants, which impedes the best possible use of resources. Machinery and equipment in this instance are generally labor-saving and require the intensive use of capital.
>
> Subsidiary companies face export restrictions to third countries. They are required to purchase capital goods and inputs contrary to the industrial plant's needs.
>
> There is interference in the production, marketing, and administration of the technology-importing company. Often contract specifications enable the supplier to fix prices and either limit or prevent research by the recipient company. It bans the use of alternate technology and sets itself up as sole purchaser of the goods produced.

In 1972, royalties collected on the transfer of technology in Mexico amounted to an average 3% of net sales, aside from the expenses caused by the obligation to purchase inputs from the technology-exporting company. The outflow of foreign exchange in 1970 to pay for the transfer of technology and additional elements amounted to some 2.5 billion pesos. As the Mexican government sees it, these circumstances have acted as a strong curb on the country's industrial development and technological progress and are the reason for President Echeverria's draft bill on the regulations of technology. The new law will require that technology-purchasing contracts be submitted to the Ministry of Industry and Com-

8. *Mexican Newsletter* (Office of the President, Mexico City), No. 6, April 19, 1972, and No. 12, November 20, 1972.

merce for consideration. A National Registry of the Transfer of Technology will be created for this purpose. It will be obligatory to register all contracts or agreements related to the transfer of technology for examination and approval. In terms of the draft bill, the Registry will supervise contracts or agreements that constitute an obligation to effect payments or provide counterservices with regard to such items as the concession of the use of trademarks, the provision of technical know-how, technical assistance of any kind, and foreign agencies or subsidiaries established in Mexico.

As specified in Article 1 of the draft bill, contracts or agreements for the import of technology will not be approved in the following cases:

> When the object is the transfer of technology freely available in the country, provided it refers to the same technology.
>
> When the price or counterservice is disproportionate to the technology acquired or constitutes an unwarranted or excessive burden on the country's economy.
>
> When they prohibit or limit the export of goods or services produced by the technology imported, in a way contrary to the interest of the country.
>
> When they prohibit the use of complementary technologies.
>
> When they impose on the importer the permanent use of personnel appointed by the supplier company.
>
> When they establish excessively long terms of validity. In no case may these terms constitute an obligation of over ten years for the importer.

Controls on royalty remittances have been imposed in many Latin American countries for almost two decades. Brazil, for example, disallows tax deductions for royalties paid to foreign firms; subsidiaries are even prohibited from paying their foreign-based parent companies. In response to balance of payment problems created by restrictions on profit remittances and to discourage income tax evasion (through the transfer of funds to third countries), Colombia, Mexico, and Chile enforce administrative regulations that reduce payments under licensing or technical service agreements.[9]

Recent efforts in some Latin American countries to improve the terms on which technology can be acquired specifically deal with: (1) the pricing of the to-be-obtained technology; (2) cost-and-benefit screening of the technology in terms of adaptability and desirability to the country/region;

9. Chudson, *International Transfer of Commercial Technology*, pp. 54–55. See also Adalberto J. Pinelo, *The Multinational Corporations as a Force in Latin American Politics* (New York: Praeger, 1973); Robert S. Ozaki, *The Control of Imports and Foreign Capital in Japan* (New York: Praeger, 1972); David Forsyth, *U.S. Investment in Scotland* (New York: Praeger, 1972); and Ciro E. Zoppo, "Toward a U.S. Policy on Nuclear Technology Transfer to Developing Countries," Southern California Arms Control and Foreign Policy Seminar, University of California, Los Angeles, July 1971.

and (3) systematic and institutionalized surveying of the worldwide availability of technology. In general, these efforts call for refusals to grant license agreements or contracts aimed at acquiring technology if this leads to prohibition or limitations of exports, the establishment of fixed prices, and the monopolization of markets.

As described above, the thrust of these policies is the strengthening of the bargaining position of the host country in the import of technology. In short, the national policies of the recipient countries are twofold: one aim is to bolster the country's private and public institutional capacity to carry out research for development and industrialization; the other is to enforce measures aimed at reducing payments for the suppliers and to increase benefits for the local recipients of the imported technology.

THE MNC AS COMMUNICATOR

In the process of diffusion of technology, the multinational corporation has become a well-organized contributing element to international communication. Such transactions—the transmission of messages as well as goods—convey values. Diffusion of technology does not occur in a sociopolitical vacuum. A system's social structure affects the diffusion of technology, and vice versa. This process of communication—in the form of technological exchange—may destroy, create, or reinforce biases in values like rationality, efficiency, progress, and the basic developmental goal of individuals and society. In an extreme case, the technological diffusion, used indiscriminately and without control, can alter the social structure of the system and may lead to what may be called technological feudalism. In many societies the composition of the power structure has been altered with the emergence and influx of the new elite, who are identified with the technological resources they command. One can hypothesize that the newest members of the political elite are technology or information experts. Thus a recent monograph on information technology and its implication concluded: "All in all, it seems obvious that development in information and communication technology will lead to greater specialization and diversity in society, also tend to exacerbate rather than ameliorate what have been rather latent differences. We thus predict increasing fractionalism in political parties, in ethnic groups and racial groups, etc." [10]

Clearly, the multinational corporation as communicator interacts with many actors in the course of diffusion of technology. Here the focus will be to illustrate four principal areas: the *individual,* the *business enterprise,* the *government,* and the *culture.*

For the individual, the multinational corporation makes available a

10. Conference Board, Inc., *Information Technology: Some Critical Implications for Decision Makers* (New York: Conference Board, Inc., 1972), p. 49.

technology which is initially highly attractive. It conveys, therefore, a new sense of well-being. The technology, be it a tractor or penicillin, brings material improvement to his life. The advent of technology may mean also a status symbol, a respect for the owner. Anthropologists working in rural Africa have reported that a radio is normally prominently displayed in the home, and often decorated.[11] Sometimes possession of an article for its status value becomes an end in itself, such as carrying cameras without film or briefcases with nothing inside.[12] Importantly, the diffusion of a given technology may confer upon the individual enlightenment about the outside world. The way in which an article such as a radio leads to such knowledge is apparent, but even other goods and services can serve this purpose. Of course, the diffusion of technology may also have secondary effects. The efficiency of the tractor may lead the farmer to develop his skill or wealth. From this may occur a spiraling consumption demand, in which expectation may be escalated far beyond the capacity for fulfillment. The effect can only be widespread discontent and resentment of the "haves." This appears to be the phenomenon occurring now in Jamaica, where natives who live in squalor have been exposed to tourists luxuriating at large chain hotels. Their resentment is being expressed in racial abuses and indifference to tourists.[13]

The multinational corporation as communicator with other *business enterprises* can stimulate, even create new consumer markets. It is also in an excellent position to capitalize on these markets. The recent study of the diffusion of technology in the semiconductor industry illustrates this ability.[14] In the production of semiconductors (components of electronic devices), capturing a large share of the market depends upon having the latest technology. Historically, American companies have been pioneers in the industry; therefore when they moved overseas, their foreign subsidiaries held an advantage over local firms in Europe. Because they could easily transfer the home technology and know-how, they early captured a large share of the market. The leading semiconductor producers in Europe had neglected to adopt a new manufacturing technique that had been available to them through licensing agreement for some eleven years; with the presence of the foreign subsidiaries, they were suddenly forced to adopt the new technology. As the study explains, "foreign subsidiaries in Europe . . . have provided an alternative to the established semiconductor leaders and imposed a discipline on the industry that assures the swift diffusion of the new technology."

11. Russell H. Bernard and Pertti J. Pelto, eds., *Technology and Social Change* (New York: Macmillan, 1972), especially p. 216, also pp. 166–99 and 202–25.
12. John C. Condon, "Some Guidelines for Mass Communication Research in East Africa," *Gazette*, 14, No. 2 (1968), p. 3.
13. The *Washington Post*, November 12, 1972.
14. John E. Tilton, *International Diffusion of Technology: The Case of Semiconductors* (Washington, D.C.: The Brookings Institution, 1971), p. 134.

Finally, the multinational corporation as a communicator with *culture* brings with itself certain values which may assume a certain priority in the recipient country's hierarchy of values. The kind of "wealth ethic" communicated by the multinational corporation has been well-expressed in the 1973 edition of *Fielding's Guide to the Caribbean:*

> Along with Coca-Cola, Betty Crocker, and Mission Impossible, we Yankees have exported southward some of the seeds of our own country's problems, juvenile delinquency, divisiveness on racial and ethnic grounds, militant radicalism.[15]

Another value that the multinational corporation can communicate to a culture is a greater affection for the culture of the originating country, at the expense of the indigenous culture. One measure of this penetration is the rapid growth and expansion of the American mass media technology and communication firms around the world.[16] The cultural-information sphere of the multinational corporation's activities must be included in the appraisal of the diffusion of technology and its global influence. Sophisticated communication methodologies, such as opinion surveys, market research, and public relations techniques are some of the chief channels that convey internationally the values and life styles of their promoters. Fashions, music, pop culture and its products, news and entertainment from the United States and some of the highly industrialized European countries are so dominant that a Mexican writer was recently prompted to say: "We are the first generation of foreigners in our own country!" The recent study on the role of the United States advertising industry around the world concluded that "with the advent of space communications, the opportunity to achieve a world-wide audience for promotional ends has not been ignored" by the multinational corporations, that "the heavy information flow produced and supported by American companies overseas makes a powerful contribution to the domestic maintenance and global extension of the business system and its values." [17] Yet it may be argued that this swift global diffusion of technology and know-how provides commonly shared cultural experience in a manner unparalleled in communication history, transmitting man's symbolic needs and expression on a world scale.

15. The *Washington Post,* November 12, 1972. See also Harvey D. Shapiro, "The Multinationals: Giants beyond Flag and Country," The *New York Times Magazine,* March 18, 1973.

16. See Alan Wells, *Picture-Tube Imperialism: The Impact of U.S. Television on Latin America* (Maryknoll, N.Y.: Orbis Books, 1972); Herbert Schiller, *Mass Communication and American Empire* (New York: Augustus M. Kelley, 1969); and T. H. Guback, *The International Film Industry* (Bloomington, Ind.: Indiana University Press, 1969).

17. Herbert Schiller, "Madison Avenue Imperialism," in Richard L. Merritt, ed., *Communication in International Politics* (Urbana, Ill.: Unversity of Illinois Press, 1972), p. 338.

CONCLUSION

Although the literature on multinational corporations has generally emphasized the importance of the system in which the process of technological diffusion occurs, little or no attention has been paid to the structural influences and determinants of the communication effect. Research is needed, for example, to identify at what points and under what conditions and working criteria the multinational corporations and the recipients of technology negotiate and reach an agreement. This requires the exploration of the values that underlie such an agreement as well as the perception of the parties as to the relative importance of these values in the decision/negotiation process.

Assuming that the social structure of a given system or country acts to impede or facilitate the rate of technological diffusion, the study of norms, social status, and hierarchy of the social system influencing the decision and behavior of individual recipients and adopters becomes imperative. Thus we can hypothesize that the power elite serves as gatekeeper in controlling the rate and kind of diffusion of technology into a system. It may prevent the diffusion of certain technological facts while favoring others that do not threaten to change its power and system structure. Once the diffusion process takes place, it is not always the new technology per se that is the main source of rising discontent, but the social structure of the country and its bureaucratic and interelite relationships that determine the nature and distribution of that technology.

To evaluate the role of the multinational corporation in the diffusion of technology, we must also focus our attention on the number of "gatekeepers" involved between the introduction of a given technology into a system and the actual adoption of that technology by the system or its members. A given technological or social innovation usually requires going through a number of important stages—such as awareness, information evaluation, trial—before it can be adopted by the recipient.[18] What are the roles and policies of both the multinational corporation and the recipient member in each of these stages? Who are the rejectors? Who are the adopters? This requires, of course, the identification and the study of such subchannels as training institutes, communication networks, and scholarship programs through which the multinational corporation may diffuse the new technology.

The multinational corporation has become one of the chief organizers

18. See Everett M. Rogers, *Diffusion of Innovation* (New York: The Free Press, 1962); Everett M. Rogers with F. F. Shoemaker, *Communication of Innovation: A Cross-Cultural Approach* (New York: The Free Press, 1971); and Joe M. Bohlen, "Research Needed on Adoption Models," in Wilbur Schramm and Donald E. Roberts, eds., *The Process and Effects of Mass Communication* (Urbana, Ill.: University of Illinois Press, 1971), pp. 798–815.

and manufacturers of the international flow of communication. The diffusion of technology through this channel takes place in a complex economy and, more broadly still, in a total, complex culture. The most interesting and useful approaches to understanding technological diffusion by the multinational corporations will be those that attempt to locate, through these contexts, the process of diffusion.

The multinational corporation and labor

NAT WEINBERG [1]

> *I remember about 15 years ago one of our local officials negotiating with Philips demanding higher wages for the technicians inside the British Company. The management replied by saying, "You have already higher wages than those paid in Holland," and the reply our official gave was, "Well, it is a bloody good job your Head Office is not in Hong Kong or you would be offering bowls of rice." [2]*

The aim of employers everywhere,[3] nationally or internationally, is to minimize labor costs and to extract the maximum possible in productivity and profits from the workers they employ. Despite frequently

1. Several points must be made clear at the outset:
   1. This chapter is an expression of my personal views and not necessarily those of the UAW, with which I was until recently associated.
   2. The subject matter of this chapter cannot be covered adequately in the space available. Accordingly, documentation, pertinent data, illuminating illustrations, qualifications on broad generalizations, and a number of quite important substantive points have had to be omitted, and certain matters have had to be considerably oversimplified.
   3. Certain proposals are advanced that, at first glance, may appear to be impossible to carry out in practice. Space does not permit presentation of means whereby the apparent obstacles could be overcome. The reader, therefore, will have to take it on faith that (a) I am not so blind as to be unable to recognize the problems involved and (b) I have thought of (what I consider to be) feasible solutions to those problems.
   4. In international matters, particularly, time spans between recognition of problems and response to them tend to be exceedingly lengthy. The reader should keep that fact constantly in mind in connection even with proposed actions that seem so obviously necessary that one might expect them to have been taken yesterday.
   5. My direct experience with the subject matter of this chapter relates to metalworking industries, primarily to autos. Although it is probably true that the International Metalworkers' Federation, and its Automotive Department in particular, is in the vanguard of trade union action in relation to international corporations, the chapter, nevertheless, admittedly deals disproportionately with those industries.
2. K. Gill in "International Companies," Report of a Conference on International Companies, Trades Union Congress, London, October 17, 1970, p. 67. He could well have added that he knew of no corporation that insisted upon forcing a wage increase on its British workers because wages in its U.S. headquarters, for example, were higher than in Britain.
3. This is an illustration of the type of generalization I am compelled to make for lack of space. There are, of course, exceptional employers who temper their pursuit of profits with a measure of concern for the welfare of their workers.

heard lip-service to the contrary, workers are treated not as human beings who are ends in themselves, but as mere instruments to be bought as cheaply as possible, to be used with ruthless efficiency and to be discarded when no longer needed. Human beings, however, do not readily accept such treatment, and history testifies that wherever employer-employee relationships develop, workers seek to unite in unions for mutual protection against abuse by their employers and for advancement of their common interests. Employers react by striving to keep their workers divided. When no longer able to deal individually with each worker, employers seek to deal separately with separate groups of their workers in an effort to play each group off against the others.

Thus unions seek to spread organization (or at least coordination among separate organizations) of workers co-extensively with the spread of market competition or coordination among the employers of their members. Managements, as long as they can get away with it, strive to maintain fragmentation and competition among their workers and to keep unions as far away as possible from top corporate policy-makers. Those management goals are likely to be abandoned only when coordination on the union side approximately matches coordination on the employer side. These matters do not change when national corporations go multinational. Both the instrumental view of human beings and the goal of keeping workers divided remain inact. Mr. Henry Ford II, who is by no means the least enlightened among corporation officials, has provided illustrations of both. Expressing the first, he said: "In South Korea, Taiwan and Indonesia we see promising markets and we see an attractive supply of cheap labor." The divisive aim was obvious when he threatened striking British Ford workers that his company would make no further investments in their country.

Thus, the rise of multinational corporations[5] confronts unions with problems that, for the most part, are new and different less in their essential character than in their scale and complexity. The transfer of familiar problems to the international arena, however, magnifies them to such a degree that they become qualitatively different.

Moreover, the transfer is occurring before the corresponding problems have been fully solved within national boundaries. In most democratic, advanced, industrialized countries large numbers of workers remain un-

4. As quoted by Tom Metz in "Ford Says More Concentration Is Planned in Overseas Markets, Especially Far East," *Wall Street Journal*, December 3, 1969, p. 12.

5. I consider "international," "transnational," or "supranational" better adjectives for the corporations under consideration than the more commonly used "multinational." The last assumes (or at least has as a possible connotation) loyalties to more than one nation. That, in turn, assumes that the interests and goals of all the nations involved are always in harmony. If the latter assumption is invalid, as obviously it is, simultaneous loyalty to all of them is impossible. The semantics are further complicated by the fact that in the Andean group of nations, for example, several *governments* may share ownership in certain corporations. Such corporations are "multinational" in the literal sense of the term.

organized; many companies have thus far succeeded in avoiding collective bargaining; and unions often have not succeeded in coordinating their policies and actions (including those relating to individual companies) among, or even within themselves. In less developed countries, unions tend to be weak, frequently to the point of almost complete impotence, and, more often than not, under severe restrictions or outright domination by their governments. In countries ruled by dictatorships, regardless of their stage of development, organizations masquerading as unions are in fact instruments of the state for the manipulation of workers and the suppression of independent action on their own behalf.

The variations in union strength and independence summarized above are the most obvious of the obstacles the unions face as they seek to coordinate their activities to counteract the centralized coordination of the hierarchically organized MNCs. Among the other obstacles are those following:

1. In a number of important industrialized countries as well as in some LDCs and in the underground movements under certain dictatorships, unions are divided along political or religious lines or both. Similar divisions exist among international labor organizations.[6]

2. Union structures differ widely from country to country. This makes it difficult to identify the units within each country's unions which are the counterparts of those in the other countries with which coordination is needed in relation to a particular MNC. Even where the proper units can be identified, the procedures of the unions involved may not in all cases readily enable those units to make the decisions needed to achieve coordinated action.

3. There are differences in the organizational situation with respect to white-collar and technical workers. In some countries they remain largely unorganized; in others they belong to the same unions as manual workers; in still others they are divided, some belonging to the same unions

6. International labor organizations are basically of two types. The first type is represented by the ICFTU (International Confederation of Free Trade Unions), composed of social-democratic-oriented and nonpolitical and nonconfessional organizations; WFTU (World Federation of Trade Unions), composed of Communist (including Soviet bloc) and Communist-oriented national unions; and the WCL (World Confederation of Labor), composed of Catholic-oriented, although no longer officially Catholic, national unions which link together so-called "national centers" such as the AFL-CIO in the United States to which in turn, are affiliated unions representing workers in various industrial and/or occupational groupings in their respective countries. Two or more separate national centers may be members of the same confederation; e.g., before the AFL and CIO merged, both belonged to the ICFTU. In some cases (e.g., The United Mine Workers of America) industrial unions unaffiliated with any national center are affiliated directly with the ICFTU. The second type of international labor organization consists of the International Trade Secretaries (ITSs), which link together the national unions representing workers in certain broad industrial or occupational categories. The ITSs have a loose autonomous relationship with the ICFTU. The WFTU and the WCL have no real counterparts to the ITSs.

and others belonging to separate unions of white collar and/or technical workers. Where there are separate unions for the latter group(s), they may or may not be affiliated with the same national federation as the manual workers' unions.

4. There are differences in bargaining procedures. In the United States, for example, separate agreements are negotiated with each auto corporation. In Germany, bargaining in the metalworking industry is on a regional basis involving all metalworking firms, including the auto corporations, belonging to the association of metalworking employers.[7] In England, bargaining for certain branches of the metalworking industry, including autos, is conducted at the national level by the Confederation of Shipbuilding and Engineering Unions with a counterpart body representing most employers in the same industries. The British subsidiaries of the U.S. auto corporations, however, bargain individually rather than through the employers' organization.

5. The subject matter covered by collective bargaining agreements differs. For example, U.S. agreements in the auto industry establish "effective" wage rates—the rates actually paid for each job. In England and Germany, minimum wages and the amounts of general wage increases are negotiated nationally and regionally, respectively, while effective wage rates are determined at the plant level—in England through negotiations with the shop stewards' body representing all the unions in the plant, in Germany with the works council, which is a statutorily created body separate from the union and representing all workers in the plant, whether or not members of the union. Matters such as working conditions, shop floor representation, and grievance procedures covered by collective bargaining agreements in the United States are dealt with by works councils or similar bodies in some other countries. Certain fringe benefits provided through collective bargaining in the U.S. are established by law elsewhere.

6. Collective bargaining agreements in some countries run for fixed terms during which strikes are prohibited. This applies to the U.S. auto industry, except that the UAW reserves the right to strike during the contract term over such matters as work pace, health and safety, and wage rates for new jobs. In certain other countries workers are free to strike at any time, whether over grievances or for changes in their agreements.

7. Legal provisions governing unions differ among countries. In the U.S., collective bargaining agreements are legally enforceable contracts. Sympathy strikes and secondary boycotts, among other things, are legally outlawed. In certain other countries (including England until recently), agreements are not legally binding and sympathy strikes, secondary boycotts, and similar actions are permitted.

8. National unions are sovereign bodies, jealous of their autonomy.

---

7. There are separate negotiations with the relatively few firms not members of the association.

Cooperation with unions in other countries is entirely voluntary. The labor movement has no international mechanism comparable to the top echelons of the MNCs, which can command obedience and adherence to a common policy or course of action from the managements of their separate national subsidiaries.

9. The bonds of labor solidarity are difficult to weld and maintain because of distance, which makes meetings infrequent and communications sporadic, and because of differences in nationality and cultural background.

The obstacles to international union coordination outlined above are certainly formidable. But so were the obstacles that had to be overcome when national unions were struggling to be born in the countries in which they now play significant roles. The earliest national unions started with no experience and no resources other than the willingness of their members to make sacrifices. There was no source to which they could turn for help; they had to make it on their own. As they gained in experience, resources, and power they were able to aid in the formation of unions in other industries; e.g., the unions that initially established the CIO helped to organize new unions in the mass-production industries.

Similarly existence of strong national unions in the industries and home countries of most major MNCs can serve as a foundation on which to build toward international union coordination. The leadership of the unions involved are aware of the dangers that the MNCs present to the welfare of their members. They know that the rapid growth and spread of the MNCs, while union coordination lags, has sharply tilted the balance of bargaining power in favor of the MNCs. They are conscious also of the obstacles to coordination.

They know, among other things, that coordination requires the surrender of a degree of autonomy by the unions involved, and certain changes, some of them major, in their customs and practices. A resolution adopted by the 1971 Congress of the International Metalworkers' Federation (IMF), for example, explicitly recognized those needs.[8]

The unions do not, by any means, underestimate either the magnitude of the challenge that faces them or the time it will take to develop an effective response. They have mapped out the steps to be taken in what they know will be a long-term process and they have embarked on the course they have charted.

The effort they have undertaken aims at three goals. The first is to halt and reverse the present trend of growing imbalance in bargaining strength in relation to the MNCs. The second is to enlist the aid of individual governments, to the extent that purely national efforts can be effective, to curb antilabor and other abuses by MNCs. The third is to

8. International Metalworkers' Federation, "Resolution on Multinational Corporations," *Minutes of the 22d Congress,* Lausanne, Switzerland, October 26–30, 1971, pp. 141–142.

subject the MNCs to international regulation covering not only labor matters but the full range of their activities that affect the welfare of world society.

The chief instruments for achieving coordination with respect to all three objectives are the International Trade Secretariats (ITSs)—although the international trade union centers (ICFTU, WCL, and WFTU) and the worker-based political parties that are highly influential in certain countries also have important roles to play.

With respect to collective bargaining, the general strategy of the ITSs concerned with MNCs includes the following elements, many of which are already being implemented in varying degrees while others await completion of the necessary groundwork:

1. Help in the organization and strengthening of unions in countries where they are nonexistent or weak, and encouragement of mergers of competing national unions in the same industries and companies.

2. Bridging ideological and religious divisions. Some progress is being made in reducing the seriousness of those divisions as factors impeding union coordination in the face of the MNCs. For example, at a recent tripartite (labor-employer-government) meeting of experts on MNCs convened by the International Labor Organization (ILO), the labor participants drawn from Socialist, Catholic, Communist, and nonpolitical, nonconfessional unions found themselves able to work together in harmony without any noticeable friction resulting from their political and religious differences.

3. Training in union procedures and techniques of workers, in countries where unionism is less advanced, by union experts from other countries.

4. Exchanges of information. The more active and effective ITSs collect, analyze, and distribute information on such matters as MNCs' finances, wage rates, working hours and overtime premiums, working conditions, benefit programs, industrial relations policies, decision-making processes, investment plans, etc. Information may be published in periodic studies, some of which are quite elaborate, or disseminated through news bulletins or magazines. Exchanges of information also take place through meetings, which may be regional (e.g., European, Asian, or Latin American), bilateral (between national unions of two countries), or worldwide and may cover a broad industrial category (e.g., metalworking), a single industry (e.g., autos or electrical equipment), or a single corporation. Knowledge of industry or company practices in other countries can be a potent union tool in mobilizing and strengthening the morale of workers and in gaining public support. Information needed by national unions to help them in particular disputes with their employers is also provided.

5. Assistance in negotiations. The UAW, for example, arranged through the IMF to send a member of its executive board to testify in

wage arbitration proceedings under Australian law involving General Motors' subsidiary in that country. The Ford Department of the UAW has sent a Spanish-speaking member of its staff to assist Latin American unions in bargaining with Ford subsidiaries in their countries. Pressure has been brought on the world headquarters of certain MNCs by unions representing the workers of the corporations' home countries to help unions negotiating with subsidiaries in other countries.

6. Assistance in strikes. This may take the form of direct financial assistance to the striking union by the ITS and by the latter's affiliates in other countries, pressure on world corporate headquarters by the union in the home country, refusal by workers in other countries to perform overtime work that would enable the corporation to make up for production lost as a result of the strike, refusals to operate machinery or to work on components transferred from the struck plant, international boycotts of the MNC's products, publicity and demonstrations directed against the MNC in other countries in which it operates or sells its products, sympathy strikes and slowdowns where legally permissible, etc.

7. Action against strategic plants. This tactic can be highly effective against corporations that integrate their operations internationally—making certain parts and components each in a separate country, bringing them together in another country for assembly, and marketing them not only in that country but in others as well. Under those circumstances, an MNC becomes highly vulnerable on an international scale to a slowdown or strike by a relative handful of workers in a single country. The ITS involved might be able to provide generous financial support to those workers if it became necessary.

8. Assistance from other ITSs. In conflicts of major importance, the ITS directly affected may be able to obtain help from others. For example, the International Transport Federation (ITF) could call upon its affiliates and their members to refuse to handle shipments to and from the MNC involved. Even if only a few of the ITF affiliates responded, they could have a devastating effect upon the production and marketing operations of the MNC. The effect on production could be particularly serious for an internationally integrated MNC.

9. Creation of worldwide corporation councils. These councils bring together and attempt to coordinate the activities of unions representing an individual MNCs' workers in all the countries in which the latter operates. Such councils have already been created for all of the major automobile MNCs. Comparable structures, although sometimes less formal, also exist or are in process of being created in other industries.

10. Synchronization of contract expiration dates. On this score, the IMF resolution previously cited says:

> As the international corporations become less dependent upon the profits drawn from any single country, the power of each national union acting alone will be correspondingly weakened. The IMF must therefore prepare

for joint action across national borders that will compel the international corporations to pay serious heed to the demands of their workers because of the danger to their profits in several countries simultaneously.

Joint action will require that unions in all countries, which bargain with the same corporation, be legally and contractually free to act simultaneously if and when the need arises. As one means to that end, common contract termination dates should be sought in those countries where collective bargaining agreements are negotiated for fixed periods.

11. Harmonization of demands. This involves presenting MNCs with identical demands in some or all of the countries in which they operate. The specific demands reflect priorities agreed upon by representatives of national unions convened under ITS (including world corporation council) auspices. The demands will frequently call for leveling up in all the countries involved to the best standards already in effect in any country in which the MNC or any firm in its industry operates. Considerable progress has already been made toward harmonization of hours of work. Next, in all probability, will come certain working conditions, e.g., relief time for assembly-line workers. Harmonization of wage rates on a worldwide scale is probably far in the future, although it has already been begun on a regional basis as between the United States and Canada and may not be too far off in the European communities. Harmonization of social insurance types of fringe benefits is complicated by differences in national legislation but, here too, some progress has already been made with respect to the United States and Canada.

12. Joint meetings with MNCs. Although the MNCs generally try to avoid anything that might be interpreted as recognition of unions on an international scale, a number of them have found it advisable to meet at the world corporation level with ITS representatives or simultaneously with unions representing their workers in several countries. Though some of these meetings amounted to little more than courtesy calls, several of them have resulted in practical actions by the MNCs. Among the subjects most likely to be discussed is the international allocation or reallocation of production by the MNC and protection or compensation for workers who may be adversely affected thereby. Another is refusal by the MNC to recognize unions in one or more countries.

13. Joint bargaining. The more successful of the joint meetings mentioned above have verged on joint bargaining, although with reference to very narrowly restricted subject matter. Both the number of MNCs involved in such meetings and the contents of the discussions are likely to broaden. True joint bargaining on a worldwide scale is probably some time off, at the very least. If and when it does arrive, it quite likely will focus at first on harmonization demands in the areas of working conditions and hours of work. Recognition of unions in countries where the MNC in question has refused recognition is another matter that may be raised. Regional joint bargaining, however, is already a fact on the North

American continent (see below) and may not be far off in the European countries (EC). A proposed new EC law intended to be applicable to so-called "European companies" would require joint bargaining where requested by the EC unions involved.

14. International agreements. International agreements of worldwide scope, of course, would have to await bargaining on the same geographical scale which, as indicated, is probably a matter for the relatively distant future. International agreements covering workers in both the United States and Canada already exist, the best-known of which is the UAW agreement with Chrysler covering approximately 128,800 workers in the United States and 13,500 in Canada. (White-collar as well as manual workers are covered in both countries.) The negotiation of these two-country agreements was facilitated, of course, by the fact that the same union operates on both sides of the border.

Unions are aware that collective bargaining alone cannot provide sufficient countervailing power to protect their members and the general social welfare against actual and potential harm from the MNCs. They know that self-interest (which all too often translates in practice as greed) is the motivating force behind corporation policies and actions, and that the corporations have far outgrown the power of the invisible hand that Adam Smith counted upon to contain business selfishness and to channel it in socially desirable directions.

Both nationally and internationally, therefore, unions look to governments to regulate corporate behavior to protect the public interest. In addition, the growing importance of the MNCs evokes new concerns. Unions see that national economic planning efforts of their governments, including planning for full employment, can be disrupted or frustrated by decisions of the MNCs relating to the allocation of investment. The MNCs can affect not only the number but the composition of job opportunities and thereby the occupational structure of the labor force. At the same time, the export of labor-intensive activities from home countries with persistently high unemployment (e.g., the U.S.) can perpetuate unemployment for the most vulnerable and disadvantaged members of the labor force. The distribution of income within countries can also be adversely affected. If, for example, the U.S., as has been predicted, were to become a service economy (i.e., a rentier economy) as a result of capital exports, the division of income as between property and employment—which means as between the wealthy and the nonwealthy—would be changed markedly. Governments are forced into competition with each other in offering concessions, subsidies, and "incentives" of various kinds—including restrictive labor legislation—in order to attract investment by the MNCs. MNCs sometimes obtain tariff protection with resulting excessive prices to workers and other consumers in host countries. MNCs can evade national taxation and foreign exchange controls through manipulation of their transfer prices. The combination of concessions and tax evasion can nullify whatever benefits might otherwise accrue to host countries from the inward flow of investment by the MNCs. The high profits that MNCs insist upon as a condition for investment in the LDCs (let alone the subsidies they exact and their evasion of tax and exchange controls) have converted some LDCs into capital exporters. That, of course, should be no surprise (either with respect to LDCs or industrialized countries) in view of the fact that one of the main arguments advanced by defenders of U.S. MNCs is that direct foreign investments make a net positive contribution to the U.S. balance of payments.

Because of the very nature of the MNCs, national governments, acting individually, are sharply limited in their ability to control the MNCs. The latter can escape many forms of national regulation through the cracks represented by national boundaries. Host countries are at a particular disadvantage[9] in attempting regulation, because they are in competition with other actual or potential hosts for the capital, managerial skills, and technologies of the MNCs.

Home countries can be somewhat more effective in curbing abuses by their own MNCs both within and outside their boundaries.[10] With respect to the latter, there is precedent in the U.S. government's application of its antitrust laws and its Trading with the Enemy Act to foreign subsidiaries of U.S.-based MNCs.

One form that home country regulation might take, which would avoid the charges of "extraterritoriality" aroused by the precedents cited, was outlined in a resolution adopted by the UAW's International Executive Board in June 1971. It proposed that government licenses be required for foreign investments (including reinvestment of foreign profits) by U.S. corporations.

The applicant for a license would be required to show that the proposed investment would serve the interests of the United States economically (with certain exceptions made for developing countries) and would be free from harmful political consequences. The licensee would have to guarantee that he would compensate in full for loss of wages, fringe benefits, seniority rights, etc., any U.S. workers adversely affected by the in-

9. The Organization of Petroleum Exporting Countries (OPEC) has shown that the disadvantage can be overcome when host countries control scarce raw materials, provided the countries can muster what is thus far a rare degree of solidarity. Where manufacturing is involved, only countries or groupings of countries that offer a large actual or potential market are in a position to exert any leverage at all on the MNCs. Even the attraction of a large market may not be sufficient; General Motors withdrew from India to escape a requirement for host country participation in ownership of its Indian subsidiary.

10. The limitations of even home country action are illustrated in a report in *Business Week* (March 17, 1973,) that Massey-Ferguson, Ltd., threatened to move its world headquarters out of Canada to escape new legislation that would tax certain forms of its overseas income previously free from Canadian taxes and that a dozen smaller MNCs had actually removed their headquarters from Canada, citing the tax change as a major reason. The Canadian government responded to these pressures by postponing the effectuation of the tax changes.

vestment, whether because of imports or decreases in exports resulting from the investment. The licensee would be required, further, to comply with a comprehensive code of good behavior in relation to workers employed in the host country.

Application of such a code, in effect, would make the MNCs transmission belts for good labor standards as they now claim to be for good managerial practices, etc. One consequence would be refusal of licenses for investments in countries that, for example, deny the right of free collective bargaining to their workers or enforce racial discrimination. Refusal of licenses on such grounds would not represent improper interference in the internal affairs of host countries any more than insistence by an MNC—as a condition for investing—on obtaining exemption from the potential host country's foreign exchange controls for dividend remittances to the parent corporation. In either case, the country involved remains free to refuse to meet the prerequisite for the investment.

The license requirement could be extended, of course, to cover a wide variety of other matters outside the specifically labor sphere, e.g., adherence in host countries to home country environmental standards.

Independently of the licensing proposal (although it could be made one of the conditions for a license), national legislation could impose financial disclosure requirements on MNCs that would materially assist the various national unions bargaining with them as well as serve other useful public purposes. Host countries, despite the competitive (with other countries) disadvantages they suffer in relation to the MNCs, in some cases, have required the disclosure of certain data by MNC subsidiaries within their respective jurisdictions. But such requirements are of limited use if the MNC varies its accounting practices from country to country. Combined with the transfer pricing problem, lack of international consistency in accounting makes it well-nigh impossible for both governments and unions to determine how much of the MNCs' total profit is properly attributable to its operation in any single country. Home countries (e.g., the U.S. through amendment of SEC regulations or, if necessary, new legislation) could require their MNCs to publish financial data calculated on a uniform basis for each national subsidiary, including the formula for determining and the amount of the corporationwide costs (e.g., research costs) allocated to each subsidiary.

In the current situation, with reform of the international monetary system a crucial issue, the U.S. has a unique opportunity to take national action to combat a major threat created by the MNCs—the trend toward international oligopoly that threatens not only workers but the world's consumers as well. Richard J. Barber has written: "A good guess is that by 1980 three hundred large corporations will control 75 percent of all the world's manufacturing assets." [11] Others have made similar projections.

11. *The American Corporation, Its Power, Its Money, Its Politics* (New York: E. P. Dutton and Co., Inc., 1970), p. 264.

Although international oligopoly grows apace, moves toward monetary reform are seriously impeded by the "dollar overhang"—the problem of how to dispose of the variously estimated 60 to 80 billion U.S. dollars in the hands of foreign governments, central banks, and private organizations and individuals around the world. Those dollars emigrated largely as a result of foreign investment by U.S. MNCs. They obviously cannot be redeemed out of the nation's limited gold holdings and it is almost certain that their holders will demand something more tangible than SDRs for their dollars.

Two problems could be alleviated simultaneously if the U.S. government would encourage foreign owners of dollars to use them to acquire the assets of the subsidiaries of U.S.-based MNCs operating within their respective national boundaries.[12] Those subsidiaries would then become independent national competitors of their present parent MNCs, thus reversing—at least temporarily—the trend toward world oligopoly.[13] At the same time, a substantial part of the dollar overhang would be removed as an obstacle to reform of the international monetary system.

An alternative that has been proposed—investment of foreign-held dollars in U.S. enterprises, old or new—would contribute to solution of the monetary problem but, through the strengthening of existing non–U.S.-based MNCs and the creation of new ones, it might aggravate the oligopoly problem.

In any case, purely national action, as noted, is sharply limited in its ability to curb abuses by the MNCs, whether in labor matters or in others affecting the general welfare of the world's peoples. The international labor movement is therefore pressing for intergovernmental action. The ultimate goal, in this regard, is adoption of a comprehensive and enforceable international code of good behavior to be applicable to all MNCs, wherever they operate. The code would apply not only to international "corporations," narrowly defined, but also to the growing number of Soviet and Soviet-bloc enterprises operating in noncommunist countries.

The goal is not as overly ambitious as it may at first glance seem. As the previously quoted IMF resolution noted:

12. Governments and/or central banks using dollar holdings for this purpose could operate the assets so acquired as publicly owned enterprises, or they could create and sell shares of stock representing full or partial ownership to private individuals within their respective countries.

13. Where the assets involved consisted of facilities whose operations were closely integrated with those owned by the same MNC in other countries, the terms of purchase would have to be carefully drawn to assure the continued viability of the acquisition. Obviously in the absence of such safeguards, the value of the assets in question would be much lower and the threat to base compensation upon salvage value, for example, could induce the MNC involved to proffer the needed assurances. The need that would otherwise arise to duplicate the facilities elsewhere in order to avoid or mend a break in the chain of integration would provide an additional inducement to the MNC to commit itself to continued purchase of the output of the sold assets.

Fortunately, unions have close ties with political parties that are, or have been and are likely to be again, the government parties in countries that play a leading role in determining the rules for economic and social relations among the world's nations.

This is true of six of the governments in the so-called "Group of Ten," which plays the decisive role in world monetary matters, and a seventh would have been added if Mitterand had won in the second round of the French elections in 1974. If some or all of those governments were to propose an international code of law to regulate MNCs, they would doubtless have the support of others who are increasingly disturbed by foreign domination of their economies and particularly of many of the LDCs, which have expressed themselves in the UN, UNCTAD, ECOSOC, and the ILO as seriously concerned with MNC abuses. The same resolution, therefore, called upon the IMF's Secretariat

> to take the initiative toward the creation of an international task force, including representatives of other trade union organizations and progressive political forces, to develop a proposal for a comprehensive code of international corporation law.

With official representatives of influential political parties (including some from the LDCs) involved in formulating the proposed code, the likelihood of its being raised and seriously considered at the intergovernmental level would be greatly enhanced.

Under the code contemplated by the IMF resolution,

> No firm [would] be permitted to carry on activities in more than one country unless it conforms to the requirements of [the proposed] international laws.

The scope of the international code—certainly in its initial form—would probably not be as broad as that of the national regulatory laws that the industrialized countries have found necessary to enact to protect their peoples from the consequences of unbridled corporate pursuit of profits. But it should be made broad enough, as quickly as possible, to cover at least the major areas in which national legislation cannot cope effectively with the power of the MNCs. Particular attention would have to be paid to such matters as subsidies and concessions (including concessions at the expense of workers) with respect to which MNCs are able to pit nation against nation in competitive bidding for their favors—thus setting in motion an international version of Gresham's law under which bad standards drive out good standards.

The international code would come into force by treaty, which would mean that it would supersede national laws in conflict with it. The treaty could pave the way for its universal acceptance by providing that, once a sufficient number of countries had ratified it, they would apply certain economic sanctions in concert to countries refusing to accept it, as well as to those accepting but violating it.

The IMF-proposed task force was called upon

> to determine among other things, whether administration and enforcement of its proposed code . . . should be entrusted partly or wholly to existing intergovernmental organizations or whether a new agency should be created for some or all of the purposes involved.

Thus, existing agencies such as the General Agreement on Tariffs and Trade (GATT), the ILO, the International Monetary Fund, etc., might each carry out certain functions or a new UN agency might be created either to take on the entire task or to share it with one or more of the existing organizations.

The issue of MNCs is already on the agenda of intergovernmental organizations. In the fall of 1972, the ILO convened a meeting of government management and labor experts, which unanimously recommended that the organization undertake a study that would include the "elements" of "principles and guidelines" for MNCs in the field of social policy.[14]

The United Nations Economic and Social Council (ECOSOC), acting partly in response to ITT's political meddling in Chile, adopted a resolution in July 1972 calling for creation of a study group on MNCs, which was charged, among other things, ". . . to submit recommendations for appropriate international action. . . ." The group officially known as "The Group of Eminent Persons," for which the writer served as consultant, recommended the creation of a permanent United Nations Commission on Multinational Corporations, supported by an information and research center, to monitor the activities of MNCs and lay the groundwork for a general agreement on multinational corporations. The group's recommendations in the labor sphere include a number of the proposals advanced by the international trade union movement.

The labor movement is not waiting, however, for the development of comprehensive rules to govern MNCs but intends, meanwhile, to take the fullest possible advantage of every opportunity that becomes available to work for specific intergovernmental regulatory measures that ultimately could be incorporated into a comprehensive code. For example, unionists will continue to work for a proposal advanced by the labor spokesman (but which was not adopted) at the ILO meeting mentioned above, for an ILO convention under which governments of home countries would obligate themselves to require "their" MNCs to adhere to existing ILO standards in all their operations, regardless of whether the countries in

---

14. "Conclusions of the Meeting," *Multinational Enterprises and Social Policy*, Paragraph 6, Appendix II (Geneva: International Labor Office, 1973), p. 176.

which they are located have ratified the conventions and recommendations in which the ILO standards are embodied. The effect would be somewhat similar to that of the code of good behavior in host countries contemplated by the UAW's proposal for licensing capital exports. Similarly, the labor movement is working for amendment of the GATT agreement, to provide for international fair labor standards. Such a provision was included in the Havana Charter for a UN International Trade Organization, which was signed by representatives of some fifty nations in 1948 but not ratified by enough of the latter to bring the organization into being.

A further illustration is widespread labor support for the proposal to allocate a substantial proportion of newly created SDRs to the LDCs. Here, the labor movement has two motivations. The first arises from the tradition of international labor solidarity, which calls for help to those suffering from depressed standards and, therefore, for assistance to the development efforts of the LDCs. The second is to relieve, by providing an alternative or additional source of external capital, the pressures that MNCs bring to bear upon LDCs to compete for investment by outbidding each other in the "cheapness" of the labor supplies they offer.

Additional instances of limited measures proposed by unionists to meet specific problems caused by MNCs could be cited. The piecemeal approach parallels the effort to establish comprehensive international regulation but it coincides with intensified work on the collective bargaining front.

Restiveness of the MNCs themselves with the complications they face as a result of the multiplicity and variety—to say nothing of overlapping and contradictions—of the national laws applicable to their operations, may facilitate the efforts of unions to establish uniform intergovernmental regulation that will take worker and general social interest into account. For example, former Under Secretary of State George Ball has recognized that ". . . Multinational Corporations and nation-states are on a collision course." [15] He has proposed:

> the establishment by treaty of an international companies law, administered by a supranational body [which, among other things, would] administer guarantees with regard to uncompensated expropriation [and] *place limitations, for example, on the restrictions nation-states might be permitted to impose on companies established under its sanction*" [emphasis added].[16]

He cites the proposed European Companies Law now being considered in the EC as a step in that direction.

15. In "Excerpts from Comments by George W. Ball," in The Probable Impact of U.S. Trade Legislation on the Foreign Operations of U.S. Companies. The Conference Board, Waldorf Astoria, New York, January 18, 1973, p. 1. Multilithed.
16. George W. Ball, "Remarks at the Annual Dinner" British National Committee, International Chamber of Commerce, London, England, October 18, 1967, p. 12. Multilithed.

In principle, the labor movement has no objection to an international companies law, but its concept of such a law differs in important respects from Mr. Ball's, and it will insist upon a quid pro quo. If companies governed by such a law are to be freed from certain national restrictions with respect to labor matters, for example, there will have to be meaningful international restrictions in their place; and the labor movement will strive to assure that these be set not at the least-common-denominator-level but in conformance with the highest possible standards. The draft of the proposed European law that Mr. Ball cited does, in fact, include certain labor provisions, which would subject companies covered by it to co-determination (i.e., worker representation on their supervisory boards) and would require them to deal with European-wide works councils, which would have veto power over management with respect to a wide range of personnel matters and the right to be consulted before decisions are made on others. It also provides for European-wide collective agreements if the unions involved desire them. A resolution adopted by the IMF in 1968 calls also for certain substantive provisions, generally along the lines of the code of good behavior under the Swedish investment guarantee program, to be made binding upon companies established under any international corporation law.[17] Moreover, in all probability, unions would insist upon meaningful representation on the supranational body, which Mr. Ball proposes to administer such a law.

Thus the efforts of the MNCs to free themselves from purely national regulation will thrust them into a bargaining position in which, in order to achieve their objectives, they will have to accede to those of the world's workers and their unions.

In pursuing the goal of international regulation of MNCs, the world labor movement is highly conscious of the main point made by Professor Raymond Vernon in his aptly titled book *Sovereignty at Bay*. The point is stated in several ways. Its essence emerges from the following quotations:

> . . . the multinational enterprise as a unit, though capable of wielding substantial economic power, is not accountable to any public authority that matches it in geographical reach and that represents the aggregate interests of all the countries the enterprise affects.

> *   *   *

> I personally am mistrustful of any large concentration of economic power, on the grounds that Lord Acton so aptly summarized: Power corrupts. Men with power have an extraordinary capacity to convince themselves that what they want to do happens to coincide with what society needs

---

17. International Metalworkers Federation, "Resolution on Multinational Corporations," *Minutes of the 21st Congress*, Zurich, May 27–31, 1968, p. 156. The Swedish Code is set forth in "Social Conditions Attached to the Swedish Investment Guarantee Scheme," Appendix 7, in *The Multinational Challenge*, ICFTU World Economic Reports No. 2, Geneva, June 24–26, 1971, pp. 72–74.

done for its good. This comfortable illusion is shared as much by strong leaders of enterprise as by strong leaders of government.

*   *   *

The basic asymmetry between multinational enterprises and national governments may be tolerable up to a point, but beyond that point there is a need to reestablish balance. When this occurs, the response is bound to have some of the elements of the world corporation concept: accountability to some body, charged with weighing the activities of the multinational enterprise against a set of social yardsticks that are multinational in scope.

If this does not happen, some of the apocalyptic projections of the future of multinational enterprise will grow more plausible.[18]

18. Raymond Vernon, *Sovereignty at Bay* (New York: Basic Books Inc., 1971), pp. 249, 272, and 284.

III

DEVELOPMENTAL DIMENSIONS

c h a p t e r   e i g h t

The diplomatic protection
of multinational corporations

RICHARD B. LILLICH

It is common knowledge that the multinational corporation of the last third of the twentieth century does not fit easily into the contemporary international legal order. Unlike its counterpart of two centuries ago—the great state trading company possessing sovereign powers and extraterritorial status—today's multinational corporation, conceptually at least, has only the legal rights of an individual or any other legal entity. Because only nation-states, not individuals or legal entities, are considered to be subjects of international law, the multinational corporation thus finds itself denied direct access to the international arena to protect its rights. Like the ill-used individual, the multinational corporation which has been harmed by a nation in which it operates, after exhausting its local remedies in that nation, must turn to the government of its own country for diplomatic protection. Only by having its claim espoused in this fashion can it obtain the advantages of international procedures.

While various remedial suggestions have been made that would short-circuit this traditional process, to date they largely have come to naught. Thus, as Professor Fatouros has remarked, the doctrine of diplomatic protection, "made to protect individuals who happened to find themselves in trouble in foreign countries, is asked to take care of the problems of multinational corporations. . . ." [1] He complains that such a doctrine should not be extended "to cover something which was really not at all in its original scope. The doctrine is inadequate. It does not fit modern ways of doing things." [2] Well-intentioned as these academic lamentations may be, they should not obscure the fact that until that distant day

1. 65 AMERICAN SOC'Y INT'L L. PROCEEDINGS 354 (1971).
2. *Ibid.*

when States decide "to allow individuals some sort of an international status; that is, to put them in some respects on an equal basis with states, having as much chance as states have to bring another state to court,"[3] not only individuals and ordinary legal entities, but multinational corporations as well, are entitled to assert whatever rights to diplomatic protection they possess. Moreover, their claims, procedurally at least, deserve the support of all persons truly concerned with the goal of a productive international economy.[4]

THE TRADITIONAL APPROACH

Assuming a multinational corporation must turn to its own state for protection, to what states does it turn? Under customary international law, an individual's claim for protection can be espoused by a state only if he is its national. The nationality of individuals, although presenting some troublesome aspects, is relatively easy to ascertain. The nationality of corporations is another matter. Because customary international law had little to say about it, states in the late nineteenth and early twentieth centuries looked to their domestic law to establish workable criteria.[5] Gradually it became accepted, perhaps because the common-law countries contributed greatly to the development of this area of international law, that for purposes of diplomatic protection corporations had the nationality of the state in which they had been incorporated.[6] Indeed, many states, the United States included, went so far as to extend diplomatic protection even to corporations substantially owned by another state.[7] This conceptualistic approach to corporate claims, which largely ignored the raison d'être of diplomatic protection—namely, the concern of states to safeguard the economic and other interests of their nationals abroad, reached ridiculous proportions when the Spanish Treaty Claims Commission, established to compensate United States nationals for losses occasioned by Spain during the Spanish-American war, actually rendered an award to a corporation in which nearly all of the stock was owned by Spanish nationals.[8]

---

3. *Ibid* at 354–55.
4. Whether their claims have substantive merit is another matter. The point being made here is that they deserve their "day in court." Failure to accord it, as Professor Weston has pointed out in the context of the compensation question, surely will discourage "that kind of investment in the underdeveloped world (and for that matter in the developed world) that will assure benefit to those countries and therefore, over the long run, to the global economic process as a whole." 2 DENVER J. INT'L L. & POL. 159 (1972).
5. I. FOIGHEL, NATIONALIZATION AND COMPENSATION 232 (1964).
6. Harris, *The Protection of Companies in International Law in the Light of the Nottebohm Case*, 18 INT'L & COMP. L.Q. 275, 285 (1969). *See generally* K. AL-SHAWI, THE ROLE OF THE CORPORATE ENTITY IN INTERNATIONAL LAW ch. 2 (1957).
7. Harris, *supra* note 6, at 275–85.
8. Crandall, *Principles of International Law Applied by the Spanish Treaty Claims Commission*, 4 AM. J. INT'L L. 806, 814–15 (1910).

By the interwar period this approach, which had, if nothing else, "the great virtue of simplicity of operation," [9] was generally accepted. Sir Eric Beckett, in a much-cited paper, made the flat assertion that "the doctrine that the nationality of a company for the purposes of International Law is, irrespective of the nationality of the shareholders, that of the country under whose law it is incorporated is the one which, it seems to me, is now really firmly established." [10] Yet even before he spoke, reaction to this rigid approach had begun. Thus, while paying it lip-service, the Department of State in 1925 acknowledged that

> it has been the long-standing practice of the Department of State to refrain from pressing diplomatically the claims of American corporations in which there was no substantial American interest. The Department does not consider it proper for the Government of the United States to seek to protect, under the cloak of American corporations, interests which are wholly alien. Unless American citizens would derive benefit from the recovery of indemnity in favor of American corporations, the Department does not consider that it would be warranted in pressing a claim diplomatically in behalf of a corporation.[11]

Applying this interest-analysis approach to a United States corporation wholly owned by its Canadian parent, the American Commissioner on the United States-German Mixed Claims Commission argued successfully that the following facts, in addition to place of incorporation, gave the claimant standing:

1. It always had had its offices in New York City.
2. Prior to its claim it had employed over 140 persons at its New York office alone.
3. Prior to its claim it had made subcontracts calling for the purchase of materials in the amount of $66 million (of which sum $60 million was to be paid to United States subcontractors).
4. At the time its claim arose it was employing directly 1000 United States laborers, while its subcontractors were employing many more.[12]

Under the generally accepted traditional approach, of course, such facts would have constituted mere "icing on the cake": incorporation in the United States would have rendered the corporate claimant eligible without further ado.

The United States' practice of requiring some effective connection other than just incorporation can be read two ways. According to some authorities, it is perfectly consistent with the traditional approach, be-

9. *See* (HARVARD) CONVENTION ON THE INTERNATIONAL RESPONSIBILITY OF STATES FOR INJURIES TO ALIENS, Explanatory Notes § 21 (3) (d), subparagraph 3(d) at 183 (Draft No. 12, 1961), which adopts the approach primarily for this reason.

10. Beckett, *Diplomatic Claims in Respect of Injuries to Companies,* in 17 TRANSACT. GROT. SOC'Y 175, 185 (1932).

11. 5 G. HACKWORTH, DIGEST OF INTERNATIONAL LAW 839 (1943).

12. *Ibid.* at 834.

cause it involves a state's self-limitation of its right to diplomatic protection, not its recognition that this right is conditioned upon any criteria other than place of incorporation. "A careful perusal of State practice," states Professor Caflisch, "reveals . . . that the restraint shown by states in this matter finds its basis in their discretionary power to grant or to withhold diplomatic protection." [13] Other authorities, such as Parry, contend that there is

> little, if any, evidence that a State may present an international claim on behalf of a corporation on the mere ground that it is incorporated under its laws. The proposition appears to rest upon the authority of John Bassett Moore, whose declaration that the matter is well settled, though frequently quoted, is unsupported by any convincing precedent. It is rendered questionable by the well-known fact that many States refuse, as a matter of declared general policy, to extend protection to corporations in which there is no substantial national shareholding interest.[14]

Although this writer finds Parry's view persuasive, fairness requires acknowledging that, as the following sections reveal, "the strict legal status of corporations and especially their effective nationality are obscure and confused." [15]

THE EFFECT OF NOTTEBOHM

Corporate claims came into their own after World War Two. Following the immediate postwar nationalizations by the countries of Eastern Europe, a steady flow of nationalizations has occurred throughout the developing world. A substantial majority of such claims, given the breakdown in international arbitration that has occurred during the past quarter-century, have not been resolved by judicial means. Though a small number have been settled diplomatically, most claims by corporations have been handled by the lump-sum settlement route, a method to be discussed in the next section. Thus, when an international judicial decision, especially one emanating from the International Court of Justice, has been handed down, it has tended to take on disproportionate weight. Such a decision was the Court's judgment in 1955 in the *Nottebohm Case*.[16]

This case, of course, turned not upon the nationality of a corporation, but of an individual, Freidrich Nottebohm, a former German national who had been naturalized by Liechtenstein before he was expelled and

13. Caflisch, *The Protection of Corporate Investments Abroad in the Light of the Barcelona Traction Case*, 31 ZEITSCHRIFT FÜR AUSLANDISCHES OFFENTLICHES RECHT UND VOLKERRECHT 162, 178 (1971).

14. C. PARRY, NATIONALITY AND CITIZENSHIP LAWS OF THE COMMONWEALTH 139 (1957).

15. Fatouros, *The Computer and the Mud Hut: Notes on Multinational Enterprise in Developing Countries*, 10 COLUM J. TRANSNAT'L L. 325, 332 (1971).

16. [1955] I.C.J. 4.

his property seized by Guatemala. Although Guatemala did not challenge Liechtenstein's right to bestow its nationality upon Nottebohm, it did raise the issue, in the Court's words, "whether the nationality conferred on Nottebohm can be relied upon as against Guatemala in justification of the proceedings instituted before the Court." [17] To determine this issue, said the Court, it had to ascertain

> whether the factual connection between Nottebohm and Liechtenstein in the period preceding, contemporaneous with and following his naturalization appears to be sufficiently close, so preponderant in relation to any connection which may have existed between him and any other State, that it is possible to regard the nationality conferred upon him as *real and effective,* as the exact juridical expression of a social fact of a connection which existed previously or came into existence thereafter.[18]

After a detailed examination of the factual context surrounding Nottebohm's acquisition of Liechtenstein nationality, the Court held that "these facts clearly establish, on the one hand, the absence of any bond of attachment between Nottebohm and Liechtenstein and, on the other hand, the existence of a long-standing and close connection between him and Guatemala, a link which his naturalization in no way weakened." [19] In the absence of any such "genuine connection," the "real and effective" nationality test precluded Liechtenstein from extending its protection to Nottebohm and hence the Court held its claim to be inadmissible.[20]

Professor Harris, in perhaps the most exhaustive analysis of *Nottebohm's* effect on corporate claims yet written, reminds us that "the rule governing the protection of companies is an extension that took place at the turn of the century of a rule that had been developed in respect of individuals. If the rule as to the protection of individuals is altered, it is tempting to regard the alteration as automatically applying to companies as well." [21] Resisting this temptation, however, he finds nothing in the Court's holding or reasoning to warrant its extension to corporations.[22] Moreover, after a brief survey of post-*Nottebohm* practice, he concludes that "there is nothing to show that the *Nottebohm Case* has had any direct or indirect effect upon the rule as to the protection of companies; what evidence there is suggests that the established rule still applies." [23] Although this view is not without its supporters, other writers have read the Court's judgment and interpreted subsequent state practice somewhat differently. Thus Dr. Brownlie, in a passage not mentioned by Harris, concludes that "as a whole the legal experience suggests that a doctrine of real or genuine link has been adopted, and, as a matter of

17. *Ibid.* at 17.
18. *Ibid.* at 24 (emphasis added).
19. *Ibid.* at 26.
20. *Ibid.*
21. Harris, *supra* note 6, at 285.
22. *Ibid.* at 285–86.
23. *Ibid.* at 288.

principle, the considerations advanced in connexion with the *Nottebohm* case apply to corporations." [24] Certainly, as Harris himself acknowledges, the *Nottebohm* test could be tailored to corporations.[25] Indeed, it has been in the single most important source of state practice since *Nottebohm:* lump-sum settlements.

THE RELEVANCY OF LUMP-SUM SETTLEMENTS

Most corporate claims since World War Two have been settled by lump-sum agreements. At last count, over 137 such settlements had been concluded by 38 claimant and respondent states, representing a substantial cross-section of the international community.[26] These agreements appear to have modified substantially, if not undercut completely, the traditional approach as expressed by Beckett. Indeed, although Great Britain continues to allow the claims of corporations without inquiry into the nationality of their stockholders, few other countries still judge a corporation's eligibility solely on the basis of its place of incorporation. Instead, the settlement agreements reveal two principal approaches which states now use to determine corporate eligibility, only one of which bears even partial resemblance to the traditional test.

The first approach, looking to the nationality of the corporation's stockholders as well as to its place of incorporation, has been adopted by the United States in its lump-sum settlements. Starting with the United States-Yugoslav Agreement of 1948, Article 2(b) which required, in addition to incorporation in the United States, that "twenty percent or more of any class of the outstanding securities . . . [be] owned by individual nationals of the United States," [27] the U.S. has increased the percentage of the corporation's "outstanding capital stock or other beneficial interest" that must be owned by such nationals to 50%.[28] Despite some initial debate over whether and how to define the required "substantial interest," United States practice uniformly supports the 50% requirement today.[29] No other country, it should be noted, follows this exact approach, although two lump-sum settlements concluded by the Netherlands lay down other requirements a corporation must meet in addition to or in place of Dutch incorporation.[30]

24. I. Brownlie, Principles of Public International Law 400 (1966).

25. Harris, *supra* note 6, at 295.

26. These agreements are the subject of a two-volume treatise, R. Lillich & B. Weston, International Claims: Their Settlement by Lump-Sum Agreements, soon to be published in the Procedural Aspects of International Law Series.

27. Article 2(b) of the United States-Yugoslav Agreement, July 19, 1948, 62 Stat. 2658 (1948), T.I.A.S. No. 1803.

28. *See, e.g.,* Article 2(b) of the United States-Rumanian Agreement, March 30, 1960, [1960] 1 U.S.T. 317, T.I.A.S. No. 4451.

29. *See generally* R. Lillich & G. Christenson, International Claims: Their Preparation and Presentation 15–17 (1962).

30. Article 1(2) of the Dutch-Czech Agreement, June 11, 1964, 556 U.N.T.S. 89 (effective Dec. 10, 1964), mentions claims by corporations "established *and having their seat* in the Kingdom of the Netherlands," while Article 2(1)(b) of the Dutch-Hungarian

The second approach to determining corporate eligibility, and the one used most frequently in the settlement agreements, treats the corporation's *siège social* as the key factor. As Dr. White has explained,

> the *siège social* of a company, as that term is understood in continental systems of law, is the place where the company exercises legal, financial and administrative controls over its operations. In France, the courts will look at the facts to determine the true siège if they think that the company's articles have conferred an artificial siège on the company. In finding the true siège the courts disregard such factors as the nationality of the shareholders, the country where the company's exploitation is carried on, and the *siège administratif* if this is separate from the main centre of control.[31]

Settlement agreements embodying this approach, either unadulterated or in some mix, have been concluded by numerous countries, including Belgium, Denmark, France, Greece, Sweden, and Switzerland.[32]

Despite one commentator's view, given after a cursory examination of certain lump-sum settlements, that "it is difficult to detect a general rule or to formulate a principle," [33] at least three observations can be made about them without indulging in overclarification. First, the place of incorporation test no longer is "firmly established," [34] if indeed it ever was. Far from receiving "wide if not universal acceptance," [35] it has been used only by Great Britain, other Commonwealth countries and, with the substantial interest requirement added, by the United States. Second, neither the place of incorporation test nor the far more popular test of *siège social* are regarded generally as exclusive tests of nationality, and hence eligibility.[36] Instead, these criteria either are coupled with a substantial interest requirement, as in the United States, or a predominant claimant state interest requirement, as in many of the settlement agreements concluded by the continental countries.[37] The end result is easily

---

Agreement, July 2, 1965, 564 U.N.T.S. 49 (effective Feb. 28, 1966), refers to claims by corporations which "existed under Netherlands law *and were already registered* in the territory of the Kingdom of the Netherlands. . . ." (emphasis added). These agreements either supplement or preempt the place of incorporation test with the test of *siège social.*

31. G. WHITE, NATIONALISATION OF FOREIGN PROPERTY 63 (1961).

32. They are discussed at length in Section III of Chapter II of R. LILLICH & B. WESTON, note 26 *supra.*

33. Ginther, *Nationality of Corporations,* 16 OESTERREICHISCHE ZEITSCHRIFT FÜR OFFENTLICHES RECHT 27, 59 (1966).

34. *See* text at note 10 *supra.*

35. F. VALLAT, INTERNATIONAL LAW AND THE PRACTITIONER 25 (1966).

36. *Cf.* Bindschedler-Robert, *La Protection Diplomatique des Sociétés et des Actionnaires,* 100 REVUE DE LA SOCIETE DES JURISTES BERNOIS 141, 164 (1964).

37. The provisions in the lump-sum settlements defining substantial or predominant claimant state interest generally are so opaque that it is impossible to discern from them the *content,* as opposed to the *existence,* of this newly emerging requirement of customary international law. de Visscher, *La Protection Diplomatique des Personnes Morales,* 102 REÇUEIL DES COURS (Hague Academy of International Law) 434, 449 (1961-I).

recognizable as a rough application of the nationality plus genuine connection test of the *Nottebohm Case* to corporate claims.

THE IMPACT OF BARCELONA TRACTION

In the *Barcelona Traction Case*[38] the International Court of Justice held in 1970 that Belgium lacked *jus standi* to present the claim of Belgian stockholders in a Canadian corporation allegedly put out of business by acts attributable to Spain. Yet, while its holding focused solely upon stockholder claims through third state corporations, "actually, some of the dicta may become of greater import than the actual holding." [39] Leading the list of significant dicta was what the Court said, or rather what it did not say, about corporate claims. Although extending the rationale of *Nottebohm* to such claims had been advocated by commentators for fifteen years,[40] the Court's judgment concluded somewhat summarily that "there can be no analogy with the issues raised or the decision given in that case." [41] Indeed, its dictum about corporate eligibility gave heavy, arguably even exclusive, stress to the traditional place of incorporation approach.

> In allocating corporate entities to States for purposes of diplomatic protection, international law is based, but only to a limited extent, on an analogy with the rules governing the nationality of individuals. *The traditional rule attributes the right of diplomatic protection of a corporate entity to the State under the laws of which it is incorporated and in whose territory it has its registered office* [siège]. These two criteria have been confirmed by long practice and by numerous international instruments.[42]

This dictum's retrogressive nature has been criticized by numerous commentators including Fatouros, who has expressed "regret that the Court has given new strength to the old concept of nationality of corporations, without any consideration of function, purpose, and such; in fact, going back to formal incorporation as the only [sic] criterion." [43]

The Court, immediately after mentioning the two criteria making up the "traditional rule," did acknowledge that

38. [1970] I.C.J. 3.
39. Rodley, *Corporate Nationality and the Diplomatic Protection of Multinational Enterprises: The Barcelona Traction Case*, 47 IND. L.J. 70, 72 (1971).
40. *See, e.g.,* van Hecke, *Nationality of Companies Analyzed*, 8 NETH. INT'L L. REV. 223, 235 (1961).
41. [1970] I.C.J. at 42. Even a commentator generally favorable to its judgment has criticized the Court for reaching this conclusion "without offering any further justification. . . ." Caflisch, *supra* note 13, at 175.
42. [1970] I.C.J. at 42 (emphasis added).
43. 65 AMERICAN SOC'Y INT'L L. PROCEEDINGS 355 (1971).

further or different links are at times said to be required in order that a right of diplomatic protection should exist. Indeed, it has been the practice of some states to give a company incorporated under their law diplomatic protection solely when it has its seat (*siège social*) or management or centre of control in their territory, or when a majority or a substantial proportion of the shares has been owned by nationals of the State concerned. Only then, it has been held, does there exist between the corporation and the State in question a genuine connection of the kind familiar from other branches of international law. However, in the particular field of the diplomatic protection of corporate entities, no absolute test of the "genuine connection" has found general acceptance.[44]

Surprisingly, given its summary dismissal of *Nottebohm*, the Court then proceeded to examine in some detail the Canadian corporation's "links with Canada," concluding that "a close and permanent connection has been established, fortified by the passage of over half a century." [45]

The Court judgment on this point confuses more than it clarifies. Rodley, for instance, reads it to "suggest that while a corporation's nationality is that of the country of incorporation, a closer connection may need to be demonstrated for the purposes of diplomatic protection." [46] Caflisch, taking a neutral position, ventures only that "the Court left open the question of corporate claims." [47] Finally, Professor Weston concludes that "what the Court comes down to saying is that, as long as you have mere incorporation in a particular nation-state, that is sufficient" for eligibility purposes.[48] The likelihood is that the matter will remain unclarified until the Court is presented with a case requiring it to rule squarely on corporate claims.

When that time comes, hopefully the Court will not ignore the teaching of lump-sum settlements as it did in *Barcelona Traction* when stockholder claims were at issue.[49] These agreements, taken as a whole, are consistent with *Nottebohm* in that they reveal a trend away from the formalistic approach to corporate claims and toward a more functional and therefore more realistic approach designed to protect the actual interests of the claimant State.[50] This trend also is reflected in Judge Jessup's separate opinion in *Barcelona Traction*, where, after discussing *Nottebohm*, he "reached the conclusion that the existence of a link between a corporation holding a 'charter of convenience' and the state granting the charter, is the key to the diplomatic protection of multinational corporate interests. . . ." [51]

44. [1970] I.C.J. at 42.
45. *Ibid.*
46. Rodley, *supra* note 39, at 82.
47. 65 AMERICAN SOC'Y INT'L L. PROCEEDINGS 347 (1971).
48. *Ibid.* at 349.
49. For a critique of the court's judgment on this point, see Lillich, *The Rigidity of Barcelona*, 65 AM. J. INT'L L. 522 (1971).
50. *See* I. FOIGHEL, *supra* note 5, at 237.
51. [1970] I.C.J. at 185.

THE FUTURE OF MULTINATIONAL CORPORATE PROTECTION

Diplomatic protection of nationals abroad is an old and honorable doctrine. Originally developed to protect individuals of the claimant state, during the past century it has been extended to cover claimant state corporations as well. Now, in a surprising "flashback" to more simple times, the International Court of Justice, ignoring the practice of recent decades, especially that found in lump-sum settlements, has adopted, albeit in dictum, what most commentators believe to be a rigidly conceptualistic approach to such claims. At best, as Rodley warns, "multinational enterprises must be content with that [diplomatic protection] of the country where they have chosen to be registered, with some uncertainty as to whether even that country will be permitted to espouse a claim without some effective connection." [52] If this dictum achieves wide acceptance in the international community, those states which have sought unsuccessfully for years to overturn the substantive concept of an international minimum standard of justice will have achieved, by one procedural ruling, almost all that they ever desired.[53] Fortunately for the international rule of law, there already is evidence that such acceptance will not be forthcoming.[54]

Admittedly, the diplomatic protection of multinational corporations is a less than adequate procedural device, as indeed diplomatic protection is generally. The following extract by Fatouros makes this point as clearly and concisely as possible:

> We have an old doctrine—that of diplomatic protection. All of us who have tried to explain the doctrine in its beautiful theoretical complexities . . . have had bitter experience of how contradictory the whole doctrine is, if seen in terms of modern international law. . . .
>
> That doctrine now, made to protect individuals who happened to find themselves in trouble in foreign countries, is asked to take care of the problems of multinational corporations, one example of which, by the way, is the *Barcelona Traction* situation. . . .
>
> I do not see why the Court should extend such a doctrine to cover something which was really not at all in its original scope. The doctrine is inadequate. It does not fit modern ways of doing things. Professor Domke . . . rightly suggested that there may be other ways of handling this whole question. It may be possible, for instance, to allow individuals [sic] some sort of an international status; that is, to put them in some respects on an equal basis with states, having as much chance as states have to bring another state to court. . . .

52. Rodley, *supra* note 39, at 86.

53. For this reason Rodley predicts "that many developing countries will applaud this decision." *Ibid.*

54. Post-Barcelona lump-sum settlements, for instance, appear unaffected by its dictum concerning corporate claims. *See, e.g.,* Article 2 of the Belgian-Rumanian Agreement, Nov. 13, 1970, [1971] Moniteur Belge 12088 (effective Sept. 9, 1971). *See also* text at and accompanying note 67 *infra*.

These are real problems; to approach them from the traditional doctrine of protection is not really very helpful. In a way, we are all guilty in that we have tried, in a traditional lawyer's way, to make the old doctrine do a lot of work which it was not really created for doing.[55]

In short, according to Fatouros, the antiquated doctrine of diplomatic protection is not capable of handling the claims of multinational corporations against foreign states and should be replaced by new procedures. Acceptable as this view may be to many observers, its implied corollary, namely, that if such procedures are not devised the respective parties must settle investment disputes in "go it bear—go it wife" fashion,[56] leaves a great deal to be desired.[57]

Among the various procedures that would obviate the necessity of protecting multinational corporations diplomatically are proposals to establish international tribunals to which they would have direct access,[58] provisions for the settlement of international investment disputes embodied in the World Bank Convention,[59] investment guaranty schemes now available in the United States and other capital-exporting countries,[60] and a liberal approach to the diplomatic protection of stockholders, the effect of which would be to render corporate claims unnecessary.[61] Unfortunately, no movement can be detected at present with respect to international tribunals; the provisions of the World Bank Convention remain unavailable to investors in many areas of the globe, including all of Latin America; investment guaranty schemes, though fine examples of remedial self-help, are essentially stop-gap measures which arguably undercut, rather than contribute to the development of, norms of universal application; and stockholder claims, given the "chilling effect" of *Barcelona Traction,* hardly can be expected to receive wider acceptance by the international community in the immediate future. Hence, for the rest of this century, diplomatic protection, or at least the possibility of its use in appropriate cases, will remain an important method of obtaining redress for multinational corporations.

This particular problem, of course, must be placed in the wider context of the continuing attack on private property in international law orchestrated by the developing countries over the past quarter-century.

55. 65 American Soc'y Int'l L. Proceedings 354–55 (1971).

56. "Many people, with no great perceived stake in the outcome, would no doubt, if asked, be inclined to say to the contestants, 'Go it bear—Go it wife.'" Metzger, *Nationality of Corporate Investment Under Investment Guaranty Schemes—The Relevance of Barcelona Traction,* 65 Am. J. Int'l L. 532 (1971).

57. *See* text at and accompanying note 4 *supra.*

58. *See, e.g.,* Sohn, *Proposals for the Establishment of a System of International Tribunals,* in International Trade Arbitration 65 (M. Domke, ed., 1958).

59. The convention, which came into force in 1966, is reprinted in 60 Am. J. Int'l L. 892 (1966).

60. *See* Metzger, note 56 *supra.*

61. For such an approach, see the comments by Professor Foighel in 63 American Soc'y Int'l L. Proceedings 42, 43, 47 (1969).

From the Universal Declaration of Human Rights[62] through the United Nations Resolution on Permanent Sovereignty Over Natural Resources[63] to the Covenant on Economic, Social and Cultural Rights,[64] the leveling of the substantive standard protecting private foreign investment is evident. When viewed with the *Barcelona Traction Case,* which effectively deprives many investors of their procedural safeguards, it becomes apparent that "the rules of the game" have changed remarkably in recent years—all to the favor of the developing countries. Acceptable or even desirable as some aspects of this change may be, it seeks to replace the rule of law with an approach to settling disputes based upon naked power, surely destructive of attempts to fashion a productive international economy. Moreover, the developing countries now seek to deprive the foreign investor, and especially the multinational corporation, of the right to fight back economically.[65] In the parlance of the ring, "rabbit punches" by nation-states are permissible, yet their multinational corporate opponents supposedly are forbidden to lift a glove in reply.

Obviously, this situation cannot and should not be accepted by the capital-exporting countries. In the present state of the international legal order, they can be expected to protect the economic interests of their nationals, in corporate form or otherwise, through all available-diplo-channels. Far from the problem being one of multinational corporations shopping "for multiple bases of diplomatic protection," [66] it is one of formulating an acceptable rule for determining which state should be allowed to make the international process available to such corporations. The nationality plus genuine connection test of *Nottebohm,* applied to corporations in the lump-sum settlements, seem the most reasonable approach. The common denominator of the investment guaranty schemes —nationality plus 51% claimant state ownership—also points to this approach. It represents, according to Metzger, "the current reality of the 'genuine link' of the *Nottebohm* case. And in international economic affairs, as much as, or more than in international political and security affairs, it pays to stay close to reality." [67] Ignored by the International Court of Justice, that lesson constitutes the message of this chapter.

62. G.A. Res. 217, U.N. Doc. A/810 at 71 (1948).

63. G.A. Res. 1803, 17 U.N. GAOR Supp. 17, at 15, U.N. Doc. A/5217 (1962).

64. G.A. Res. 2200, 21 U.N. GAOR Supp. 16, at 52, U.N. Doc. A/6316 (1966).

65. G.A. Res. 3016, adopted on December 18, 1972, by a vote of 102 in favor, 0 against, with 22 abstentions (including the major developed countries), and reprinted in 12 INT'L LEGAL MATERIALS 226 (1973).

66. Rodley, *supra* note 39, at 86. Multinational corporations make investment decisions, *i.e.,* shop around, for many reasons, but obtaining diplomatic protection surely is not one of them.

67. Metzger, *supra* note 56, at 541. "[M]ere local incorporation is far too slender and neutral a connection to motivate capital exporting countries to expend the extraordinary time, energy, and international political capital needed in pressing an international claim. The respondent developing country likewise cannot be expected to accept such a minor connection as constituting the 'genuine link' necessary to confer standing to present an international claim. . . ." *Ibid.* In short, Barcelona Traction "establishes an unworkable standard." *Ibid.*

chapter nine

Capitalism, communism, and multinationalism

IRVING LOUIS HOROWITZ

CAPITALIST, COMMUNIST, AND MULTINATIONALIST IDEOLOGIES

A recent advertisement in *The New York Times* (October 1, 1972), placed by the World Development Corporation, reads as follows:

> A well-known party is looking for revolutionary ideas. It may come as a surprise, but the communists are no longer claiming they've invented every good idea under the sun. On the contrary, they're eagerly hoping that Westerners may have invented a few before them. The fact is that the communists—in particular the East Europeans—are building a broad consumer society. They're in a hurry. And they're in the market for advanced technology in a staggering number of fields. The point is this: if you own the patented or proprietary technology that East European countries need, you could work out some highly profitable arrangements. Sell technology to the communists? Can it even be done? The answer is that today it finally can be done. And is being done. In fact, over the past couple of years, major American corporations have been doing it with increasing frequency. Naturally, the technology must be non-strategic. Exactly how do you go about it? You go about it with infinite patience. As you can imagine, selling American technology in Eastern Europe is a highly complex economic, political and technical problem. Obviously, it's absolutely crucial to develop the right contacts and the right communication. That's where we, World Patent Development Corp. come in. For years now, we've maintained close technological contacts with the proper governmental agencies in all East European countries. Because of our unique position, we've been able to locate markets and negotiate licensing agreements for the sale of almost every kind of technology. Conversely, we're also presiding over the transfer of East European technology to the West. In fields ranging from synthetic copolymers to pollution control equipment. From advanced textile equipment to natural cosmetics.

This is a far cry from Cold War rhetoric; and helps place in perspective the obvious thaw *cum* rapprochement reached between Nixon and Kissinger for the American side and Brezhnev and Kosygin for the Soviet side. For the emergence of the multinational corporation is the paramount economic fact of the present epoch, and helps to explain current trends in the political sociology of world relations.

The overriding ideological posture of the twentieth century has been the Manichean struggle for supremacy between capitalism and communism. From this posture flows the utopian fantasy of the chief protagonists: that the struggle will be resolved by the conquest of communism and equality over capitalism and inequality. A further consequence has been the derivation of a counterutopian literature reversing good and evil, excoriating communism for creating a totalitarian nightmare that could only be halted by a total allegiance to democratic life as expressed by the present moment in Western history—the "West" serving as a banal euphemism for capitalist nations.

Two real-life events of macroscopic proportions broke this ideological-utopian barrier: first, the rise of a Third World in Africa, Asia, and Latin America with the attendant pluralization of economic forms, political systems, and social doctrines; and second, the rise of multinational corporations which are primarily loyal to industrial growth and financial profitability rather than to any one national regime. In other words, multinationalism, like recent Third World "isms," has commitments that, whatever their ultimate nature, ostensibly have taken us beyond a model premised on a showdown struggle between old capitalism and new communism; or to use the oracular vernacular, classical democracy and modern totalitarianism.

The historical fact is that the phase of Third World nation-building that extended from 1945 to 1970 has resulted in a fully crystallized world system (Horowitz, 1972). (See References at the end of this chapter.) More speculative and contentious, because it is of more recent vintage, is the function and role of the multinational corporations in this world system, and their impact on capitalist-communist dichotomous relations. It is curious, but a fact nonetheless, that despite the amount of information available on the multinationals, little attention has been given to how this industrial phenomenon affects United States' relations with the Soviet Union, and by extension, the structure of capitalism and communism as competing world empires.

THE NATURE OF MULTINATIONALISM

On the assumption that the term "multinational" may still be strange to some, let us try a simple definition: a multinational corporation is one that does a sizable portion of its business outside the borders of the nation in which it has its primary headquarters. One important argument against this definition is that the multinational is simply and historically an extension of the national corporation, doing business abroad. By that definition, nothing qualitative has changed, rather the volume of commodities sold abroad has increased. Here, multinationalism is simply viewed as imperialism by another name. The difficulty with this argument is that everything novel about the present situation is omitted for the sake of maintaining the myth of economic determinism.

It is true that the multinational is an old phenomenon that has achieved new dimensions in recent years. Many firms, such as Singer

Sewing Machines, National Cash Register, Unilever, General Motors, etc., have been conducting overseas business for many years; it is however the fusion of these older firms with more basic (in the sense of having the capacity to produce high-level technology) industrial firms, such as Xerox Corporation, IBM, British Petroleum, Phillips of the Netherlands, International Nickel, etc., that has tipped the balance within them from national to international corporate participation.

But what we witness now is more than old wine in a new bottle. That which is new about multinationals can be summarized as follows: Firms that in the past maintained classical imperial relations—i.e., importing raw materials and exporting finished commodity goods at superprofits—have new arrangements. Now they share research and development findings, and also patent rights distribution; manufacture in the economic periphery at lower costs rather than producing the same goods in the cosmopolitan center (which has the additional payoff of quieting nationalist opposition); develop profit-sharing arrangements between local firms and foreign firms, which involves training and tooling. Beyond that, one finds a reverse multinationalism, one based on raw materials rather than on finished goods. Thus, the oil-rich countries of the Arab Middle East form a bargaining collective to do business directly with major oil companies of the West. Thus there takes place bartering and bargaining between public-sector multinationals, such as the Arab oil states joined by Venezuela, with private-sector multinationals such as the powerful oil corporations of America and Western Europe (see Tanzer, 1969).

That which is new about the multinational is not simply the transcendance of the nation-state boundaries to do business, an old ploy of corporations in wealthy nations, but more profoundly, a reduction in profits through increased payment of high prices for raw materials (like petroleum) and the acceptance of lower prices and hence less profit for finished manufactured goods (such as automobiles). This is the aspect of multinationals which most sharply points to the need for a modification of classical and new forms of Marxism-Leninism alike, because the very essence of politics as a reflexive form of national and economic exploitation is exactly what is reversed. What we have now is economics as a reflexive form of political exploitation and domination.[1]

1. The connections and conflicts between the international economy and the national polity is of considerable intrinsic interest to the study of multinationalism; however, it is tangential for the purposes of this study. It also has the advantage of being perhaps the best research area in the field of multinational corporate analysis, thanks in no small part to the work of Raymond Vernon (1971) in calling attention to the impact of multinational corporations and national sovereignties. Other works which have taken up this issue that deserve attention are those of Eisenhower and Frundt (1972) which adopts a more radical stance than that of Vernon but nonetheless raises the same fundamental set of considerations. For the specific impact of multinationals on United States foreign relations, see Ray, 1972: 80–92.

THE BUYING OF WESTERN CAPITALISM
BY EASTERN SOCIALISM

The post–World War Two thrust of nationalism prevented any undue optimism about the capacity of socialism to triumph as a world system and as an international ideology. Indeed, so intense did nationalist sentiments become in Third World areas of Asia, Africa, and Latin America that the Soviets, after much hesitation, had to readjust their policy and ideology, and finally recognize a third way, something more than capitalism and less than socialism (Thornton, 1964); or in my own terms, a cross between a Keynesian economic mechanism and a Leninist political machinery. But in that act of recognition, the dream of an international proletarian revolution, with or without a Soviet vanguard, gave way to more parochial dreams of peoples' democracy and socialist republics that would no more dare try to transcend nationalist sentiments than would the older capitalist regimes in Western Europe. Between 1945 and 1970, the nationalist thrust profoundly diminished belief in a socialist utopia.

When internationalism finally did make its move, it did so in corporate rather than proletarian guise. The multinational corporation, pointing to an international brotherhood of the bourgeoisie and the bureaucracy, to a transcendant class loyalty considerably beyond the national aspirations of even the United States or other principal capitalist social systems, discredited the socialist utopia no less than had the earlier nationalist phase. For the multinational is a giant step toward an international economy no less remote from the socialist brotherhood than national socialisms. The multinationals offered a basket of commodity goods that the socialist states, no less than the Third World states, desire to have. The relative ease with which such multinationals of the capitalist sector penetrated the societies and economies of the socialist sector stands in marked contrast to the difficulties involved in concluding the most elemental treaty arrangements between East and West at the policy and political level. Doing things in a businesslike way has become as much a touchstone for rational efficiency in the Soviet Union as in the United States. The culture of multinationalism permeated Eastern Europe and the Soviet Union long before the actual economic penetration, with the mass consumer demands of the Soviet public following the Stalin period. It is plain to see therefore, that multinationalism, like nationalism in an earlier era, has stymied the socialist utopia at the very same time that it has improved the commodity conditions of the socialist nations.

One need only consider the extensive trade agreements reached between the United States and the Soviet Union in September 1972 to gauge the velocity and the extent of multinational penetration.

White House adviser Henry Kissinger, negotiating in Moscow between September 11 and 14, achieved substantial progress in trade talks with the Soviet Union. The White House got a report from Mr. Kissinger of a "great breakthrough" that could result in completing a broad multibillion-dollar agreement with the Russians ahead of the original target date, the end of 1972. On September 14, the U.S. Department of Agriculture confirmed a private sale of 15 million bushels of American wheat to Communist China, the first to that nation in many years. A few days earlier, the Boeing Company announced sale of 10 of its 707 jetliners to the Red Chinese for 125 million dollars in cash. The chairman of Occidental Petroleum Corporation, Armand Hammer, said in Moscow on September 14 that details of the trade pact his firm had signed in June with the Soviet Union were being arranged. Among other things under consideration, said Mr. Hammer, were sales of chemical fertilizers and construction of a 70-million-dollar U.S. trade center in the Russian capital, complete with a 400-room hotel . . . reports from Moscow indicate that the overall trade agreement now being negotiated could increase business between the two countries to as much as 5 billion dollars a year by 1977. At present, U.S.-Russian trade amounts to about 220 million dollars annually. That figure, however, does not include around a billion dollars in purchases by the Russians of American grain in recent weeks. Still remaining to be resolved before final agreement on the overall trade pact was the issue of Lend-Lease debt owed the U.S. by Russia since World War II. The sticking point is said to be over the amount of interest due. Agreement also was reported near on a maritime pact that would guarantee to U.S. and Russian merchant ships at least a one-third share each of the cargoes involved in the billion-dollar grain sale to Russia (*U.S. News and World Report,* October 10, 1972).

The question then becomes: Can the Soviet Union maintain its basic commitment to *production development* rather than to *consumption modernization* in the face of foreign business penetration? Obviously the Russians and to a lesser degree, the Chinese, think the answer is affirmative. However, the inexorable logic of consumer orientations is toward satisfying immediate needs of a social sector able to pay, rather than delaying such gratifications in favor of long-range goals of economic equality at home, and certainly rather than fulfilling ambitious goals of national liberation abroad.

The political potential of multinationals, even those dominated by the United States, are revealed by their use in East European nations like Rumania and Hungary. One finds Pepsi Cola Corporation, Hertz Rent-a-Car Agencies, Pan American and ITT-supported hotels in the center of Bucharest, and of course the most conspicuous multinationals in such a country, Western-dominated commercial airlines. Such firms, doing business on a licensing basis in East Europe, open up channels of communication to the West. And if a socialist republic's dependence on the Soviet Union is lessened more symbolically than in reality, it nonetheless has the effect of displaying the physical presence of the West in

Eastern Europe. Beyond that, it permits higher numbers of international conferences at which Westerners participate and interact with participants from China and the Soviet Union. In short, the multinational firm encourages a country like Rumania to strive to become a Switzerland of the East Socialist bloc; a place where Israelis, Albanians, Russians, and Chinese interact freely and to the greater benefit of the open-ended socialist regime. In such a context, to speak of the corrupting influence of multinationals is a Puritan Divine's ravings against autonomy. In the East European setting, national sovereignty is strengthened rather than weakened by the existence of the multinational corporations. This is, of course, at considerable variance with the impact of multinationals in a Western European context. For example, the combined power of Dutch multinationals (Royal Dutch Shell, Unilever, KLM Airlines, Phillips) is much stronger than the standard vehicles of political life in the Netherlands. Indeed, Holland shows how national sovereignty can be weakened rather than strengthened by multinationalism.

The idea of a single world market has so deeply permeated Soviet socialism that the USSR is now in the position of accepting as part of its own economic codebook the rules on any given day of the much-reviled free market economy. The recent "wheat deal" between the super-powers indicates an increasing sophistication by Soviet "business" in precisely these areas of market management and manipulation. It sent forth twenty buying teams which each negotiated independently and without any apparent coordination. But of course, it was exactly a high level of commercial orchestration that enabled the USSR in one fell swoop to fulfill an agrarian internal need for wheat, and buy a surplus amount at a low cost for resale on the world market at a high profit. The Soviets in this way have become part of the "paper economy" —for the wheat deal involves the movement of money no less than the transfer of a basic crop.

The Soviets have done as well in the area of natural gas as in wheat negotiations. In 1966, they negotiated with Iran to purchase gas that had previously been flared off in the fields because there was no market for it at that time. In turn, the Iranians received Soviet financing and assistance to construct the necessary pipelines and associated equipment as well as a steel mill. While the Iranians gained a valuable steel plant, the Soviets began negotiating its sale of the Iranian gas to both East and West European nations. These deals culminated in sales equal to the total Iranian gas supply. The Soviet purchase price from Iran for the natural gas was 19 cents per thousand cubic feet, while its sale price was nearly double that price, or 37 cents. This deal, profitable as it was to the Soviets, was equally advantageous for the United States, who without this gas arrangment would have had to pay 87 cents per thousand cubic feet to Algeria for such gas purchases (Vinnedge, 1972:558–59). In short, the rise of sophisticated multinational dealings

across East and West boundaries clearly services the major powers at
the expense of Third World nations.

THE SELLING OF EASTERN SOCIALISM
TO WESTERN CAPITALISM

The fundamental antagonism within the socialist bloc has been
the development of an industrial society without a corresponding mod-
ernized society. The Soviet Union can mount trips to outer space, but
cannot satisfy consumer demands for automobiles; it can launch supersonic jet aircraft, but cannot supply the accoutrements of personal satis-
faction to make such travel enjoyable. It can mass-produce military hard-
ware, but cannot individualize stylistic consumer components. In every
aspect of socialist society, the duality between industrialism and mod-
ernism has emerged as a central factor. In this, the socialist sector is
the opposite of the Third World, where modernization is purchased
at the cost of development; where production is increased with relatively
low technology inputs, and product is exchanged for commodity goods
produced in the advanced capitalist sector. Both the Second World and
Third World need and want consumer goods from the First World. The
Third World pays for such consumer goods with agrarian goods, while
the Second World wants to pay for such consumer goods with industrial products.

The lessening of tension since the end of the Stalin era in 1952 has
taken the form of opening consumption valves in the Soviet Union, and
hence maintaining tight political, statist controls. The wider the valves
are opened and the more demands for immediate consumer gratification
must be met, the stronger is assumption that the stability of the socialist
bureaucratic regimes will become correspondingly greater. Multinational
penetration must therefore be seen as part of a general commitment of
the Soviet leadership political quietude through economic gratitude.

The most obvious commodity that the Soviets have to sell is not
agrarian products, and certainly not consumer goods—both of which
are in profoundly short supply within the socialist orbit. They have
a high technological sophistication, built up over more than fifty years
of emphasis on industrialization at the expense of nearly every other
economic goal. To an increasing degree, American companies looking
for ways to reduce costs in their own research and development are
buying the latest Soviet technology. The trend is most apparent in the
metallurgy field, as is made clear in the following report, filed jointly
by Boris E. Kurakin, spokesman for the official Soviet buyer, Licensin-
torg; and Henry Shur, president of Patent Management (*The New York
Times,* August 25, 1972).

> The Soviet Union constitutes the world's largest single concentrated source
> of high technology with proven industrial results which eliminate the risk

of costly R. & D. efforts for United States industry. The U.S.S.R. demonstrably excels in many areas of metallurgy, production and fabrication of metals and welding.

Another recent *New York Times* (April 17, 1972) report indicates that as the Soviet Union moves closer to a consumer-oriented society, its attitudes toward banking and savings have tended to show a corresponding transformation.

Because consumer goods are purchased largely through Western-dominated multinationals, the character of international banking communism has drawn closer to international banking capitalism—in short to the essence of banking principles, profits from interests on loans secured by equity arrangements.

Coming into existence is a banking network that has the capacity to raitonalize multinational exchanges. Banking capitalism links up with banking socialism precisely because banks are involved in similar international activities and investment in profitable enterprises. In the absence of direct industry-to-industry contacts, given East-West structural constraints at the manufacturing level, the banking system is the fluid that pumps life into an East-West economic *detente*. And it is this detente that permits arms reduction negotiations to take place in an atmosphere of cordial political *entente*.

THE FUSION OF CAPITALISM AND SOCIALISM AS SOCIAL SCIENCE IDEOLOGY

The multinationalist framework has already demonstrated a cultural impact on an East-West accommodation beyond any level reached in the past. Led by the United States and the Soviet Union, scientific academies of a dozen nations have set up a "think tank" to seek solutions to problems created by industrialization and urbanization of societies. Such problems as pollution control, public health, and overpopulation are to be studied by an International Institute of Applied Systems Analysis with overseas headquarters in Vienna, Austria. Even the broad composition of this new knowledge industry reflects multinational thinking. Its director will be a professor of managerial economics at Harvard, and its council chairman will be a member of the Soviet Academy of Sciences, Jerman M. Gvishiani, and incidentally the son-in-law of Premier Aleksei N. Kosygin (*Science,* October 13, 1972). In this remarkable display of East-West fusion, representatives from Czechoslovakia, Bulgaria, Poland, and East Germany will be joined by representatives of Japan, Canada, Great Britain, West Germany, and Italy. The director of the program, Dr. Howard Raiffa, indicated that the accumulated findings of management techniques, particularly as these have evolved in the aerospace industry, would be applied to a wide variety of health and welfare problems in Eastern Europe. He noted that a "likely first task would be concerned with energy: an analytical study of short and long range projections of the world supply of energy sources, future technologies and hazards of each source" (*The New York Times*, October 5, 1972).

It is evident from the tone and substance of these preliminary guidelines for this international think tank that it will be technocratic and nonideological in nature; in short, the perfect cultural and educational coefficient to the rise of a multinational framework.

The rise of a multinational cultural apparatus has been made possible by the widening exchange of contact between scientists, scholars, and performers from East and West alike. But underneath such widening contacts, indeed its presupposition, has been the declining fervor of ideology. Both Marxism and Americanism have yielded to considerations of efficiency and effectiveness, and with this, a vigorous effort to provide methodological guidelines that would provide accurate and exchangeable data. The new technology, with its potential for simultaneous translation and rapid publication, has also served to bring East and West together. This coalescence occurs precisely in areas of intellectual activities relatively uncontaminated by inherited ideological sore points. Hence it is that such subjects as futurism, computer technology, machine learning, etc., by virtue of their newness, permit widening contact points. But of course it is precisely these areas too that are most significant from the viewpoint of multinationalist exchanges of goods and services.

MULTINATIONALISM AND THE END OF CLASSICAL IMPERIALISM

The rise of multinationalism corresponds to a transformation in the nature of imperialist relations. What commenced as the classical military occupation of foreign territories in the pre-imperial, colonial period, shifted to the export of banking and industrial wealth owned by the advanced powers, and exchanged for the mineral wealth and natural resources of the peripheral colonized area. Whatever the merits of economic arguments concerning the relative value of agricultural and industrial products, the historical fact is that underdeveloped areas were, and remain, characterized by an agrarian base and the export of raw materials, and the import of finished goods and commodities. But over time this pattern has broken down: first, the failure of masses to participate in this system—i.e., the selective distribution of commodities— created huge riots and revolutions in overseas developing areas. In this way, the contradictions between the national middle classes and the rest of these underdeveloped societies made classical imperialism subject to intense pressures by indirection. National liberation and socialist movements of various types and structures simply invalidated the classical model of colonialism.

This overseas climate has become increasingly unfavorable to the signs and symbols of imperial enterprises, while desperately demanding more of the goods and uses of these same foreign firms (Boddewyn and Cracco, 1972). Hence, the multinationals become involved in bridging the gap between revolutionary nationalism and establishment internationalism. It does this by acquiescing to the symbolic demands of nationalists and revolutionists, while satisfying the very real economic demands of the conservative middle-sector elements in Third World societies.

The rise of the multinational corporation has given an increased weight to Lenin's initial focus on imperialism, albeit in a manner perhaps not entirely foreseeable by the master builder of Russian Bolshevism. At the turn of the twentieth century, the basic imperial powers engaged in banking-industrial capitalism were the United States, England, France, Germany, Japan, and Russia. After the Soviet revolution, the Marxists postulated that Russia was taken out of the imperialist orbit for all time. After World War One it was further postulated that the imperialist powers redivided Europe so as to limit and minimize German participation in the Imperial Club. After World War Two, this same set of theories further declared that the back of Western European capitalism had been broken, and that certainly both German and Japanese capitalism had been brought to heel. Now, a quarter-century later, we have witnessed a certain Grand Restorationism, of which the multinational corporation is merely the advance guard. For what we now witness is precisely the same cluster of nations that prevailed at the turn of the century controlling the overwhelming bulk of the international economy. The mix has certainly changed; it is now far more favorable to the United States than in 1900. But it is also, curiously, far more favorable to Japan than at the turn of the century.

The multinationals, by serving to alter the fundamental relationships between the bourgeoisie of advanced countries and the bourgeoisie of the peripheral countries, has also served to change the terms of the international game. The difficulty with much Marxian thinking in the current era is the supposition that dependence and underdevelopment are the handmaidens of backwardness, whereas in fact what one observes increasingly throughout the Third World is a correlation of dependence *and* development. And this is as true of Soviet penetration in Cuba as it is of United States penetration in Brazil. For what is involved is the internationalization of the notion of the senior and junior partner arrangement, which more fittingly and accurately describes present developmental realities than does the conventional model of superordination and subordination. By internationalizing capital relations, multinationals have also internationalized class relationships. Obviously, the situation with Soviet satellites is more complex, because all trade and aid relations are filtered through a grid of political and military tradeoffs; yet the same principle clearly obtains. This means that multinationalism permits development while at the same time maintaining a pattern of benign dependence.

This new situation is made perfectly plain by Richard Barnet (1972:237) in drawing our attention to the elimination of world war as a mixed blessing; one that permits world order within a multinationalist context sanctioned by the major powers.

> While it is claimed by the apologists for the multinational corporation that the peaceful division of the world is the most "rational" way to exploit resources, expand productivity, and promote the good life for the greatest number, the interests of the great corporate units conflict with the basic human needs of a majority of the world's population. The supreme value pursued by the new breed of corporate managers is efficiency. This is an improvement, to be sure, over glory, *machismo*, and the excitement of winning, which, it will be recalled, are so important to the national security managers. For those who can make a contribution to the rationalized world economy there will be rewards. But the stark truth is that more than half of the population of the world is literally useless to the managers of the multinational corporation and their counterparts in Soviet and Chinese state enterprises, even as customers.

It need only be added that since this inutility of large masses to the multinational and state enterprises has no apparent mechanism for realizing their own aspirations through official channels, new forms of political and economic competition emerge in this epoch.

THE REEMERGENCE OF PROLETARIAN INTERNATIONALISM AS A FUNCTION OF MULTINATIONALISM

The strangest, or certainly the least anticipated, consequence of the multinational corporation is the reappearance of militant unionism. The emergence of worker resistance to the multinationalist attempt to seek out the cheapest supply of labor as well as raw materials wherever that condition might obtain is still in an infant stage, but clearly on the rise. Highly paid West German optical workers must compete against lowly paid workers from the same industries in Eastern Europe. Auto workers in Western Europe find themselves competing against workers in Latin America producing essentially the same cars. Chemical plants of wholly owned United States subsidiaries are put up in Belgium and England, to capitalize on the cheaper wage scales of European chemical workers and to gain greater proximity to retail markets. Even American advertising agencies are protesting the manufacture of commercials in Europe. Such stories can be repeated for every major multinational firm and every nation.

One can well appreciate the rationale offered by the multinationals.

They can take advantage of the protectionist system of closed markets in the United States while pursuing an antiprotectionist approach for trading abroad. They can thereby derive the payoffs of having the American worker as a customer at high price while employing overseas workers at low wages. As Gus Tyler (1972:56–57) has observed: "For all these reasons—cheap labor, tax advantages, protected markets, monopoly control—as well as for other reasons of proximity to materials or markets, the giant conglomerates of America are moving their investments massively overseas. The result has been a rising threat to American employment and trade: jobs have not kept up with either our growing population or market: exports have not kept up with an expanding world trade." In a fierce critique, he sees the situation created by multinationalism as destructive of nationalism no less than unionism.

This new situation, whatever the merits or demerits of the rationalizing capacity of multinationals, has created a partially revivified working class, that unlike its responses to earlier periods shows greater class solidarity than cross-class national solidarity. Certainly, in the major wars of the twentieth century, the working classes have lined up solidly behind nationalism and patriotism; and in so doing have frustrated just about every prediction made on its behalf by left-wing intellectuals. Now, precisely at that moment when so much left-oriented rhetoric has itself become infused with an anti–working-class bias, we bear witness to the emergence of proletarian militance; this time as a function of self-interest rather than lofty ideology.

The organization of working-class life is still along national lines; but when confronted with middle-class internationalism—*i.e.*, as represented by the multinationals—it must either create new trade union mechanisms or revitalize old and existing ones.

It is intriguing to note how a relatively insular trade union movement such as the British Trades Union Congress (TUC) has vigorously responded to multinationals as a threat. It has put forth demands for making union recognition a precondition for setting up foreign subsidiaries in the United Kingdom; and likewise to have organizations such as the Organization for Economic Cooperation and Development (OECD) serve as an agency for funneling and channeling working-class demands on wider multinationals.

But while British responses have been legalist and proffered through government agencies, European workers on the mainland have become more direct and forthright in their dealings with multinational-led strike actions and corporate lockouts.

This renewed working-class activity has had a stunning effect on East-West trade union relations. It is axiomatic that socialism does not tolerate or permit strikes because, in the doctrine of its founders, socialism is a workers' society, and a strike against the government is a strike against one's own interest. The concept of working-class international action between laborers in "capitalist" and "socialist" countries has been virtually nonexistent. Nevertheless, such is the force of multinationalism that even these deep political inhibitions are dissolving. We may be entering an era of working-class collaboration across systemic lines not unlike the coalescence between the bourgeois West and bureaucratic East.

> Recent work stoppages and unofficial "wild cat" strikes in Poland, Yugoslavia, Sweden, Germany, Belgium, Switzerland, Holland, United Kingdom, Italy, and elsewhere, emphasize the growing opposition to centralized union authority and policies. By their nature, the national centres, like national governments, are best (perhaps uniquely) suited to deal with problems in the marginal areas of the lowest paid, least trained and poorest organized. For this reason, they tend to emphasize narrowing of the gap between the highest and lowest paid categories and raising of millions of working poor up into the middle-income brackets. This is an aim upon which there is universal agreement in principle and much sanctimonious moralizing. Practice is another thing entirely. In an economy which is disaggregating and in which challenges to central authority are being mounted everywhere, the levelling precept runs counter to the current of social change (Levinson, 1971:209–10).

Several important features of this special variant of proletarian internationalism must be distinguished: (1) It cuts across national lines for the first time in the twentieth century. (2) It cuts across systemic lines, being less responsive to Cold War calls for free labor or socialist labor than at any time in the post–World War Two period. (3) The vanguard role in this effort is being assumed by the workers in the better-paid and better-organized sectors of labor; in the specialized craft sector more than the assembly-line industrial sector. (4) While new mechanisms are being created to deal with multinational corporations, the more customary approach is to strengthen the bargaining position of available organizations, such as the International Metal Workers' Federation and the International Federation of Chemical and General Workers Unions.

What we have then is an intensification of class competition, but on a scale and magnitude so unlike the conventional national constraints. It is still difficult to demonstrate or to predict whether such class struggles can be as readily resolved short of revolution in the industrial areas as the previous epoch was resolved in the national areas. In effect, if Marxism as a triumphal march of socialism throughout the world has thoroughly been discredited, it manages to rise, phoenixlike, out of the bitter ashes of such disrepair. The intensification of class struggles at the international level remains muted by the comparative advantages of multinationalism to countries like Japan and the United States. But if such comparative advantages dissolve over the long pull of time (and this is beginning to happen as less developed nations play catch-up), then the quality of class competition might well intensify.

THE THEORY OF BIG-POWER CONVERGENCE
AND MULTINATIONAL REALITIES

Multinationalism has served to refocus attention on the theory of convergence; that set of assumptions whichs holds that over time, the industrial and urbanizing tendencies of the United States and the Soviet Union will prevail over systemic and ideological differences and form a convergence, or at least enough of a similitude to prevent major grave international confrontations (see Brzezinski and Huntington, 1964:429–30). The convergence theory does not postulate that the two systems will become identical, but rather that what will take place is a sort of political twin-track coalition network. Convergence more nearly represents a parallelism than a true coming fusion. In this sense, multinational corporation interpenetration is quite distinct from convergence, because involved are the linkages of the two super-states at the functional economic levels, but with a continued disparity at the political organization level. Convergence theory perhaps implied too much in the way of parallel lines; because as in geometry, parallel lines do not necessarily meet in politics. In an interpenetration such as that being brought about by the multinationals, systems of society do indeed meet and cross over. The lines of intersection are clearly evident as the data show; and the implications of such a development extend far beyond a formal proof for any doctrine of political science or economics.

The evidence for the convergence theory has been generally made much stronger by the rise of multinationals. And without entering into an arid debate about whether capitalism and socialism can remain pure and noble if this can take place, the empirics of the situation are clear enough: the United States (whatever its economic system can be called) and the Soviet Union (whatever its system can be called) have shown a remarkable propensity to fuse their interests at the economic level and collapse their differences at a diplomatic level for the purpose of forming a new big power coalition that dwarfs the dreams of Metternich for a United Europe in the ninteenth century. Indeed, we now have a situation in which the doctrine of national self-interest has been fused to one of regional and even hemispheric spheres of domination by the two major world super-powers (Weisband and Franck, 1971).

The issue of systemic convergence is certainly not new. Geographical size, racial and religious similitudes, even psychological properties of the peoples of the USA and the USSR, all conspire to fuse American and Soviet interests. What has been in dispute is whether such root commonalities would be sufficient to overcome longstanding differences in the economic organization of society, ideological commitments, and political systems of domination. This argument remained largely unanswered and unanswerable as long as the mechanism—the lever—for expressing any functional convergence remained absent. The unique contribution of multinationalism to the debate over convergence between the major super-powers is precisely its functional rationality; its place in contemporary history as the Archimedean lever lifting both nations out of the Cold War. Multinationals take precedence over political differences in prosaic but meaningful ways. They serve to rationalize and standardize international economic relationships. They demand perfect interchangeability of parts; a uniform system of weights and measurements; common auditing languages for expression of world trade and commerce; standard codes for aircraft and airports, telephonic and telegraphic communications; and banking rules and regulations that are adhered to by all nations. Convergence takes place not so much by ideological proclamation (although there has even been some of this) but primarily by organizational fiat; that is, by seeming to hold ideological differences constant while rotating every other factor in international relations.

What lies ahead? Even as we enter the multinational era, questions arise as to the efficacy of this resolution to world society. Some critics see the social structures of modern business as being in contradiction with the larger value complex of society (Brown, 1972:131); while crusaders see the multinational corporation as the beginning of a true internationalism (Turner, 1971, 185–87). Most recently, it has been suggested that the multinationals may resolve certain issues in relationship to the underdeveloped regions and the Third World as a whole. It has recently been suggested (Adam, 1971:63) that beyond the multinationals might be the antimultinationals, or regional organizations serviced by public institutions.

> The polar opposite of the world corporation is the antimultinational corporation. The latter is a public institution which organizes many industries across one region, substituting regionalization for internationalization. The boundaries of an enterprise are thus to be contained by the boundaries of the political unit, in order to render possible the control of the enterprise, the elimination of oligopolistic waste and regional imbalances. Owing to the aeronautical and electronic revolutions which greatly reduce costs of communication, regional groupings can obtain new knowledge easily and cheaply; this increases their chances to preserve their economic independence.

The difficulty with this small-power formula is that regionalism already exists, in the form of the European Common Market, the Latin American Free Trade Federation, Comecon, etc. These agencies, while serving the nation-states who are the member-states, reveal precisely the indebtedness to political pressures to power blocs that the multinationals serve to move beyond. The ideology of antimultinationalism as superstatism thus becomes a special variant of world political readjustments. And if it may serve to keep in check the multinationals, it does so at the expense of any real movement beyond the current Metternichean phase.

If multinationalism is not exactly the fulfillment of an egalitarian dream, the return to more parochial forms of socioeconomic organizations are clearly no real improvement.

PAX AMERICANA PLUS PAX SOVIETICA: THE POLITICS OF MULTINATIONALISM

The politics of multinationalism is not so much an illustration of convergence as it is an example of pragmatic parallelism. One has only to compare and contrast the position of Michael Harrington (1972: 570) on Nixon's program with the Weisband-Franck (1971:37–38) approach to Brezhnev's program to see how this parallelism operates—with or without a broad solution to theoretical disputations on convergence.

Harrington points out that underlying the Nixon-Kissinger position is a shared metaphysical belief that the division of the world is both necessary and desirable.

> Internationally, then, Nixonism has a profoundly conservative, shrewd yet utterly flawed approach. It seeks a Metternichian arrangement among the superpowers, Capitalist and Communist, according to which change would be relegated to controllable channels. In pursuit of this goal it is, unlike the moralistic policy of Dulles, willing to strengthen the power of its enemies if only they will accept the model of a global equilibrium. Nixonism is rhetorically dedicated to the virtues of the global division of labor but actually committed to utilizing America's state power to socialize the enormous advantage of our corporations on the world market. . . . Capitalist collectivism, in other words, wants to make a deal with bureaucratic collectivism to preserve the status quo.

Weisband and Franck, aside from assigning causal priority to this doctrine to the West, assert nonetheless the similitude of the Brezhnev approach toward peaceful coexistence as big-power sovereignty over smaller areas.

> The Brezhnev doctrine, which continues to govern the policies of the Warsaw Pact governments, to some degree represents a tradeoff or division of the world by the Soviet Union and the United States into spheres of influence or "regional ghettos." Not that our policy-makers in Washington planned it that way: little or no evidence has been adduced to show that the U.S. government ever willfully intended to trade control over Latin America for recognition of absolute Soviet dominance over Eastern Europe. Nor can it be said that any actions we have taken in relation to Latin America are the same as Russia's brutal suppression of Czechoslovakia. . . . What we do wish to assert is that virtually every concept of the Brezhnev doctrine can be traced to an earlier arrogation of identical rights by the United States vis-à-vis Latin America. . . . It is important to realize that the search for new norms in the world must begin with a

clear understanding that we, as much as the Russians, bear responsibility for conceptualizing the Brezhnev norms. . . . In the Soviet view, regional determination and prerogatives take precedence over those of the international community including the United Nations.

Curiously enough, the connection between international politics and the rise of multinationalism was clearly articulated, even by the above prescient commentators on international affairs. Lesser analysts seem to prefer to think of the new Nixonism as some sort of magical mystery tour; a transformation of high spiritual beliefs into policy matters. My contention is that the current foreign policy initiatives of Henry Kissinger derive precisely from a new American policy-making realization of changes in corporate relationships as necessitating an end to the Cold War, and establishing a new detente based on economic realities. President Nixon, throughout the 1972 year, clearly articulated such a geopolitical realignment based on economic realities.

As early as January of 1972, Nixon articulated the point of view which he sustained on his diplomatic initiatives in Moscow and Peking.

We must remember that the only time in the history of the world that we had any extended periods of peace is when there has been a balance of power. It is when one nation becomes infinitely more powerful in relation to its potential competitor that the danger of war arises. So I believe in a world in which the United States is powerful. I think it would be a safer world and a better world if we have a strong, healthy United States, Europe, Soviet Union, China, and Japan, each balancing the other, not playing one against the other, an even balance.

The peculiar linkage is China, because it alone has yet to participate fully in the multinational system. Further, it can be said to be by far the poorest of the countries with which power balance has to be sought. But with that admittedly crucial exception, and this can be argued to be a requirement of political tradeoff preventing an undue Soviet impact on the Western world and an undue Japanese presence in the Eastern world, what Nixon has outlined is quite clearly the politics of multinationalism, and not of capitalism triumphant or socialism defeated. The trade and aid agreements between East and West during this period serve to confirm the accuracy of this appraisal. Even China has entered the multinational race with its increased sale of specialized consumer goods to the United States and its purchase from Boeing Aircraft of an international fleet of advanced jets.

This new Metternichian arrangement among the super-powers is precisely a repudiation of the earlier moral absolutism of anticommunism and anticapitalism. In a sense, and one step beyond an acknowledged end of the Cold War, such a geopolitical redistribution also serves to solve a major problem of the multinational corporation, its transcendence of the limits and encumbrances placed by national sovereignty. By an international linkage of the super-powers, the problems of multinational regulation, which looms so large in the established literature, can be rationalized, if not entirely resolved by appeals to commercial rationality rather than to political sovereignty.

The thesis presented by George Kennan (1972:13) that the end of the Cold War came about as a result of a series of victories of the United States over the Soviet empire is simply untenable. The plain fact is that Stalinist foreign policy was remarkably legalistic in its foreign policy, whatever its extralegalities were internally. Beyond that the Soviet empire has neither dissolved nor shrunk. Current Soviet policy, especially as it affects Eastern Europe, can only be described as extremely aggressive. It is precisely the absence of victory, of a thoroughly stalemated situation, that led the major powers to reconsider their collision course—a course that could threaten both empires at the expense of outsider factions in the Third World, China, and even nonaligned nations like India, waiting in the wings to pick up the pieces.

What has happened in rapid succession is arms control agreements, direct executive rapprochement, new trade and purchasing agreements, exchanges of research and development technology in basic fields. These have signaled the real termination of the Cold War. Multinationalism, in its very extranation capacities, has served to rationalize this new foreign policy posture on both sides. Terms like "have" versus "have-not" states have come to replace and displace an older rhetoric of capitalism versus socialism, not simply as an expression of the uneven international distribution of wealth, but as an indication of the current sponginess of any concept of capitalism or socialism. It is precisely the inability of the Cold War to be resolved through victory that has led to a feeling on the part of the leadership in powerful states that the coalition of the big against the small, of the wealthy against the impoverished, and yes, even of white-led nations against colored-led nations, that can best guarantee the peace of the world, and the tranquilization of potential sources or rival power like China in the East or Germany and France in the West. With one fell swoop the mutual winding down of the Cold War settles the hash of rival powers and determines the subordinate position of the Third World War for the duration of the century. The cement for this new shift in fundamental policy is the multinational corporation. An end to ideology? No. An end to capitalist and communist rhetoric? Possibly. An end to the Cold War epoch? Yes. Good riddance to bad rubbish.

REFERENCES

ADAM, GYORGY, *The World Corporation: Problematics, Apologetics and Critique.* Budapest: Hungarian Scientific Council for World Economy, 1971.

BARNET, RICHARD J., *Roots of War.* New York: Atheneum Publishers, 1972.

BODDEWYN, JEAN, and ETIENNE F. CRACCO, "The Political Game in World Business," *Harvard Business Review* (January–February 1972).

BROWN, LESTER R., *World Without Borders*. New York: Random House, 1972.

BRUYN, SEVERYN T., "Notes on the Contradictions of Modern Business," *Sociological Inquiry*, 42, No. 2 (Spring 1972), 123–39.

BRZEZINSKI, ZBIGNIEW, and SAMUEL P. HUNTINGTON, *Political Power: USA/USSR*. New York: The Viking Press, 1964.

EISENHOWER, DAVID, and HENRY FRUNDT, *A Proposal to Study the Impact of Multinational Corporations or American Foreign Policy* (mimeographed). New Brunswick, N.J.: The Rutgers Multinational Research Group, 1972.

HARRINGTON, MICHAEL, "The Anatomy of Nixonism," *Dissent*, 19, No. 4 (Fall 1972), 563–78.

HOROWITZ, IRVING LOUIS, *Three Worlds of Development: The Theory and Practice of International Stratification*. New York and London: Oxford University Press, 1972, second edition.

KENNAN, GEORGE F., "Interview with George F. Kennan," *Foreign Policy*, No. 7 (Summer 1972), pp. 5–21.

LEVINSON, CHARLES, *Capital, Inflation and the Multinationals*. London: George Allen & Unwin, 1971.

RAY, DENNIS M., "Corporations and American Foreign Relations," *The Annals of the American Academy of Political and Social Science*, 403 (September 1972), 80–92.

Science, "East-West Think Tank Born," October 13, 1972.

TANZER, MICHAEL, *The Political Economy of International Oil and the Underdeveloped Countries*. Boston: Beacon Press, 1969.

THORNTON, THOMAS PERRY, ed., *The Third World in Soviet Perspective*. Princeton, N.J.: Princeton University Press, 1964.

TURNER, LOUIS, *Invisible Empires*. New York: Harcourt, Brace, Jovanovich, 1971.

TYLER, GUS, "Multinational Corporations vs. Nations," *Current*, No. 143 (September 1972), pp. 54–62.

VERNON, RAYMOND, *Sovereignty at Bay: The Multinational Spread of U.S. Enterprises*. New York: Basic Books, 1971.

VINNEDGE, HARLAN H., "Another Rum Deal With Russia," *The Nation*, 215, No. 18 (December 4, 1972), 558–59.

WEISBAND, EDWARD, and THOMAS M. FRANCK, *World Politics: Verbal Strategy Among the Superpowers*. New York and London: Oxford University Press, 1971.

c h a p t e r   t e n

The multinational corporation, U.S. foreign policy, and the less developed countries

JAMES R. KURTH

COMPETING EXPLANATIONS OF U.S. FOREIGN POLICIES

How can the major U.S. policies toward underdeveloped countries be explained? Why, for example, did the United States in 1965 undertake a massive military intervention in Vietnam and then persist in the divisive enterprise for eight years? Why did it undertake other, lesser interventions at the Bay of Pigs, in the Dominican Republic, and elsewhere in the 1960s? Why, conversely, did it undertake economic pressures but little more against the Allende regime in Chile in 1970 to 1972? And why does it now undertake sizable programs of military sales, military aid, and military advisors throughout much of the underdeveloped world?

The problem with such questions about the making of U.S. foreign policies is not that there are no answers but that there are too many answers. Around nearly every major U.S. policy toward underdeveloped countries, there has grown up a cluster of competing explanations, a thicket of theories, which prevents us from having a clear view of the making of those policies. Did Vietnam, for example, result from rational calculations about communist threats to international stability, or from distorted information from parochial bureaucrats and military officers, or from the determination of successive presidents to avoid political costs like those that followed "the loss of China," or from corporate pressures to preserve economic interests, or from some combination of these factors? Generally, we can distinguish in the academic and journalistic literature on U.S. foreign policies four broad, major, competing explanations of these policies: the strategic, the bureaucratic, the democratic, and the economic.[1]

Strategic explanations are familiar enough: they argue that U.S. foreign policies result from rational calculations about foreign threats to American security and to international stability. Not surprisingly, policy-makers and officials offer strategic explanations. They are less favored, however, outside official circles. Bureaucratic explanations see foreign policies as the outcome of bureaucratic politics, competition between bureaucracies, especially the State Department, the CIA, and the military services; or as

---

1. Other explanations are possible, for example, an idiosyncratic or psychological explanation and a stylistic or cultural one, but these are of less prominence in the literature.

the output of bureaucratic processes, standard operating procedures within bureaucracies. Many liberals favor bureaucratic explanations; for them, the problem is, as the title of a book by John Kenneth Galbraith puts it, "how to control the military." [2] Democratic explanations see foreign policies as the outcome of electoral politics—e.g., a president's efforts to avoid being vulnerable to campaign charges that he "lost" this or that country to the communists. Some liberals are drawn to this kind of explanation; for them, the problem is, as the title of an essay by Theodore Lowi puts it, "making democracy safe for the world." [3] Economic explanations see foreign policies as the result of *aggregate* economics, the needs of the capitalist system; or, in a less sweeping formulation, as the result of *corporate* economics, the needs of particular corporations, especially those that are multinational or military-industrial. Radicals favor such explanations; for them, the problem is not how to control the military but how to control the economy.

This essay is an effort to analyze economic explanations for the major U.S. policies toward underdeveloped countries in the period since World War Two. These policies include:

1. Military interventions or limited wars: Korea 1950–1953, Lebanon 1958, Dominican Republic 1965–1966, Vietnam 1965–1973, and the associated interventions in Laos 1965–1973 and in Cambodia 1970–1973.
2. Advisory interventions: China 1946–1947, Greece 1940s, Vietnam and Laos early 1960s, Bolivia 1967.
3. Proxy interventions: Iran 1953, Guatemala 1954, Cuba 1961, British Guiana 1963.
4. Military alliances: Rio Pact, SEATO, military agreements with CENTO, bilateral treaties with South Korea, Taiwan, and the Philippines, and the military assistance programs for these allies and for other underdeveloped countries.[4]

We will also consider certain cases of nonintervention, that is, no military intervention by the United States despite the failure of its other methods to prevent a communist or procommunist government or, in Laos, division of the country: China 1948–1949, Vietnam (Tonkin) 1953–1954, Iraq 1958, Cuba 1959–1962, Laos 1961–1962, and Chile 1970–1972.

CAPITALISM AND IMPERIALISM

Economic explanations emphasize the economic system as the determinant of a nation's foreign policy; i.e., the role of industrialism, capi-

2. *How to Control the Military* (New York: New American Library, 1969).
3. "Making Democracy Safe for the World," in James N. Rosenau, ed., *Domestic Sources of Foreign Policy* (New York: Free Press, 1967).
4. This list is a minimal one. It could be expanded to include less intensive cases, such as the advisory assistance in Venezuela, Guatemala, and Peru in the 1960s, or less plausible cases, such as the alleged proxy interventions in Brazil in 1964 and in Bolivia in 1971. The list also excludes the economic assistance programs.

talism, and the great corporations and the demand for foreign markets, investment opportunities, and raw materials. Leading economic theorists of U.S. foreign policy are William Appleman Williams, Harry Magdoff, and Gabriel Kolko.[5] Their intellectual ancestors are Hobson, Lenin, and Rosa Luxemburg.[6]

Among the contemporary theorists, Harry Magdoff offers the most systematic argument, particularly in his *The Age of Imperialism*. Like the others, Magdoff argues that U.S. foreign policy is determined by economic interests, particularly the interests of the large multinational corporations in their search for foreign investment opportunities, markets, and raw materials. To back up this proposition, and to a greater degree than other economic theorists, Magdoff presents data on the amount and rapid growth of American investments and banking abroad, on the dependence of the United States on foreign raw materials, and on the high proportion of corporate profits derived from foreign investments. The vast foreign interests of the multinational corporations result, Magdoff says, in a U.S. foreign policy that is expansionist, even interventionist, and he quotes Bernard Baruch on "the essential oneness of economic, political and strategic interests." But Magdoff is not very specific on this critical point of the foreign policy consequences of the multinational corporations. He discusses U.S. aid programs at length but not particular U.S. interventions (or noninterventions). Yet it was the U.S. interventions in underdeveloped countries and especially the one in Vietnam that gave Magdoff's book its popularity and indeed, by his own account, prompted him to write it.

Not surprisingly, Magdoff's work has provoked a barrage of criticism. Here the most systematic argument is offered by Robert W. Tucker, who dissects Magdoff's figures for domestic profits (nonfinancial corporations and after taxes) and foreign profits (including financial corporations and before taxes), criticizes Magdoff for "comparing these incomparables," and much reduces the weight of foreign profits relative to domestic ones.[7] Another point is counterfactual: Tucker asks if a socialist America would have a foreign policy fundamentally different from that of capitalist America, and he answers in the negative. If true, Magdoff is turned on his head (and Baruch probably returned to his original

5. William Appleman Williams, *The Tragedy of American Diplomacy*, 2nd rev. ed. (New York: Delta, 1972) and *The Roots of the Modern American Empire* (New York: Random House, 1969); Harry Magdoff, *The Age of Imperialism: The Economics of U.S. Foreign Policy* (New York: Monthly Review, 1969); Gabriel Kolko, *The Politics of War* (New York: Random House, 1971), *The Limits of Power* (New York: Harper and Row, 1972), and *The Roots of American Foreign Policy* (Boston: Beacon, 1969).

6. J. A. Hobson, *Imperialism: A Study* (London: George Allen and Unwin, 1902); V. I. Lenin, *Imperialism, The Highest Stage of Capitalism* (New York: International, 1969); Rosa Luxemburg, *The Accumulation of Capital* (New York: Monthly Review, 1966).

7. *The Radical Left and American Foreign Policy* (Baltimore: Johns Hopkins Press, 1971), p. 128, note 4.

position); "the essential one-ness of economic, political and strategic interests" would mean that economic interests are rooted in strategic ones
rather than the reverse.

Factual and counterfactual criticisms such as Tucker's raise an important problem for economic theorists of U.S. foreign policy. What
kinds of evidence can they bring to bear in support of their causal propositions? Here they confront a serious difficulty. The traditional sources
of evidence in foreign policy analysis are (1) memoirs and interviews,
(2) newspapers, (3) bureaucratic documents, normally after a period of
twenty-five years, and (4) congressional hearings and votes. But the very
choice to rely on these sources of evidence contains biases toward certain
explanations, none of which are economic.

Thus, presidential memoirs and interviews usually will yield a strategic explanation, advisors' memoirs, interviews, and newspaper leaks
a bureaucratic one, and congressional records an approach emphasizing the separation of powers and democratic factors.

AGGREGATE ECONOMIC ANALYSIS
AND U.S. FOREIGN POLICIES

Given these problems with the traditional sources of evidence in
foreign policy analysis, it is not surprising that economic theorists have
turned elsewhere to find evidence in support of their arguments. Their
classical source for empirical data has been the aggregate statistics on
U.S. direct foreign investment, published by the U.S. Department of Commerce.[8] Accordingly, we present some such aggregate statistics here, for
different areas and for different years since World War Two, including
1971, the latest year for which data are available at the time of this
writing (see Table 1).

One striking feature of this data is the much greater expansion of
U.S. investment in developed countries than in underdeveloped ones.
The investment in developed countries grew from $5.7 billion in 1950
to $58.3 billion in 1971, or by a factor of ten; the investment in Western
Europe grew even faster. Conversely, the investment in underdeveloped
countries grew from $5.7 billion in 1950 (the same amount as in de-
veloped countries) to $23.3 billion in 1971, or by only a factor of four;
the investment in Latin America grew even slower. At first glance, this
would suggest that even if U.S. foreign investment is a major determinant of U.S. foreign policy, the investment in underdeveloped countries is
not.

Such a conclusion does not logically follow, however. First, as Thomas
Weisskopf has pointed out, "although the *value* of U.S. direct private
investment is now much higher in the developed than in the under-

8. These statistics are normally published each autumn in the *Survey of Current
Business*; the publication date is getting progressively later and the data now appears
in the November issue.

Table 1.   VALUE OF U.S. DIRECT FOREIGN INVESTMENT (millions of dollars)

	1950	1960	1970	1971
All areas	11,788	32,778	78,178	86 001
Developed countries	5,697	19,328	53,145	58,346
Canada	3,579	11,198	22,790	24,030
Europe	1,733	6,681	24,516	27,621
Japan	19	254	1,483	1,818
Australia, New Zealand, and South Africa	366	1,195	4,356	4,876
Underdeveloped countries	5,735	12,032	21,448	23,337
Latin America	4,576	9,271	14,760	15,763
and other Western Hemisphere (excluding Canada)				
Africa (excluding South Africa)	147	639	2,614	2,869
Middle East	692	1,139	1,617	1,657
Asia and Pacific	320	983	2,457	3,048
(excluding Japan, Australia, New Zealand)				
International, unallocated	356	1,418	3,586	4,318

Sources: 1950 and 1960 data: U.S. Department of Commerce, *Survey of Current Business,* August 1962, pp. 22–23.
1970 and 1971 data: *Survey of Current Business,* November 1972, pp. 28–31.

developed countries, there is much less of a difference in the level of *income* from that investment." [9] Thus, in 1971, total earnings from U.S. investment were $10.2 billion; earnings from developed countries were $5.3 billion or 52%, while earnings from underdeveloped countries were $4.3 billion or 42%. [10] Indeed, the difference is reversed for the category of "interest, dividends, and branch earnings," which corresponds roughly to earnings repatriated to the U.S. In 1971, these totaled $7.3 billion; the amount from developed countries was $3.1 billion or 42%, while the amount from underdeveloped countries was $3.7 billion or 51%. Phrased differently, for underdeveloped countries in comparison with developed ones, a much higher proportion of earnings is repatriated to the U.S. rather than reinvested in the host country. The relative weight of earnings from underdeveloped countries, of course, was even heavier in the earlier years.

Moreover, much of the U.S. investment in developed countries is dependent upon the petroleum sector, either directly (in the sense that of $58.3 billion invested in developed countries in 1971, $13.0 billion or 22% was in the petroleum industry) or indirectly (in the sense that much of U.S. manufacturing in Western Europe runs on Middle Eastern oil).

Given these aggregate data on U.S. foreign investment and given the important weight of the underdeveloped countries in them, various analysts have argued that U.S. investments in underdeveloped countries are a primary determinant of U.S. foreign policies toward these countries. The results, it is said, are foreign policies that are protective both of

9. Thomas E. Weisskopf, "United States Foreign Private Investment: An Empirical Survey," in Richard C. Edwards, Michael Reich, and Thomas E. Weisskopf, eds., *The Capitalist System* (Englewood Cliffs, N.J.: Prentice-Hall, Inc., 1972), p. 431.
10. *Survey of Current Business* (November 1972), pp. 28–29.

these investments and of opportunities for their future expansion, which therefore are profoundly counterrevolutionary in their intent, and which undertake foreign interventions and military alliances in pursuit of these ends.

An aggregate economic analysis such as this is subject to criticism, however. First, there is the familiar if oversimplified argument that although U.S. foreign investment seems large in absolute terms, it is in fact of small moment relative to the massive size of the aggregate U.S. economy, with its trillion-dollar GNP.[11] Second, an aggregate economic analysis is an amorphous political analysis; aggregate statistics give us little sense of which groups with which interests push for which policies. There is, accordingly, some advantage in moving beyond aggregate to corporate economic analysis.

CORPORATE ECONOMIC ANALYSIS
AND U.S. FOREIGN POLICIES

Let us consider the three largest American industries—the automobile, oil, and aerospace industries—and the largest corporations within them. These largest corporations are the ones listed among the top fifty in the annual *Fortune* "Directory of the Top 500 Industrial Corporations"; in 1971, the latest year for which data are available at this writing, the top fifty corresponded roughly to those with over $2 billion in annual sales. In that year, the largest corporations within the three industries were those listed in Table 2.

THE AUTOMOBILE INDUSTRY:
FOREIGN INVESTMENT AND THE NATO ALLIANCE

The automobile industry clearly has had an interest in an open door for U.S. foreign investment in developed countries. Throughout the period since World War Two, the automobile corporations have had major investments in Canada and in Western Europe, especially in Britain and West Germany, and therefore have had an interest in maintaining and expanding these investments. In addition, in the last decade or so, the automobile corporations have made major investments in certain underdeveloped countries, especially Mexico and Brazil.

In order to get a complete sense of the importance to particular corporations of their foreign investments in particular countries, we should present systematic comparative data for all large corporations, for all host countries, and for several years. Unfortunately, the corporations refuse to make such data available, allegedly because the information would be useful to competitors. It is particularly difficult to get comparative data for investments in particular host countries. However,

---

11. For a sophisticated rebuttal to the argument, see Frank Ackerman, "Magdoff on Imperialism: Two Views," *Public Policy* (Summer 1971), pp. 525–31.

Table 2. LARGEST AUTOMOBILE, OIL, AND AEROSPACE CORPORATIONS

Industry and Corporation	Sales in 1971
Automobile industry	
General Motors	$28.3 billion
Ford	16.4 "
Chrysler	8.0 "
Oil industry	
Standard Oil of New Jersey	$18.7 billion
Mobil Oil	8.2 "
Texaco	7.5 "
Gulf Oil	5.9 "
Standard Oil of California	5.1 "
Standard Oil of Indiana	4.0 "
Shell Oil	3.9 "
Atlantic Richfield	3.1 "
Continental Oil	3.0 "
Occidental Petroleum	2.4 "
Phillips Petroleum	2.4 "
Union Oil	2.0 "
Aerospace industry	
Boeing	$3.0 billion
Lockheed	2.9 "
North American Rockwell	2.2 "
McDonnell Douglas	2.1 "
United Aircraft	2.0 "
Ling-Temco-Vought (conglomerate)	3.4 "

Source: *Fortune*, May 1972, p. 190.

global data which we shall present below, first for the automobile industry (Table 3) and then for the oil industry (Table 4), give some indication of the importance to particular corporations of their foreign investments. The data are for 1965 and 1967, the latest years for which minimally comparable data are available.

Table 3. FOREIGN OPERATIONS OF AUTOMOBILE CORPORATIONS

	Percent Foreign 1965			Percent Foreign 1967			Number of Countries with Production Facilities
	Sales	Assets	Earnings	Sales	Assets	Earnings	
General Motors	18	12	10	14[a]	15[a]	7[a]	24
Ford	22[a]	27[a]	12[a]	36	40	92[b]	27
Chrysler	25	26		21[a]	31[a]		18

[a] Excludes Canada.
[b] Ford's profits in the U.S. in 1967 were substantially reduced by an auto strike.
Blank space means data not available.
Sources: 1965 data: N. Bruck and F. Lees, *The Bulletin* (Institute of Finance, New York University), April 1968, pp. 83–85. 1967 data: Sanford Rose, *Fortune*, September 15, 1968, p. 100.

Given these foreign investments, what are the implications for the foreign policy of the automobile industry? The implications are probably not very dramatic. Because the automobile corporations have had most of their foreign investments in countries with developed economies and democratic polities (Canada, Britain, West Germany, France, Australia, and recently Japan), their direct interests in U.S. foreign policy presumably have not included the various forms of foreign intervention—military, advisory, or proxy. Rather, they would have been strong supporters of the NATO alliance, which serves their investments not only as the protective shield against Soviet armies but also as a bargaining chip against nationalist parties.

Of course, with their growing investments in countries with underdeveloped economies and potentially unstable polities, the automobile corporations might be expected to develop a direct interest in a U.S. foreign policy that can threaten foreign intervention. However, they had not developed very far in this direction at the time they were confronted with the election of Allende in Chile in the autumn of 1970. ITT, in association with members of the CIA, tried to organize American corporations in Chile to cooperate in economic disruption, which in turn could be used by elements of the Chilean military to justify a coup against former president Allende. (ITT ranked ninth on the *Fortune* list in 1971, with annual sales of $7.3 billion.) But on October 7, 1970, W. R. Merriam, an ITT vice-president in charge of the corporation's Washington office, wrote to another ITT vice-president, "repeated calls to firms such as GM, Ford, and banks in California and New York have drawn no offers of help." Two days later, Merriam wrote to John McCone, director of the CIA from 1961 to 1965 and since then a director of ITT.

> Practically no progress has been made in trying to get American business to cooperate in some way so as to bring on economic chaos. GM and Ford, for example, say that they have too much inventory on hand in Chile to take any chances and that they keep hoping that everything will work out all right. Also, the Bank of America had agreed to close its doors in Santiago but each day keeps postponing the inevitable. According to my source, we must continue to keep the pressure on business.[12]

(The "source" to which Merriam referred was "our contact at the McLean Agency," i.e., the CIA.)

Because GM and Ford subsequently lost their Chilean properties anyway, they may be less hesitant toward any future challenge from a Marxist government in the future. At any rate, the Chilean affair demonstrates conclusively that particular corporations do actively pursue a foreign policy of proxy intervention.

12. "Memos Reveal ITT Operations in Chile," *NACLA's Latin America and Empire Report* (North American Congress on Latin America), April 1972, pp. 13, 14. This issue reprints in full many of the ITT documents on Chile, which have been excerpted in major newspapers such as *The New York Times.*

THE OIL INDUSTRY: FOREIGN INVESTMENT AND FOREIGN INTERVENTION

Throughout the period since World War Two, the largest of the oil corporations (Standard Oil of New Jersey, Mobil Oil, Texaco, Gulf Oil, Standard Oil of California) have had major investments in the Middle East and, for some, in Venezuela. However, these corporations also have had major investments in developed countries, especially in Canada, Britain, West Germany, and recently Japan, in a pattern similar to that of the automobile corporations.

Again, some indication of the importance to particular corporations of their foreign investments is given by the following data for 1965 and 1967 (see Table 4).

The oil corporations, like the automobile corporations, have been supporters of the NATO alliance, but that is hardly an interesting observation. More importantly, because the oil corporations are so dependent upon investments in countries with underdeveloped economies and potentially unstable polities, they presumably have had a direct interest in a U.S. foreign policy that could threaten and, if necessary, carry out the various forms of foreign intervention—military, advisory or proxy. In fact, of course, the only actual such intervention in an oil-producing country was the proxy intervention in Iran in 1953.

Table 4. FOREIGN OPERATIONS OF OIL CORPORATIONS

	"Percent Foreign 1965"			"Percent Foreign 1967"			Number of Countries with Production Facilities 1967
	Sales	Assets	Earnings	Sales	Assets	Earnings	
Standard Oil, N.J.	68	52	60	68	56	52	45
Mobil Oil	49	43	52		46	45	38
Texaco	35ᵃ		25ᵃ				
Gulf Oil		33	29		38	29	48
Standard Oil, Cal.	35ᵃ	9ᵃ	43ᵃ				

ᵃ Excludes Western Hemisphere.
Blank space means data not available.
Sources: 1965 data: Bruck and Lees, *The Bulletin*, pp. 83–85. 1967 data: Rose, *Fortune*, p. 100.

Since the nationalist Libyan coup of 1969 and since the later series of agreements between the oil corporations and the oil countries, the polities of oil in the Middle East has dramatically changed.[13] As a result, U.S. intervention in the area in pursuit of oil interests seems rather unlikely in the future, even a proxy intervention, unless it be in one of the sheikdoms of the Persian Gulf. And what will become the new foreign policy of the oil industry is hard to discern.

13. For a good account, see M. A. Adelman, "Is the Oil Shortage Real? Oil Companies as OPEC Tax-Collectors," *Foreign Policy*, 73 (Winter 1972–73), 69–107.

THE AEROSPACE INDUSTRY: FOREIGN EXPORTS AND FOREIGN ENEMIES

Unlike the automobile and oil industries, the aerospace industry has not had an important interest in investing abroad. The determination of several foreign governments to maintain their own national aerospace industry (Britain, France, Sweden and, to a lesser extent, West Germany, Italy, and Japan) and the security restrictions imposed by the U.S. government have been among the causes. As such, there is some merit in drawing a distinction between multinational corporations and military-industrial ones.[14] However, most of the large aerospace corporations have had a significant interest in exports to foreign countries in the period since World War Two. This has been especially the case with (1) Boeing with its 700 series of commercial airliners; (2) Lockheed with its F-104 Starfighter fighter-bomber and its C-130 Hercules military transport; and (3) McDonnell Douglas with its A-4 Skyhawk fighter-bomber and recently its F-4 Phantom fighter-bomber. In addition, a much smaller aerospace corporation, Northrop (sales of $600 million in 1971), has produced almost entirely for the foreign market since the mid-1960s, with its F-5 series of fighters.[15]

It is not possible to present for the aerospace corporations global data on foreign operations fully comparable to that for the automobile and oil corporations. The data that exists, however, indicates that the foreign operations of the largest aerospace corporations normally account for 5% or less of the corporation's total operations.[16] (Although in 1965 the foreign earnings of North American were 9% of its total earnings, and the foreign sales of United Aircraft were 13% of its total sales.)

Through the U.S. government's military assistance and military sales programs, certain aerospace corporations have produced aircraft for the armed forces of several underdeveloped countries.[17] The major examples are: (1) Lockheed, whose C-130 Hercules has been delivered to more than a dozen underdeveloped countries, the largest numbers going to Iran, Brazil, and, during the "peace is at hand" phase in the autumn of 1972, South Vietnam; (2) McDonnell Douglas, whose A-4 Skyhawk has been delivered to Brazil and Argentina and whose F-4 Phantom has been delivered to Iran and South Korea; and (3) Northrop, whose F-5 series also

14. For a discussion of the relations between the two kinds of corporations, see Jonathan F. Galloway, "The Military-Industrial Linkages of U.S.-Based Multinational Corporations," *International Studies Quarterly* (December 1972), pp. 491–510.

15. Aerospace corporations, aerospace systems, and their export destinations are discussed in various annual editions of *Jane's All the World's Aircraft* (New York: McGraw-Hill).

16. N. Bruck and F. Lees, "Foreign Investment, Capital Controls, and the Balance of Payments," *The Bulletin* (Institute of Finance, New York University), April 1968, pp. 83–91.

17. For details, see annual editions of *Jane's All the World's Aircraft*; annual editions of *The Military Balance* (London: International Institute for Strategic Studies); and *The Arms Trade With The Third World* (Stockholm: Stockholm International Peace Research Institute; Almquist and Wiksell, 1971).

has been delivered to more than a dozen underdeveloped countries, the largest numbers going to Iran, Saudi Arabia, South Korea, Taiwan, and South Vietnam. As such, these three aerospace corporations have had a direct interest in the U.S. military assistance and military sales programs in underdeveloped countries. But until 1972, this was only a minor factor for the major corporations (Lockheed and McDonnell Douglas) and a major factor for only a minor corporation (Northrop). In any event, their direct interest did not prevent Congress from imposing restrictions on the sale of supersonic aircraft to Latin America from 1967 to 1973.

The main foreign policy interest of the aerospace industry has been of course the identification and preservation of a foreign enemy, most particularly the Soviet Union and more broadly communism. It is this which maintains by far the largest source of demand for the industry's products, i.e., the U.S. armed forces. And given the character of the Soviet Union, this has not been difficult to do.

The automobile, oil, and aerospace industries are the three largest American industries, but certain other industries contain corporations which fall within the top fifty of the *Fortune* Directory and which have a high percentage (more than 20%) of their operations abroad.

Given the aggregate and corporate economic interests discussed in this and the preceding section, one can hypothesize that U.S. policymakers adopt certain principles, called decision rules, operational codes, or ideological tenets, which guide them in their foreign policy choices. We shall consider one such possible principle which might be called the procapitalist imperative and which has been used, in one form or another, by economic theorists to explain U.S. foreign policies.

THE PROCAPITALIST IMPERATIVE AND U.S. FOREIGN POLICIES

At their simplest, economic theorists have argued that U.S. foreign policy toward an underdeveloped country is determined by a sort of procapitalist imperative which seeks to protect existing American investments and markets within the country itself. The procapitalist imperative, however, has been readily extended in two dimensions: from local areas to regional ones and from actual interests to potential ones.

LOCAL AREAS AND ACTUAL INTERESTS

The simplest form of the procapitalist imperative has been used to explain several major U.S. foreign policies toward underdeveloped countries since World War Two. Thus, the proxy intervention in Guatemala in 1954 has been explained by the interests of the United Fruit Company, including the fact that several U.S. policy-makers had close connections with the company: John Foster Dulles, who was Secretary of State, had been for many years a legal counsel for United Fruit; Henry Cabot Lodge, the U.S. Ambassador to the U.N., was on the company's board of directors;

and John Moors Cabot, the Assistant Secretary of State for Inter-American Affairs, was a large shareholder in the company. Similarly, the proxy intervention in Cuba in 1961 has been explained by the $1 billion American investment there. The proxy intervention in British Guiana in 1963 has been explained by American investments in bauxite. The military intervention in the Dominican Republic in 1965 has been explained by American sugar interests, again including the fact that several U.S. policymakers or advisors had close connections with major sugar corporations: at the time, Ellsworth Bunker was chairman, president, and had been for thirty-eight years a director of National Sugar Refining Corporation; Adolf Berle had been chairman and was still a director of Sucrest Corporation; and Abe Fortas also had been a director of Sucrest.[18]

LOCAL AREAS AND POTENTIAL INTERESTS

If the actual American investments and markets within a country at the time of intervention were small, then the emphasis of the explanation can be on potential ones. Thus, the advisory intervention in China in 1946 to 1947 could be explained by dreams of, in the phrases of the time, "oil for the lamps of China" and "four hundred million customers." The proxy intervention in Iran in 1953 was quickly followed by the entry of American oil corporations. The alleged proxy intervention in Brazil in 1964, far more indirect and less assignable than those in Guatemala and Iran, was quickly followed by a major mining concession to the Hanna Mining Company and by major increases in the already large American investment in Brazilian manufacturing ($700 million in 1964; $1.4 billion in 1971).

REGIONAL AREAS AND ACTUAL INTERESTS

A more complex form of the procapitalist imperative is regional rather than local in focus. Here, U.S. policy toward a country is explained by existing American investments and markets within a substantial region. The loss of the country through its takeover by a communist or revolutionary nationalist regime would lead, by variations on the domino theory, to the loss of the region itself and perhaps of even more. Thus, it has been argued, the military intervention in Korea preserved Japan and its markets and that in Lebanon preserved the Middle East and its oil. Similar regional explanations have been applied to the advisory interventions in Greece in the 1940s and in Bolivia in 1967. And, of course, interventions covered by the local procapitalist imperative (i.e., Guatemala, Cuba, the Dominican Republic) can be covered by the regional one too.

REGIONAL AREAS AND POTENTIAL INTERESTS

Finally, the most extended form of the procapitalist imperative has been applied to the most extensive example of U.S. intervention: the advisory

18. See James Petras, *Politics and Social Structure in Latin America* (New York: Monthly Review, 1970), pp. 235–36.

intervention in Vietnam and Laos in the early 1960s and the later military escalation in Vietnam, Laos, and Cambodia. Here, what was presumably preserved was the entire region of Southeast Asia and its vast economic potential.

The regional form of the procapitalist imperative has also been used to explain the American system of military alliances with underdeveloped countries: the Rio Pact, SEATO, the military agreements with CENTO, the bilateral treaties with South Korea, Taiwan, and the Philippines, and the military assistance programs for these allies and for other underdeveloped countries.

As an explanation of U.S. foreign policies, the procapitalist imperative as extended has the important virtue of generality: it can be applied to each of the major U.S. foreign policies toward underdeveloped countries in the period since World War Two.

That virtue, however, is not achieved without cost. To most people—professional scholars, college students, ordinary citizens, or government officials themselves—the procapitalist imperative and other simple economic explanations lack plausibility as decision rules for U.S. policymakers. That such great events could be explained by such narrow conceptions simply seems incredible. Moreover, as we have observed, there exists virtually no documentary evidence to support the proposition that U.S. leaders calculate their policies in such economic terms. Consequently, the more sophisticated economic theorists, such as Williams, Magdoff, and Kolko, have cast their economic propositions in a more complex form: they see the capitalist economic system generating an ideological superstructure which lends political legitimacy and moral energy to the system's foreign policies, and the content of the American ideological superstructure has been anticommunism. When recast into anticommunist form, the procapitalist imperative is slightly narrowed in regard to its targets (no longer including certain nationalist expropriating regimes) but greatly broadened in regard to its support (now including many American classes and groups). And as an explanation of U.S. foreign policies, it rings much more true.

Even when recast, however, the procapitalist imperative retains at least two important problems which commonly afflict various theories of foreign policy. One is the problem of *overprediction:* the theory would have predicted events which have never occurred. A second is the problem of *overdetermination:* other theories can also explain the events and can do so just as well or better. In the space of this article, we will only be able to deal with the first.[19]

A theory that can explain everything may explain too much. The procapitalist and anticommunist imperatives surely would have predicted

19. I have discussed the problem of overdetermination at greater length in my "A Widening Gyre: The Logic of American Weapons Procurement," *Public Policy* (Summer 1971), pp. 373–401; and in my "United States Foreign Policy and Latin American Military Rule," in Philippe C. Schmitter, ed., *Military Rule in Latin America* (Beverly Hills, Calif.: Sage Publications, forthcoming).

U.S. military intervention against the Chinese communists sometime in 1948 to 1949, after the failure of the earlier advisory intervention and for the sake of those "four hundred million customers." Given the perspective of the procapitalist and anticommunist imperatives, the most interesting question about the advisory intervention in China, the proxy intervention at the Bay of Pigs, and the economic pressures on Chile would be not "why did they occur?" but "why were they not followed by full military intervention?". Indeed, the imperatives would have mispredicted as many or more military interventions that did not occur as they would have correctly predicted military interventions that *did* occur (Korea 1950 to 1953, Lebanon 1958, which they might not have predicted, the Dominican Republic 1965 to 1966, Vietnam 1965 to 1973, and the associated interventions in Laos and in Cambodia).

Efforts could be made to interpret these six noninterventions in strictly economic terms. I believe, however, that such efforts would prove unsuccessful. In order to salvage the economic theory from the desert of nonintervention, we will have to add to the economic explanation elements from the bureaucratic and the democratic.

BUREAUCRATIC AND DEMOCRATIC CONSTRAINTS ON ECONOMIC COMPULSIONS

The noninterventions we have mentioned suggest that there have been historical limits to the operation of the procapitalist and anticommunist imperatives. But what was it that imposed these limits? Let us look at the six cases more closely.

In three of these cases (China, Tonkin, and Laos), the source of the communist threat was in a strong revolutionary movement, which included conventional military forces as well as guerrilla forces, and there was consequently the clear prospect that a military intervention would become a long and bloody war. In these three cases, the military intervention was blocked by one or more elements in the American bureaucracy, particularly by the army or by the State Department. In addition, in these three cases, there was opposition to military intervention by important leaders of Congress, and the president thought that there would be strong opposition by the public at large.

In the other three cases (Cuba, Chile, and Iraq), the source of the communist threat was in a firmly established government, and there was almost no prospect that important groups in the target country would welcome and support a U.S. military intervention (even if they might not oppose it with vigor); as such, military intervention would have been wholly lacking in political legitimacy. In these three cases, the military intervention was blocked by an element in the "American Creed," the axiom of self-determination, and the president again thought that these would be strongly opposed by the public at large.

As for Vietnam, in 1965 the presence of communist conventional forces as well as guerrilla forces was a matter of debate. But by that time the presence or absence of such conventional forces was not the major variable in determining the outcome. Even if communist conventional forces had been as clearly present and as clearly successful as they had been in China and Tonkin, the American bureaucracy this time would not have blocked the U.S. military intervention. For in the years from 1961 to 1964, the massive buildup of American conventional forces under Kennedy and McNamara had utterly changed the situation of the army and the way its leaders would calculate. This change was made easier by the change in army leaders, the appointment of the politically facile Generals Taylor and Westmoreland. Thus, by 1964, the liberal coalition of Democratic politicians such as Kennedy and Johnson, bureaucratic politicians such as Rusk and McNamara, and academic politicians such as McGeorge Bundy and Walt Rostow had removed the first block to massive military intervention, the U.S. Army.

There was still, however, block number two, the American democracy, the Congress, and the public. And then in 1964, as accounts of the Tonkin Gulf Incident and the Pentagon Papers demonstrate, the same liberal coalition of Democratic, bureaucratic, and academic politicians removed that second block, by stealth and by deceit, much as their hero, Franklin Roosevelt, had done twenty-seven years before with secret operations by the U.S. Navy against German submarines in the autumn of 1941.

But now the American intervention in the Vietnamese War has come to an end. What would the economic theorists predict about the future of U.S. foreign policy? Presumably, they would predict U.S. intervention wherever there should develop a serious threat to American corporate interests, perhaps in the Philippines in a year or two, perhaps in the Persian Gulf not long after. Yet, just as liberals have misrepresented the direction of bureaucratic and democratic factors, so have radicals underestimated their strength. For after the experience of Vietnam, which has restored the professional caution of the army and the skeptical attitude of Congress and the public, U.S. military intervention in underdeveloped countries seems unlikely, at least for the remainder of the 1970s.

The impact of the multinational corporations on the international system

THEODORE A. COULOUMBIS AND ELIAS P. GEORGIADES

The ability to assess the impact of the MNCs on the international system rests on the effectiveness with which we can describe or define the system. The literature on international relations is replete with attempts at definition—which have been referred to as "grandstand" theories or systemic conceptualizations.

Stanley Hoffmann has described the contemporary international system as an existential "state of war." [1] The absence of central authority and force, the plurality of autonomous centers of decision-making, and the incidence of war viewed as the "continuation of politics" for vigorous bargaining and ultimate arbitration, all lead him to his dreary analogy of the world system as playing "roulette in the cellar." The roulette ball is thermonuclear, the players (governments) are encumbered by the hustling and bustling of interested bystanders (public, press, business, labor, students, and other pressure groups), and the game is one of low gains, high costs, and onerous risks.

Hoffmann, more recently, has moderated his power political conception of the international system *qua* international "political" system. He concedes that

in an age dominated by the expansion of science and technology . . . the competition between states takes place on several chessboards in addition to the traditional military and diplomatic ones: for instance, the chessboards of world trade, of world finance, of aid and technical assistance, of space research and exploration, of military technology, and the chessboard of what has been called "informal penetration." [2]

These chessboards tend to tilt international politics more to the side of competition and away from conflict. Hoffmann, however, gives us precious little advice on how to study the interactions and mutual effects among these various chessboards.

Raymond Aron, in his seminal work *Peace and War*, defines the in-

1. *The State of War: Essays in the Theory and Practice of International Relations* (New York: Praeger, 1965). For Hoffmann's formal definition of the international system, see his "International Systems and International Law," in Klaus Knorr and Sidney Verba, eds., *The International System* (Princeton, N.J.: Princeton University Press, 1961), p. 207.

2. Hoffmann, "International Organization and the International System," in *International Organization*, XXIV, No. 3 (Summer 1970), 401.

ternational system as follows: "I call an international system the en-semble constituted by political units that maintain regular relations with each other and that are all capable of being implicated in a generalized war." [3] Aron, further, enjoins international relations students to focus on the diplomat and the soldier (once more an attempt to reify the nation!) as executants of international affairs. The risk of war motivates the cal-culation of national means, and mutually rational objectives pursued by independent actors in an anarchic world system can easily lead to war.

Although Aron was one of the first theorists to discuss the existence of a "transnational society," [4] he feels that the ideological and power con-frontations of the post–World War Two period have considerably eroded the potency and potential impact of transnational relations. He concludes, therefore, that

> it is doubtful if this restoration of transnational society has modified es-sentials: heterogeneity, with regard to the principle of legitimacy, the form of the state and the social structure, remains fundamental. The Christian community has only a limited scope because political faith is stronger than religious faith, the latter having become a strictly private matter; lastly, no organization, whether political, syndical or ideological, can unite Soviet and Western citizens unless it is in the open or clandestine service of the Soviet Union. *The heterogeneity of the inter-state system irremediably divides transnational society.*[5] (Emphasis added.)

Given the traditionalist impressionistic description of the international system, can we estimate the impact of multinational corporations upon it? The authors submit that the answer is "not yet." One must first look into the "black box" of multinational corporations and search for the types and subdivisions therein. Is, for instance, the following definition of an MNC adequate? "A multinational corporation, in contrast to a domestic corporation, is a company that controls production facilities in two or more countries." [6] Admittedly this definition is too broad and

3. *Peace and War* (New York: Doubleday, 1966), p. 94. Aron goes on to say that "units taken in their calculation of forces, by those governing the principal states, are full-fledged members of an international system." However, in this context it is doubtful whether he meant such transnational actors as the MNCs.

4. Aron defines "transnational society" as follows: "A transnational society reveals itself by commercial exchange, migration of persons, common beliefs, organizations that cross frontiers and, lastly, ceremonies or competitions open to the members of all these units. A transnational society flourishes in proportion to the freedom of exchange, migration or communication, the strength of common beliefs, the number of non-national organizations, and the solemnity of collective ceremonies" (*Ibid.*, p. 105).

5. *Ibid.*, pp. 105–106. For the distinction between homogeneous systems and hetero-geneous systems, Aron credits Panayis Papaligouras, *Theorie de la Société Internationale*, thesis at the University of Geneva, 1941.

6. In Bernard Mennis and Karl P. Sauvant, "Multinational Corporations, Managers and the Development of Regional Identifications in Western Europe," in *The Multi-national Corporations*, in *The Annals* of the American Academy of Political and Social Science, 403 (September 1972), 23, note 2.

inclusive to be useful for our purposes. Should we, for example, differentiate MNCs as to function? Should MNCs involved with weapons industries be lumped together with those in petroleum, energy, chemicals, food, plastics or finance? Should one differentiate between "ethnocentric" MNCs that are nationally controlled versus those precious few "geocentric" MNC's that tend to lose their nationality and owe their highest loyalty to the corporation? [7] Should we classify MNCs in terms of the locus of control or of decision-making? Should we classify them in terms of dependency to or independence from various nationally pursued foreign policies? Invariably it is difficult to devise a precisely operational scheme to classify the various types, but it is vital to continue research on this topic.[8]

Hans Morgenthau's[9] impressionistic conception of the international system allows us, perhaps, to move a step further toward the meaningful conceptualization of the MNC's role in the international system. The grand master conceives the world in terms of the adjustment or balance of power, where power is defined in terms of conflicting and self-adjusting national interests. The concept of national interest and the institution of the nation-state are not, however, considered timeless and permanent by Hans Morgenthau. It is only the pure concept "interest" (of individuals or groups of varying size and organization) that is a permanent and timeless characteristic of the "political process". The national interest is either a compromise among conflicting group interests within nations or the articulation of "establishment" interests, reified and legitimized as national interests.

It is precisely the interplay between group and national interests that supplies us with a powerful conceptual device with which to assess the impact of MNCs on national action and by extension on international interaction. Of course this is more easily said than done. Numerous studies have been conducted designed to assess the impact of business (including MNCs) on U.S. foreign policy.[10] Approaches, mostly in re-

7. For a widely quoted typology of MNCs in terms of ethnocentricity, polycentricity, and geocentricity, see Howard V. Perlmutter, "The Tortuous Evolution of the Multinational Corporation," *Columbia Journal of World Business,* 4, No. 1 (January–February 1969), 9–18. Perlmutter concludes that most MNCs are ethnocentric in nature. Another very suggestive definition, if adequately operationalized, is Sidney Rolfe's, who defines an international company as "one with foreign content of twenty-five percent or more"; "foreign content" is defined as "the proportion of sales, investment, production, or employment abroad." See his "International Corporation in Prospective," *Atlantic Community Quarterly,* 7, No. 2 (Summer 1969), 260.

8. For an outstanding effort to define MNCs and develop specific criteria of multinationality, illustrating the great complexity of this exercise, see A. J. N. Judge, Multinational Business Enterprises, *Yearbook of International Organizations,* Brussels, 1968, p. 1189 ff.

9. Hans J. Morgenthau, *Politics Among Nations,* 4th ed., rev. (New York: Alfred Knopf, 1967).

10. Raymond Vernon, *Sovereignty at Bay* (New York: Basic Books, 1971); Jack N. Behrman, *U.S. International Business and Governments* (New York: McGraw-Hill, 1971); Seymour J. Rubin, "Multi-national Enterprise and National Sovereignty: A Skeptic's Analysis," *Law and Policy in International Business,* 3, No. 1 (1971), 1–41.

visionist literature, range from studies tracing the feedback of managerial personnel and other symbiotic arrangements between the foreign policy establishment and the business world,[11] to studies professing as an article of faith the "equation" of America's national interests with Big Business Interest.[12] The results are not yet scientifically convincing, and by the time they are, the system is quite likely to have changed in the meantime.

Morgenthau offers us a second conceptual outlet with which to evaluate the role of the MNCs in the international system.[13] He sees the international system in terms of power (defined as ability of A to control the mind and actions of B), resulting in some form of stable or unstable "balance of power." Among the elements of power he includes size, population, geographic characteristics, military and industrial capability of states, and a number of intangible factors, such as quality of leadership, morale, national character, national cohesiveness, and others.[14]

The MNCs—especially the ethnocentric ones—unquestionably play an important role in strengthening the capabilities of given states, especially in the sectors of military-industrial preparedness. But the effect of the geocentric MNCs on the capabilities of nations—assuming that their activities and benefits are approximately equally distributed among the participating nations—is probably negligible or nil. On the other hand, the potential effect of geocentric MNCs on the structure of the international system is likely to be immense, unless the nation-states agree to curb genuinely multinational corporate development.

Moving now to the more "systematic" behavioral literature, we find that the international system has been described as bipolar and/or loose-bipolar,[15] multipolar,[16] and bimultipolar.[17] The bipolar literature not only reifies decision-making at the state level but does so at the bloc (East and West) level. Political and national diversity are deemphasized, while integrated military alliance capabilities and ideological exclusivism

11. Richard Barnet, *The Economy of Death* (New York: Atheneum, 1969).

12. See Gabriel Kolko, *The Roots of American Foreign Policy* (Boston: Beacon Press, 1969); Henry Magdoff, *The Age of Imperialism* (New York: Monthly Review Press, 1969).

13. By way of reminder, it should be noted that most well-known writers on international relations failed to foresee the rising role of the MNCs in world politics. Morgenthau is not an exception in this category. His theoretcal framework, however, could be stretched to account conceptually for the MNCs. For a brief overview of the international relations and comparative politics literature, see Jonathan F. Galloway, "Multinational Enterprises as Worldwide Interest Groups," *Politics and Society*, 2, No. 1 (Fall 1971), 1–5.

14. See Charles O. Lerche and Abdul A. Said, *Concepts of International Politics* (Englewood Cliffs, N.J.: Prentice-Hall, Inc., 1970), pp. 59–76. These authors, under the rubric of "capability," provide a very fine framework which operationalizes Morgenthau's "elements of power."

15. Morton A. Kaplan, *System and Process in International Politics* (New York: Wiley, 1957).

16. Karl W. Deutsch and J. David Singer, "Multipolar Power Systems and International Stability," *World Politics*, XVI, No. 3 (April 1964), 390–406.

17. Richard N. Rosecrance, "Bipolarity, Multipolarity and the Future," *The Journal of Conflict Resolution*, X, No. 3 (September 1966), 314–27.

are greatly emphasized. Recent trends, such as polycentrism in the communist camp and Gaullism in NATO, are undermining the bipolar conception of the world. On the other hand, to the degree that multinational corporate activity facilitates "regional" and "polar" economic integration rather than "global" integration, it is contributing further to the structure of bipolarity, or at most, tripolarity (in terms of East, West, and the Third World). A cursory view of the clusters of multinational corporate activities seems to strengthen this view.[18]

To the degree that multinational business concerns bridge the East-West gap, one could argue that such MNC activity would be eroding bipolarity and contributing to the process of global integration. The scarcity by comparison, however, of such East-West multinational corporate activity leads, once more, to the conclusion that economic activity is following the pattern of the post–World War Two division of the world along power/ideological lines. So once more we must conclude that the global integration pretensions of MNCs are unfairly exaggerated, while a very good case can be made for MNC contribution in regional, up to a certain level, integration, especially in the Atlantic area. Thus MNCs reflect to a greater extent and magnify or modify to a lesser extent the dominant features of the international system.[19]

Finally, Richard Rosecrance's conception of bimultipolarity is an intelligent, if limited, refinement of the evolving international system, pointing out that in strategic terms the world is still bipolar, but that it is fragmented politically and to a lesser extent, economically. The MNC, only to the degree to which it increases East-West interdependencies, could be considered contributive to lessening divisions (and resultant tensions) at the strategic level. Within geographic or alliance regions the MNC is, on the other hand, contributive to lesser political and economic diversity and a gradual development of the infrastructure which could eventually "spill over" [20] to regional political unions. The authors are

18. For a thorough survey conducted by Booz, Allen, and Hamilton, showing in detail the regional flow of U.S. investments, see John B. Rhodes, "U.S. Investment Abroad: Who's Going Where, How and Why," *Columbia Journal of World Business,* VII, No. 4 (July–August 1971), 33. The data supports the polarizing contention above. The lion's share of the investment pie has been dished out to the Western European region, at least until recently.

19. For further exposition of the thesis "that transnational actors and processes are dependent upon peculiar patterns of interstate relations," see Robert Gilpin, "The Politics of Transnational Economic Relations," *International Organization,* XXV, No. 3 (Summer 1971), 398–419.

20. The literature on functional integration studies is voluminous. For two excellent critical reviews, see Roger D. Hansen, "Regional Integration: Reflections on a Decade of Theoretical Efforts," *World Politics,* XXI, No. 2 (January 1969), 242–71; and Ernst B. Haas, "The Study of Regional Integration: Reflections on the Joys and Anguish of Pretheorizing," *International Organization,* XXIV, No. 4 (Autumn 1970), 607–48. See also Peter J. Katzenstein, "Hare and Tortoise: The Race toward Integration," *International Organization,* XXV, No. 2 (Spring 1971), 290–97. For the purposes of this article we do not go into the distinction between functionalists and neofunctionalists.

somewhat sceptical, however, about the rather utopian expectations of the functionalist "spill-over" assumptions. There is probably more evidence that functionalist cooperation tends to follow political accommodation rather than vice versa. Spill over could be appropriately paraphrased, therefore, as spill under.[21]

Most of the international relations literature discussed above tends to reify the political aspects of the nation-state and to eliminate much of the complexity of viewing the effects of transnational actors on various national interests and attitudes. International relations theorists emphasize traditional interstate politics which form only one dimension—to be sure the dominant one—of the international system today. As a result this literature (as exemplified above) is relatively ill-suited conceptually to account for the impact of transnational economic/business group-actors on the international system.

James Rosenau, in reviewing the state of foreign policy in the fields of political science and international politics, has alerted us with great concern to the erection of conceptual "jail cells" surrounding each field. For instance, political science studies polities with little concern (ceteris paribus) for external inputs and the international environment around the polity under study. International politics, on the other hand, studies phenomena such as war, peace, alliances, diplomacy, strategy, and conflict management without concern for the domestic considerations and inputs to the formation of foreign policies. So far much of Rosenau's work has conceptualized efforts at synthesis of domestic and international politics and the breakdown of conceptual jails by advancing work on domestic sources of foreign policy, intervention, penetrated political systems, and linkages.[22]

Rosenau has defined a "linkage" as "any recurrent sequence of behavior that originates in one system and is reacted to in another." [23] He has then proceeded to fragment this highly inoperational conceptual baggage to myriad subdivisions, thus creating what we could call a conceptual Tower of Babel. Yet, despite its imprecision, we feel that the concept of linkage (defined quite precisely) can become a useful device in assessing the impact of MNCs and other transnational actors upon the international system. "Transnational linkage," to modify Rosenau's concept somewhat, could be defined as a cluster of transnationally shared values, properties, or processes by a multinational group of people. This concept can indeed become a very useful device which will allow us to

21. For an exposition of the "logic of diversity" (Hoffmann) as it is contrasted with the "logic of integration" (Haas), see Stanley Hoffmann, "Obstinate or Obsolete? The Fate of the Nation-State and the Case of Western Europe," *Daedalus*, 95, No. 3 (Summer 1966), 862–915.

22. See James N. Rosenau, *The Scientific Study of Foreign Policy* (New York: Free Press, 1971). This is a compendium containing most of Rosenau's essays from over a ten-year span.

23. Rosenau, "Toward the Study of National-International Linkages," James N. Rosenau, ed., *Linkage Politics* (New York: Free Press, 1969), p. 45.

develop a set of meaningful interdependency indices, thus evaluating the impact of transnational activities, including those of the MNCs as linkage agents, on the international environment.[24] Other such activities would include formal and informal transnational linkages, such as those of private international organizations, religious movements, transnational revolutionary organizations, ideological movements, functional international labor organizations, Olympic-type and other athletic arrangements, and perhaps even international rackets of the MAFIA type.[25]

This leads us to the integration, communication, or "transnational flow" type studies of the kind pioneered by Karl W. Deutsch, Ernst Haas, Leon Lindberg, Philippe Schmitter, Bruce Russett, Joseph Nye, and others.[26] Here, if we discount the bias or value in favor of "integration" or "security community" as an end, we find a conceptual approach that allows for vigorous and systematic collection of data that can be packaged in highly operational concepts. For instance, using a variation of Nye's model for assessing regional integration trends,[27] we can start collecting data on transnational flow variables on (a) *economic indicators,* such as trade investment and services; (b) *social indicators,* such as tourists, air passengers, guest workers, cultural groups, students, multinational managers, and other elites crossing borders; and (c) *political indicators,* such as attitudes of publics and elites, numbers of cooperative or conflictual incidents, multilateral institutional arrangements, or governmental expenditures for multilateral intergovernmental activities. It is only after the painful and systematic collection of data on such and other transnational flow activities that inductively derived patterns can be discerned

24. For a heuristic attempt to develop some typologies of "transnational politics" defined as "those political processes between national governments (and international organization) that have been set in motion by interaction within a transnational society," see Karl Kaiser, "Transnational Politics: Toward a Theory of Multinational Politics," *International Organization,* XXV, No. 4 (Autumn 1971), 790–817.

25. For a pioneering study of transnational actors and politics, see the anthology edited by Robert O. Keohane and Joseph S. Nye, Jr. *Transnational Relations and World Politics* (Cambridge: Harvard University Press, 1972). This anthology was originally issued as *International Organization,* XXV, No. 3 (Summer 1971).

26. The relevance of transactional flow analysis for the study of international processes has been the subject of considerable controversy. For an exposition of the literature and an exploration of the utility, as well as shortcomings, of transaction analysis, see Donald J. Puchala, "International Transactions and Regional Integration," *International Organization,* XXIV, No. 4 (Autumn 1970), 732–63. For an examination of some theoretical and methodological problems involved in the measurement and interpretation of international transactions, see James A. Caporaso, "Theory and Method in the Study of International Integration," *International Organization,* XXV, No. 2 (Spring 1971), 228–53; and Cal Chard and Susan Welch, "Western European Trade as a Measure of Integration: Untangling the Interpretations," *Journal of Conflict Resolution,* XVI, No. 3 (September 1972), 378–82.

27. Joseph S. Nye, "Multinational Enterprises and Prospects for Regional and Global Political Integration," in *The Multinational Corporation,* Annals of the American Academy of Political and Social Science, 403 (September 1972), 118.

and empirically based hypotheses can be advanced which will be designed to project and predict the likely flow of activity and behavior of relevant variables.

Otherwise we are left with quite misleading quantitative impressions regarding the "explosive growth" of MNCs or other international dependency transactions. In effect, unless these figures are viewed relatively and compared against domestic activities or as percentages of GNP (which has also been growing), we find ourselves floating in a chamber of conceptual weightlessness. For instance, Modelski finds that in "1914, the grand total of direct foreign investment (say $10 billion in 1914 book values) may have reached perhaps 8 or 10 percent of the world gross product. By 1965, foreign investment (say $100 billion in 1965 values, nearly two thirds of it American) may have been less than 5 percent of world product." [28] Deutsch has similarly demonstrated that despite the phenomenal growth of transnational expenditures over time, there has been an even more phenomenal growth in intranational expenditures rendering, relatively rather than absolutely, a greater degree of ethnocentricity in our half of the twentieth century as compared with the first half.[29]

There are certain rudimentary Marxist characteristics in the style and approach of analysis in the linkage and integration/functionalism types of analysis. The fundamental unit of analysis of traditional international theory—the nation-state—is questioned or even considered imperfect and undesirable by these analysts. Marxism advances "class" rather than "nation" to central analytical importance and has assumed a transnational solidarity among workers (the proletariat) while it has relegated nation and nationalism to the status of "opiates" allowing capitalists and a satiated and insensitive bourgeoisie to exploit the duped and doped workers. Marxism, in theory, at least, aims at a world order, without governments and nation-states. In one way, the Marxist dream could be considered equivalent to the "one world" dream of some integrationists, functionalists, and world federalists. Functionalist/integrationist scholars also focus on the importance of economic interactions upon political processes and institutions and proceed from the assumption that continuing economic growth behavior (such as generated by the MNCs) will have decisive integrationist effects on the politics and structures of the international system.

The integrationist/functionalists can argue that the growth of a new class of multinational business and managerial elites will result in the development of multinational labor unions which—in order to bargain effectively against a multiheaded-type management—will resort to the

28. George Modelski, "Multinational Business," in *International Studies Quarterly*, 16, No. 4 (December 1972), 411.
29. Karl W. Deutsch, "The Impact of Communications upon International Relations Theory," in Abdul A. Said, ed., *Theory of International Relations: The Crisis of Relevance* (Englewood Cliffs, N.J.: Prentice-Hall, Inc., 1968), pp. 74–92.

multinational strike.[30] Genuinely multinational bargaining has been employed in Europe against the multinational managements of companies such as Philips and Brown Boveri.[31] A number of countries such as Holland and Germany forbid "sympathy" strikes. But the trend among labor unions will be to increase pressure on their own governments so as to secure genuinely multinational bargaining institutions against the transnationally organized managements they will have to contend with. Alternatively, the labor unions will lobby for regulation of further growth of MNC activity that might escape their control.[32] If this trend continues, then the third level in the labor versus management conflicts—the government—will have to assume multinational regulatory functions and devise appropriate institutions in order to fulfill its mediating and arbitrating roles. All this, to the delight of the functionalist/integrationists, will probably move the international system toward a more genuine federationism.

As in the case of the functionalists and earlier, the Marxists, the apologists of MNCs might be overstating their case. National governments will not be content in the role of mere observers to their own demise, which the MNC apologist, the functionalist, and the Marxist models assign to them. It is more likely that nation-states will successfully demand to stay in the center of action. Their role in the affairs of socioeconomic sectors including MNC affairs will remain pivotal, not marginal. They will insist in being full participants in the transnational processes generated and affected by the MNCs. As such, they will inject into these processes such traditional considerations as national interest, power politics, prestige, propaganda, domestic welfare, and so forth. In short, the phenomenon of MNCs will not remain immune to traditional international politics. In the multinational corporation–nation-state interaction within the international system, the politicization of the former will be much greater than the commercialization of the latter.[33]

This train of thought leads us to the concluding portion of this essay. We feel that the nation-state system will not go down without a fight against its multinational predators—if indeed, it goes down at all. Regulatory techniques are likely to be developed which will lead to the digestion of the MNCs by the ulcerous stomach of the international system.

---

30. See Stephen Hugh-Jones, "Today the Multinational Company. And Tomorrow? The Multinational Strike," *Vision* (November 1970), p. 34.

31. *Ibid.*

32. For example, see "Labor Organization to Investigate Multinational Corporations," *The Washington Post*, September 7, 1972, pp. E-1 and E-4.

33. In a recently published study focusing on seven U.N. specialized agencies and UNCTAD, the authors Robert Cox and Harold Jacobson conclude that the trend in the future will be for greater politicization (rather than international bureaucratization) of these functional specialized agencies. "The nation-state," they remind us, "is the only available instrument capable of controlling multinational corporations and other external influences on the national economies." See their *Anatomy of Influence: Decision Making in International Organization* (New Haven: Yale University Press, 1973), p. 434.

The pressures for international regulation and coordination of the MNCs will come from many disparate quarters. However, in each case the most effective and organized instrument to assume international regulatory control is, and will remain for some time, the nation-state (and its government). Pressures on the nation-state will emanate from labor unions which will seek protection against the multinational managements.[34] There will also be pressures—paradoxically—on the nation-state from the MNCs themselves and their international professional associations[35] while seeking good terms against nationalization, expropriation without appropriate compensation, opportunity for appeal, and the like. Less developed countries and forum-type international organizations such as UNCTAD will also continue to lobby for adequate redistribution of the world's income and against extractive, or what might be considered high-risk and high-profit MNC operations in the Third World.[36] Further, the socialist nations, should they as in the case of Yugoslavia open their doors to capitalist (profit-oriented) MNC enterprises, would, as a minimum, insist on strict governmental overseeing of such enterprises. Other predictable but anomic transnational groups (or public interest lobbies) will intensify their pressure tactics and voice continuous protest regarding the global social costs,[37] such as ecological pollution, maldistribution of wealth, and culture shock caused by abrupt introduction of technology in traditional societies, all resulting from inadequately controlled MNCs. Others have voiced and will continue to articulate serious concern about the erosion of traditional democratic control which can arise from the activities of independent-minded MNCs—especially in the area of foreign policy.[38]

When all is said and done, and despite great efforts and considerable successes by the MNCs to transform themselves into functionally and geographically diversified conglomerates, to change the mentalities of their managers away from ethnocentrism and toward globalism, to command uniformly the loyalties of their employees, to provide lifetime career

34. See Richard L. Barovick, "Labor Reacts to Multinationalism," *The Columbia Journal of World Business*, 5, No. 4 (July–August 1970), 40–46.

35. William M. Evan, "MNCs and IPAs: An International Organization Research Frontier," *International Associations*, 24th Year, No. 2 (February 1972), pp. 90–99; Jonathan F. Galloway, "Multinational Enterprises as Worldwide Interest Groups," pp. 1–20.

36. Peter B. Evans, "National Autonomy and Economic Development: Critical Perspectives on Multinational Corporations in Poor Countries," *International Organization,* XXV, No. 3 (Summer 1971), 675–93; Stephen Hymer, "The Multinational Corporation and Uneven Development," in A. Kapoor and Philip D. Grub, eds., *The Multinational Enterprise in Transition* (Princeton, N.J.: The Darwin Press, 1972), pp. 438–44.

37. See Fuad Ajami, "Corporate Giants: Some Global Social Costs," *International Studies Quarterly*, 16, No. 4 (December 1972), 511–29.

38. See Karl Kaiser, "Transnational Relations as a Threat to the Democratic Processes," *International Organization*, XXV, No. 3 (Summer 1971), 706–20. The U.S. Senate Foreign Relations Committee has established a subcommittee, under Senator Frank Church, expressly devoted to the study of the impact of MNCs on U.S. foreign policy.

patterns and lucrative retirement programs, to develop distinctive company styles, doctrines, and procedures (crudely analogous to national character and ideologies), to negotiate directly with host governments, and generally to seek a status of multifunctional self-sufficiency (thus resembling societal microcosms)—despite all of these attainments, the MNCs in our opinion lack a fundamental characteristic which will quite probably not permit them to challenge the nation-state. And this characteristic is "territoriality." [39] Whether a multinational corporation executive works for IBM, Singer, Unilever, Volkswagen, or Hitachi, he lives in a nation-state which possesses some sovereignty, greater authority, and even greater control capacity over its environment. MNCs have no jails, no courts and executioners, no passports, no armies, and very, very few weapons. In the last analysis, national governments control an overwhelming concentration of power and authority that would allow them to break up any MNC, provided there were adequate cause for such an operation.

The problem of how to deal with or regulate the MNCs internationally is a high-agenda item for most national governments despite the fact that their full impact on the international system cannot be adequately projected to date. The first question that should be posed concerns the scope, structure, and functions of international regulatory arrangements or structures designed to moderate, license, monitor, police, and even sanction, where necessary, the MNCs of the world.

Prior to moving to more formal regulatory arrangements, national governments and other interested units will have to agree on such points as the following:

1. the form any new agency should take;
2. the proper role of the various MNCs, governments, ombudsmen, and international civil servants, represented in the above agencies;
3. control techniques and mechanisms to be employed;
4. the extent of the agencies' authority;
5. operational and management questions;
6. legal personality of agencies;
7. financing provisions for the agencies;
8. relations with other intergovernmental or nongovernmental international organizations.

In Giovanni Angelli's work, the inevitability of transnational interaction is considered too complex to be left to fate.

---

39. It is interesting to note that even those who were forecasting a premature "demise" of the nation-state were soon to revise their views and allow for its continued lease on life. See John Herz's two relevant articles, "Rise and Demise of the Territorial State," *World Politics,* IX, No. 4 (July 1957), 473–93, and "Territorial State Revisited," *Polity,* 1, No. 1 (Fall 1968), 11–34. For a provocative proposition that both the nation-states and the MNCs are ill-suited modes of organizing human societies, and that they should be replaced with alternative visions of world order, see Robert L. Heilbroner, "The Multinational Corporation and the Nation-State," *New York Review of Books,* February 11, 1971, pp. 20–25.

National independence is now largely an illusion—particularly in the Atlantic world. The price of our interdependence is constant interference in each other's affairs. The real question is whether this interference will take place by means of uncoordinated and conflicting national actions or through mutually agreed solutions in international organizations.[40]

One can at best only speculate as to the modus operandi that should be followed with respect to the MNCs. There is the strategy of doing nothing[41] and allowing Adam Smith's "invisible hand" and Darwin's "survival of the fittest" to take care of the situation for us. A second strategy is to leave the regulation to a special agency to be chartered and financed by the UN. MNCs could give strong teeth to such an agency (as well as to the UN) provided that international agencies would be allowed to tax the multinational corporations for a portion of the international organization budget. A third strategy is to prompt the countries involved in clusters of MNC activity to develop appropriate multinational agencies (of semiprivate and semipublic nature) outside the purview of the United Nations. The cases of companies such as Intelsat,[42] Eurochemic and Eurofima,[43] or even GATT,[44] are good examples of prototypes that could be followed for this strategy.[45]

If we are right in expecting to witness a number of efforts at the systemic or subsystemic level to deal with or regulate the impact of the MNCs on the present international system, then we can go one step further and say that as a result of these efforts the international system will increase its level of institutionalization.[46]

National and transnational actors will tend more and more to channel their interaction through routinized procedures at the international level. To the extent that such institutionalization will reflect or encourage

40. As quoted in *Newsweek*, December 11, 1972.

41. See Kenneth N. Waltz, "The Myth of National Interdependence," in Charles P. Kindleberger, ed., *The International Corporation: A Symposium* (Cambridge, Mass.: The MIT Press, 1970), pp. 205–26.

42. See David Wilson, "Space Business: The History of INTELSAT," *The Yearbook of World Affairs*, 1968, George W. Keeton and George Schwarzenberger, eds. (New York: Praeger, 1971), pp. 72–86. Also Stephen E. Doyle, "Communication Satellites: International Organization for Development and Control," *California Law Review*, 55 (1967), 431–47.

43. See H. T. Adam, "Eurofima," *European Yearbook*, III, 70–91. (This article is in French, but it is followed by a five-page summary in English.)

44. See Paul M. Goldberg and Charles P. Kindleberger, "Toward a GATT for Investment: A Proposal for Supervision of the International Corporation," *Law and Policy in International Business*, II (1970), 295–325.

45. For an excellent argument that MNCs require new and creative modes of regulation both at the national and international level, and for some suggestions toward possible directions of evolution, see Detlev F. Vagts, "The Multinational Enterprise: A New Challenge for Transnational Law," *Harvard Law Review*, 83, No. 4 (February 1970), 739–92.

46. It is Samuel P. Huntington's thesis that institutionalization can be viewed as an indicator of political development and modernization. See his "Political Development and Political Decay," *World Politics*, 17, No. 3 (April 1965), 386–430.

standardized, ordered, and efficient problem-solving patterns among the various actors of the international system, we might say that as a consequence of the MNCs the international system will move toward a new level of sociocultural development,[47] to borrow an anthropological concept.

Institutionalization, of course, does not imply either uniformity or centralization. On the contrary, we expect numerous *transnational arenas* to be developed depending on the issue-area the actors are interacting upon. For example, one might inquire as to whether indeed electronics and communications technologies, as compared to oil and energy industries or tourist, airlines, and chain-food industries, operate on quite distinct and often unrelated policy arenas.

There are, therefore, powerful conceptual and analytic reasons for one to employ Theodore Lowi's concept of "policy arenas" to the study of the interplay between MNCs and the international system. By using the "policy arena" typology one will thus arrive at the "characteristic political structure, political process, elites, and group relations" [48] of each policy arena and classify them according to whether they are perceived and acted upon as being "distributive," "redistributive," or "regulative."

Piecemeal, reactive institutionalization will also bring about a rise in the frequency with which the actors of the international system will disagree on procedural or substantive questions. This implies that we may be witnessing an international system whose participants will be increasingly aware of their interdependencies or individual vulnerabilities.[49] To paraphrase John Herz, if weapons have penetrated the "hard shell" of sovereignty, MNCs (and other transnational actors) are continuously penetrating the durable "soft shell" of sovereignty. Moreover one would expect, as Hoffmann aptly reminds us, a continued effort by each actor, but especially the nation-state, to attempt to manipulate these interdependencies for maximum actor benefit.[50]

So despite the fact that we forecast the nation-state will win the bout against the growing "threat" of MNCs, the "winner" will emerge substantially changed. Therefore, processes of strategy and diplomacy will no longer be the only ones typifying international transactions. The diplomats and soldiers will be given a run for their money by the managers and the bankers.

47. Darcy Ribiero, *The Civilizational Process,* transl. Betty J. Meggers (Washington, D.C.: Smithsonian Institution Press, 1968).

48. Theodore J. Lowi, "American Business, Public Policy, Case Studies and Political Theory," *World Politics,* XVI, No. 4 (July 1964), 677–715. For an extension of Lowi's framework, see Robert H. Salisbury, "The Analysis of Public Policy: A Search for Theories and Roles," in Austin Ranney, ed., *Political Science and Public Policy* (Chicago: Markham, 1968), pp. 151–75.

49. See Edward L. Morse, "The Transformation of Foreign Policies: Modernization, Interdependence and Externalization," *World Politics,* XXII, No. 3 (April 1970), 371–92; and Oran R. Young, "Interdependencies in World Politics," *International Journal,* 24, No. 4 (Autumn 1969), pp. 726–50.

50. See Hoffmann, "International Organization and the International System," p. 403.

c h a p t e r   t w e l v e

A view of the future

HOWARD V. PERLMUTTER

THE MULTINATIONAL CORPORATION: DECADE ONE
OF THE EMERGING GLOBAL INDUSTRIAL SYSTEM

INTRODUCTION

Predicting the future of the multinational corporation is a hazardous activity. Aggregating the consequences of the future that MNC executives seek to create is less adventurous. The former activity is optimally based on a testable theory of the evolution of the global industrial system, which historians of the year 2000 can evaluate.[1] The latter presumes that the study of the self-fulfilling prophecies increasingly shared by business and political leaders is not wholly a wasted effort. There is, we believe, a growing consensus that some forms of the MNC will successfully survive for several more decades. In this perspective (and we believe for twenty years beyond) the MNC is an irreversible, irresistible, and inevitable phenomenon. But if one gives any credence, as we do, to the countervailing forces of the next ten years from governments, unions, and the wider public, the transformations of MNCs as we know them today may be as interesting as their durability through time.

In this essay we consider the MNC in the present decade (Decade One in the tables) of what is here called the *emerging global industrial system,* the network of commercial, financial, and industrial activities which are beginning to cover the planet Earth. The global industrial system, we hasten to add, exists in a less integrated but nevertheless potent global political system. We assume however that for the remainder of the 1970s the MNC can be conceptually described as a *leading system* in the global industrial system, with the nation-state and trade unions as *lagging* systems. Political and trade union leaders remain puzzled as to the most effective manner to regulate or exploit MNCs without diminishing unduly the MNCs efficiency in generating wealth and goods and services.

LOOKING FORWARD AND BACKWARD
WITH GLOBAL SYSTEMS VIEW

Our three-decade view of the emerging global industrial system gives us a perspective for analyzing the MNC in the next decade in two time-related vantage points: (1) looking forward from today, wherein we attempt to identify and extrapolate from some seemingly dominant processes in the first decade considered. Here the focus is on the MNC in ad-

1. See H. V. Perlmutter, "The Multinational Firm and the Future," *The Annals of the American Academy of Political and Social Science,* 403 (September 1972).

vanced, less developed, and socialist countries; (2) looking backward from the year 2000 to Decade One, wherein we attempt to ascertain what latent, emergent processes—though barely distinguishable today—might become dominant in the decades ahead. By the year 2000, the global industrial system is hypothesized as a cohesive, relatively unitary, and highly regulatable network. How will we get from here to this distant future without understanding the seeds of the future in the present?

Whatever the merits of this analytic approach, we are explicit about the underlying processes we infer to be at work in our global industrial system. As it becomes more interdependent, nation-states must find a balance between *sovereignty-sharing* and *surrender,* and *sovereignty-affirmation* will become quite difficult and painful to achieve.[2] There will be some *value changes* and *expectation shifts* in the various stakeholders and claimants of the MNC—for example, from employees, customers, and suppliers of funds. Some of these value changes can be ascribed to the shift from industrialism to post-industrialism. Given the difficulties nation-states have in managing the complexities of a turbulent global industrial system, defensive and maladaptive strategies are likely to be chosen first by political leaders (protectionism).

The global industrial imperative, which impels all nations to link in some way to the global industrial system in order to remain viable, and to utilize global technology, leads to a large number of MNCs in rich countries and very few based in poor countries. At the same time, the global *political* imperative requires that power embodied in the MNCs' wealth cannot continue unleashed and unconnected to the citizenry of various nation-states.

LOCATING DECADE ONE IN AN EVOLUTIONARY GLOBAL INDUSTRIAL SYSTEM

The reader may begin by referring to Table 1, which describes our three-decade view of the emerging global industrial system. In understanding this view, it is important to note the following facts:

1. Decade One (Stage One) is an era in which primary loyalties are home country oriented or ethnocentric, and in which the MNC is overtly under attack but covertly sought. In this decade, the public policy environment of the MNC could be described as varying from ethnocentric-protectionistic to geocentric (global) laissez-faire.

2. Decade Two (Stage Two) is an era in which bi- and trinational MNCs begin to take form. Public policies are likely to range from regiocentric-protectionistic to geocentric laissez-faire, with the regiocentric regulatory process on MNCs (e.g., in the EEC).

3. Decade Three (Stage Three) is an era in which many institutions have found that they must be more geocentric than regiocentric or ethnocentric. The MNCs become *regulated* by various kinds of intergovernmental and global institutions and claimants.

2. See F. Emery and Eric Trist, *Toward a Social Ecology* (London: Plenum Press, 1973).

Each industrial sector is likely to evolve at a somewhat different rate, so that by the year 2000 a geocentric regulatory scenario for some indus-

Table 1. THE EMERGING GLOBAL INDUSTRIAL SYSTEM

STAGE I. THE ERA OF NATIONAL GLOBAL SYSTEMS (1970–1980)

A. *In advanced countries:* Governments encourage buildup of large national private and public firms with multinational interests. Regional and global industrial constellations built up.

B. *In less developed countries:* Governments build up control of national economic-industrial systems in selected areas with interconnections to advanced MNCs.

C. *In socialist countries:* Governments seek a wider transideological zone on a country-by-country basis while working on Comecon multinationals and industrial system constellations.

STAGE II. THE ERA OF BI- AND TRINATIONAL AND REGIONAL GLOBAL SYSTEMS (1980–1990)

A. *In advanced countries:* Bi- and trinational companies with global interests emerge (such as Dunlop-Pirelli, Unilever, Royal Dutch Shell). The regional corporation will serve as a dual headquarters for U.S. and Japanese firms.

B. *In less developed countries:* Emergence of bi- and trinational companies in GISCs (Global Industrial System Constellations) with advanced MNCs; also a few LAFTA (Latin American Free Trade Association) multinationals.

C. *In socialist countries:* The transideological firm sanctioned. Comecon plus West European companies merge. Many participate in GISCs.

STAGE III. THE ERA OF GEOCENTRIC AND GEOCENTROID GLOBAL SYSTEMS (1990–?)

A. *Key Actors:*
  1. Multistate supergiant transideological firms
  2. Stateless supergiant transideological firms
  3. Global industrial-financial-commercial-service system constellations and coalitions.

B. *Other Actors:*
  1. State-owned MNCs
  2. Regional private and mixed MNCs
  3. Micro-MNCs
  4. Millions of small non-MNCs
  5. A very few large non-MNCs?

C. *Supporting infrastructures:*
  1. Regional and interregional central banks, and a worldwide central bank
  2. A global financial system—global banking constellations
  3. Incorporation possibilities in UN or world central bank
  4. A global patent, tax authority
  5. World boards for firms with representation of various claimants

6. World annual reports with financial, social, ecological impacts of all key actors

7. Worldwide shareholding or some new concept of investment

D. *Other infrastructures:*

1. Global cities and regional cities

2. Global educational systems and global universities

3. Global telecommunication-transportation system—persons, ideas, things

4. Global arms reduction in relation to global security system

tries is more likely than for others; e.g., advanced technology versus steelmaking. Table 2 describes this kind of variation.

Table 2.   THE EMERGING GLOBAL INDUSTRIAL SYSTEM BY INDUSTRIAL SECTOR

	Slow Evolution Sectors	Moderate Evolution Sectors	Rapid Evolution Sectors
Stage I	1970–1985	1970–1980	1970–1975
Stage II	1985–2000	1980–1990	1975–1985
Stage III	2000–2020	1990–2000	1985–1990
	Steel	Automobiles	Computers
	Construction	Chemicals (heavy)	Aerospace
	Agriculture	Containerization	Software
	Natural fibers	Paper	Telecommunications
	Wood products	Pharmaceuticals	Petrochemicals
	Coal mining	Petroleum	Semiconductors
		Heavy electric equipment	Tourism
		Synthetic fibers	
		Publishing	

It will be noted that the appearance of multiple interlinking joint ventures between firms of different nationalities around the world becomes a new corporate form beginning in Decade One. We call these quasi-companies *global industrial system constellations* (GISCs).[3]

PROPOSITIONS ABOUT THE TOTAL GLOBAL INDUSTRIAL SYSTEM IN DECADE ONE

Our manner of exposition is rather condensed. Some suggestive anecdotes will illustrate the concepts of the future likely to be held by present and future political, industrial, and trade union leaders. In addition, some overall trends in the total global industrial system and in turn the advanced and developing countries and socialist countries will be described.

The eight propositions in Table 3 have two parts: section A, wherein we infer from existing trends what *dominant* trend there will be looking

3. See Perlmutter, "Notes on the Design of NISC's, RISC's, GISC's," Wharton School (Mimeograph), 1972.

Table 3. PROPOSITIONS ABOUT THE TOTAL GLOBAL INDUSTRIAL SYSTEM IN DECADE ONE

Prop.		Prop. (continued)	
I A	As Decade One passes, there will be an erosion of some of the more *overt* forms of ethnocentrism in large MNCs and a preference for varying dosages of poly-, regio-, and geocentrism. But *covert* ethnocentrism will persist in MNCs and range from ambivalent to virulent in nation-states.		*zation* among those firms who decide to "go it alone" in the global industrial system. This applies especially to small and medium-sized firms whose distinctive competencies must be progressively defined more from a *regional* than from a *national* point of view.
I B	There will be more experimentation with creating truly geocentric institutions from the outset in some industrial and service sectors called the "rapid evolution sectors" (Table 2). The expansion of a global domain will be an increasingly legitimate concept for the seas, space, and planets.	III B	A new breed of *micro-* and *mesomultinational* will emerge which permit world scope with limited resources.
II A	As Decade One passes, more MNCs will increase their information and capability for dealing simultaneously with non-neighboring (from a geographical point of view) subsystems of the global industrial system to form *some* rational GISCs, but *more* regional industrial system constellations (RISCs).	IV A	As Decade One passes, there will be increasing *differentiation* between nation-states as regards their effectiveness in *multinationalizing*. The slower the rate of legitimized multinationalization of a nation-state, the greater the slippage between that nation-state, its own MNCs, and the global industrial system.
II B	More MNCs will act as if future quasi-unitary states of the global industrial system are inevitable, leading to both managerial expertise in GISC creation and an awareness of its hazards.	IV B	Political leaders will discuss future forms of intergovernmental *rule-establishing* in the regulation of MNCs; they will have limited success in *rule-implementation* in Decade One. (Unilateral efforts at regulation of MNCs are more likely to be preferred.)
III A	As Decade One passes, there will be greater need for *size*, *product*, or *geographical speciali-*	V A	As Decade One passes, increasingly effective counterforces from trade unions will come at the regional level and with coalitions in some developing countries; e.g., through world councils, international

Table 3 (continued)

Prop.		Prop. (continued)	
	collective bargaining. The effectiveness of this activity will be limited, in Decade One, to a few industries.	VII A	As Decade One passes, MNCs will experience a vacillation between two extreme public policy poles, ethnocentric-protectionism and geocentric laissez-faire. The former is more likely in the first half of Decade One, the latter by the latter half.
V B	The ideological split in the world trade union movement will become a more chronic source of tensions for the East-West domain of industrial cooperation.		
		VII B	New formulations of a geocentric-regulatory scenario will be made, but not implemented (see Prop. IV B).
VI A	As Decade One passes, the need for asymmetry reduction in the global industrial system will be hampered by rising polycentric nationalism in the less developed countries and the weakening legitimacy of advanced country MNCs as the allocators of production, capital, technology, labor, markets.	VIII A	As Decade One passes, an uneven internationalization of the stakeholder demands and expectations about the MNC will take place. The main MNC posture will be defensive, reactive, and begrudging at first, accommodating later.
VI B	New mechanisms for guaranteeing reciprocity and asymmetry reduction will be tried between advanced and developing country enterprises (see the GISC).	VIII B	The international communication between claimant-stakeholders should arise. The internationalization of the claimant system should vary by claimants.

forward to the 1980s; and section B, wherein we infer by looking backward from the year 2000 what emergent processes are likely to begin to be evidenced in Decade One.

The principal character of the eight propositions is that MNCs, wherever they are, including those evolving in LDCs and socialist countries, begin to experience the constraints and opportunities of competing in an international context. In this period MNCs have no *effective* countervailing forces and achieve a de facto legitimacy given the national preference for monolateral action.

But the increasing public exposure of the MNC and sometimes demystifying investigations is causing an increasing sensitivity of MNCs to those claimants who "squeal the loudest." The U.K. government's investigation of the Swiss Hoffman Laroche on its transfer pricing is an example. Although size helps an MNC to survive the various misfortunes it can experience, giantism also guarantees that the MNC cannot go unnoticed.

PROPOSITIONS ABOUT THE ADVANCED COUNTRIES IN THE GLOBAL INDUSTRIAL SYSTEM IN DECADE ONE

We turn to a set of propositions focused on the advanced industrial countries of Western Europe, the U.S., and Japan. As Decade One passes, the domain of interdependence will expand in this trilateral, tripolar system where mutual penetration is perceived by firms in each area as requisite to survival, growth, and profitability (Props. I, II in Table 4).

The deepening commitments of larger MNCs to multinationalism will be matched by a reluctance to give up ownership (e.g., control to "foreigners"). But most executives will continue *in theory* to favor a rational, geocentric management system in marketing, finance, and production. The adaptive strategies of middle-sized and smaller firms should be different, given their limited resources (Prop. V A 2, 3 in Table 4). "Internationalism" may be favored, e.g., through continued reliance on export licensing.

The responsiveness of some nation-states to the MNCs' role in the emerging global industrial system leads to such questions as: "Can Sweden, with its smaller enterprises, afford to go it alone in the global industrial system of the 1980s?" "To what degree will the future of France depend on transnational industrial zones involving Belgium, Germany, Switzerland, Italy?" (See Props. V B, VII B in Table 4). The concept of the *multinationalization of the nation-state* should begin to get consideration as some nations move from defensive to cooptive orientations regarding their own and foreign MNCs (Prop. IX A in Table 4).

THE U.S. MULTINATIONAL IN DECADE ONE

Results of research on U.S. multinationals at Wharton's Worldwide Institutions Group revealed the following perceptions by executives when they were asked what their policies would likely be in the 1970s:

1. Approximately 60% of the 45 companies sampled anticipated catastrophic or permanent damage from a total pullout of all their foreign operations.
2. An ethnocentric-protectionist world would hurt U.S. MNC profits and sales, but clearly *not* benefit the U.S. in exports, level of employment, repatriation of earnings.
3. The main result of an ethnocentric-protectionist world for U.S. MNCs would be to strengthen their regional operations in the EEC and Japan to make them more independent of operations in the U.S.

Table 4. PROPOSITIONS ABOUT THE ADVANCED COUNTRIES IN THE GLOBAL
INDUSTRIAL SYSTEM IN DECADE ONE

Prop.		Prop. (continued)	
I A	As Decade One passes, a trilateral interregional consultative system will emerge between the U.S., W. Europe, and Japan in spite of or because of interregional rivalry. This will be the "rich countries' club."	IV A	As Decade One passes, vacillation between preference for polycentric and regiocentric strategy should increase sophistication in dealing with environmental differences in the EEC and the blocs in developing countries (ANCOM, CARIFTA, CACM).
I B	A variety of countervailing forces will arise from LDCs and socialist countries aiming to weaken collusive potentialities of "the rich countries' club."	IV B	MNCs will begin to become more aware of the need for an interregiocentric strategy, particularly for the advanced countries.
II A	As Decade One passes, a doctrine of reciprocal, balanced, and mutual penetration will gain force, requiring an increasingly heavier direct as opposed to portfolio investment in the U.S., Japan, and Western Europe to make up for the U.S. lead.	V A 1	As Decade One passes, an increasing proportion of the larger MNCs will become simultaneously committed irreversibly to global expansion and aware that at some future date their resources will be limited, and it will be difficult to go it alone in the global industrial system.
II B	The advanced countries MNC will attempt to develop a code of international behavior. This code will have limited legitimacy in LDCs and socialist countries.	V A 2	An increasing proportion of middle-sized MNCs will become irreversibly committed to *regiocentrism* and aware of their shortages of resources for building a competitive *global* strategy.
III A	As Decade One passes, a more rapid erosion of ethnocentric primacy will take place by function and product than in ownership, in large and middle-sized MNCs.	V A 3	An increasing proportion of smaller firms will become committed (even if not irreversibly) to international expansion.
III B	New, innovative ideas will develop about spread of ownership at the country, regional, and corporate level. This should lead to new ideas about financial accountability of MNCs.	V B	Smaller nation-states will try to define those areas of the national economy where their

Table 4 (continued)

Prop.		Prop. (continued)	
	MNCs are likely to be competitive worldwide, leading to a disposition to favor regiocentric strategy.		ating interdependent systems between the advanced countries and selected LDCs on the basis of perceived reciprocity. Mutual distrust is likely to continue.
VI A	As Decade One passes, there will be an increasingly unsystematic character to the widening of the transideological domain of East-West cooperation. A polycentric strategy is likely to prevail on both sides on the first half of Decade One.	VIII B	New organizations will be designed to produce *equal power* relations with LDCs and advanced countries.
VI B	More efforts will be made to require regiocentric strategy from Western cooperations (led by USSR).	IX A	As Decade One passes, some nations among the advanced countries will move from defensive, autarchic, xenophobic attitudes toward foreign investment to cooptive, cooperative postures in building geocentric centers of excellence, such as global cities.
VII A	As Decade One passes, MNCs from the advanced countries are likely to develop the most sophisticated design of cooperation in global systems using financial, commercial, and industrial modular systems. This should threaten the regiocentric concept of EEC political leaders.	X A	As Decade One passes, the mutual penetration strategies of Japanese, Western Europe, and U.S. firms will produce threats and some defensiveness.
VII B	Nation-states, especially in the EEC and with the help of MNCs, will help to design transnational industrial zones.	X B	The rise of the MNC in the advanced countries will encourage a renewal of Marxian analysis of the finality of the emerging global industrial system.
VIII A	As Decade One passes, some progress will be made in cre-		

4. A geocentric laissez-faire and/or geocentric regulatory world, which most U.S. multinationals anticipate by the 1980s, would lead to accelerated movement of U.S. MNCs toward an integrated worldwide enterprise system.

It is to be noted that in identical research conducted in Sweden, Swedish multinationals respond in roughly the same way.

QUALITATIVE AND QUANTITATIVE DETERMINANTS
OF THE TRANSFORMATION PROCESS:
A MICROVIEW

Before attempting to understand some of the aggregate phenomena of Decade One, we need to understand how a given firm is "lured into" the global industrial system. A firm rarely approaches going multinational in a systematic way. A set of projects and opportunities overseas are found. After an overseas organizational structure is built, turning back becomes progressively more unthinkable.

The "global strategy thinking" is frequently an afterthought. More often there is the belief that (1) expanding overseas must continue and (2) there are more profits, resources, markets, abroad than at home.

The primary impulse is to identify the firm as American, French, Swedish, or Japanese "with increasing stakes overseas." But at some as yet undefinable point the "we" becomes more diluted. This point is accelerated as a function of the degree of vociferousness of foreign *claimants,* who say, "In what sense are you still Swedish, if the proportion of your resources are greater outside of Sweden? You must identify with *our* interests as employees, customers, governments, unions."

When these claims are embodied in foreign laws and connected with host-country penalties, a transformation process gets underway. The next ten years in the advanced countries are seen as a period of "takeoff" for their firms into multinationalism, the irreversibility increasing by the end of the 1970s. Two kinds of data are relevant here:

1. Estimates by U.S. and European executives concerning the percentage of research and development, sales, profits, financing, production, personnel management, and labor expected by 1980.
2. Estimates by MNC executives concerning the shifting competitive environment in which they live worldwide, especially the coalitional potential of competitors.

Table 5 approximates the figures agreed on by a group of senior executives.

THE EEC AS A SETTING FOR MULTINATIONALS IN DECADE ONE

Seven trends appear to be prominent in the 1970s for the EEC:

1. More realization that the EEC is not large enough to build for the world scale, if it is treated exclusively.
2. More attempts to build European companies will be undertaken, among the middle-sized companies.
3. An increasing mixture of private and public enterprise continues, especially where national interests are safeguarded in some industrial sector.
4. Greater attempts to develop more egalitarian forms of collaboration with former colonies.

Table 5. QUANTITATIVE ESTIMATES OF % OF INCREASE IN VARIOUS INDICES OF MULTINATIONALIZATION OF A EUROPEAN FIRM

	1970	1975 (estimate)	1980 (estimate)
% sales			
outside home country	30	50	75
% profits			
outside home country	35	55	70
% production			
outside home country	25	50	65
% R & D			
outside home country	10	30	50
% personnel			
% management of non-home nationality	0	20	40
% labor of non-home nationality	20	50	70
% financing			
outside home country	20	75	85

5. A greater interest in building counterforces to the European giants and their monopolistic tendencies while recognizing that these firms must meet the U.S. and Japanese challenge (the rise of European antitrust).

6. Greater attempts, however, to build relationships with Eastern Europe on a more polycentric pattern at the outset, with regiocentrism taking hold by the end of Decade One.

7. The rise of European multinational union activity to newer, more sophisticated ventures however limited in their impact.

The dynamics of the EEC multinational enterprise activity is important to understand, especially because it is regarded as a potential model for other regional common markets, for example in Latin America, the Caribbean (CARIFTA) and Central America (CACM), and the Andean group of Peru, Bolivia, Ecuador, Colombia, and Venezuela (ANCOM).

DEFENSE OF THE LARGE EUROPEAN MNC IN DECADE ONE

Decade One has a typical style of defense of the MNC. Where attacks on its legitimacy occur by the home government and threats are made to limit its independence and ownership, the basis for justification appears rather clear.

The defense of capitalism offered by St. Gobain-Pont a Mousson (SGPM), is instructive. The four areas under attack were "bigness," "multinationality," "monopolistic character," and "capitalism." These were justified in these ways: (1) *Bigness:* This is required in order to remain competitive in the world market. Bigness is relative. "SGPM is France's fifth largest firm, thirtieth largest in the EEC, and falls in the bottom rank of the 100 largest in the world." (2) *Multinationalism:* "SGPM is not multinational in its legal structure, as its headquarters is in one nation. It is international with regard to markets, financing sources, use of Anglo-Saxon accounting methods (revealing its transparency and nakedness) and composition of personnel. And it is essentially French—directly subject to (implying sometimes victimized by) French government policies and French laws." (3) *Monopolism:* SGPM, because of its products, is fully exposed to risks of a market economy. It can help "prevent Europe from being overrun by non-European manufacturers [presumably U.S. and Japanese]." (4) *Capitalism:* SGPM claims that workers and communities benefit more from expanded operations than investors, given the meager dividends paid to French shareholders.[4] Two points should be emphasized: (1) Decade One Multinationals still profess loyalty to the home country and to home-country claimants, especially communities and workers. But justifying responsibilities to foreign workers and communities is more difficult. (2) Nevertheless, there is a growing hint that other foreign claimants have rights expressed through such processes as the internationalization of customers, personnel, financing, and production.

PROPOSITIONS ABOUT THE LESS DEVELOPED COUNTRIES IN THE GLOBAL INDUSTRIAL SYSTEM IN DECADE ONE

We view the relationships between MNCs and LDCs as primarily *conflictual,* defensive, and above all ambivalent in Decade One. Thus formulating propositions for the great variety of LDCs is quite difficult because fluctuations in this kind of positive and negative relationship may produce quite different outcomes at any time in any given country (e.g., Chile versus Malaysia).

As Table 6 indicates, MNCs have their areas of ambivalence, as do LDCs. "Is it worth the trouble to stay in Latin America during this period?" asks one American chief executive who has sold out most of his Latin American operations. "We must learn to live without MNCs in order to regain our sovereignty," says a Latino political leader. "Now we are prepared to invite selected MNCs to come to our country. After independence we were able to eliminate the foreign firms we didn't want," says an Algerian political leader.

The areas of ambivalence are a measure of the unstability of LDC-MNC relations in Decade One. But they are also indicative of a painful learning process between these two classes of institutions whose resources are unequal. Witness the positive reaction of the U.N. assembly to one late Dr. Allende's accusation that U.S. MNCs try to subvert the sovereignty of LDCs, while foreign investment is still sought.

LDCS AS LEARNING SYSTEMS

Learning can be seen as the constructive management of ambivalence to achieve new mutually satisfactory, realistic, and distortion-free relation-

---

4. *Business International,* February 23, 1973, p. 60.

Table 6. SOME AMBIVALENCE AREAS FOR MNCS AND LDCS IN DECADE ONE

For MNCs	For LDCs
1. Markets too small for economies of scale.	1. Though it is politically desirable to attack MNCs, is it possible to go too far?
2. Can get agreement with this government but how about next?	2. Campos' "independence of beggars" thesis is that the poor united don't gain much. How much to let ACs in?
3. Retroactivity of restrictive legislation.	3. Finding own models for development—Brazilian, Mexican, Venezuelan—but how much dependence on ACs is politically possible?
4. "Fadeout" thinking threatens managerial control and investments with long-term view.	4. MNC products not always suitable for LDCs—priorities of LDCs may be different, e.g., not labor-intensive or too "luxury"-oriented.
5. How to continue to justify MNCs' benefit to development as LDC aspirations increase in proportion to the best deal obtained by other HS countries.	5. LDCs want capital-intensive technology to maintain worldwide competitive niches, but can LDCs afford this policy?
6. Demand for joint ventures by government may be backfiring as local talent becomes increasingly scarce.	6. How much R&D capability does an LDC need and where will it come from?
7. Extractive industries deal with xenophobic psychological climate which is hard to change.	7. Do foreign subsidiaries cause a drain on balance of payments?
8. Hard to export from LDCs when they are not willing to import.	8. How to influence MNC regarding investments that require continuing technology inputs?
9. Promoting LDC managers to key positions before they are ready is a risk.	9. What to do with foreign firm whose worldwide marketing capabilities are required, but LDC wants managerial control?
10. Host oligarchy are allies of private investment but they are under attack themselves.	10. Supporting inefficient local industries not a favor to consumers.
11. Local investment is threatened by MNC alliance with government and may try to subvert foreign investment.	11. Many sectors wholly owned by MNC yet how to get them out, short of nationalization? How to retain their managerial efficiency?
12. Investments are hostages in LDC despite initial attractive incentives by HS governments.	12. How far to get involved in complementation agreements with other countries, vs. go-it-alone strategy?
13. Can MNC afford to do R&D in LDC?	13. How to deal with new trends in home countries who want to nullify host country incentives and prevent runaway plants?
14. Home country is ambivalent about motives for investment in foreign countries.	14. How to bargain with the giant multinationals as equals?

ships. LDCs are in the position of learning how to cope with foreign investment. The learning process is evidenced in ten decision areas (1) local equity, (2) local content, (3) profit and royalty remittances, (4) personnel restrictions, (5) expropriations and nationalization, (6) borrowing restrictions, (7) tax discrimination, (8) acquisitions, (9) investment and investment barriers, and (10) export pressures (see Table 7).

Countries, as they improve their bargaining power, can be expected to increase their demands on each of these areas when the primary modality changes from *economic dependency* (Pattern I) to *economic nationalism* (Pattern II), from accepting foreign-owned subsidiaries to outright nationalization.

Decade One for the LDCs is primarily an exercise in moving from Pattern I to Pattern II, from dependence on U.S. MNCs to efforts at interdependence among LDCs as in the Andean Common Market and Carifta. In *Business Latin America,* February 1973, we note:

> CCM, [Caribbean Common Market] to be created out of the existing Caribbean Free Trade Association (CARIFTA), is . . . on the way to becoming a reality . . . time for startup: May 1, 1973. Building blocks are: (1) agreement to use the Brussels Nomenclature and Brussels Definition of Value for its common outer tariff (COT). (2) A basic outline of harmonized fiscal incentives program for all CCM countries. Trinidad-Tobago were given three years to phase in as a MDC (more developed country)—the other MDC's, Jamaica, Guyana, and Barbados, are expected to follow Trinidad's decision. Incentives exist for using 50% or greater local content, export, and special rebates for selling non-traditional exports.

THE COOPTIVE PATTERN—
LDC PATTERNS OF MOBILIZING THE GLOBAL INDUSTRIAL SYSTEM

Decade One has begun to produce some subtle experiments in which the global systems resources are mobilized by LDCs. The question is, in how much conflict will the host LDC be about the massive foreign presence it recruits? Must LDCs perceive MNCs' presence as neocolonialism or a manageable industrial system—Pattern I or Pattern III? A hostage or a Trojan horse? Unconflicted mobilization of MNC resources by LDCs is perhaps illustrated by the case of Malaysia. As Singapore runs out of space and manpower, Kuala Lumpur has begun to build a piece of the global industrial system in its territory. Already more than 300 international companies have invested about $250 million in Malaysia. They include Dunlop, Shell, Colgate-Palmolive, Dow Chemical, Yawata Steel, Mitsui, Volvo, Toyota, Philips, Monsanto, and Alcan Aluminum. It will be noted that a selection of the advanced countries' MNCs are on the list—not those of one particular nation. Is this a step function in Malaysian economic development, or will it be perceived as a new form of imperialism in Decade One?

Table 7. MNC-LDC PATTERNS

	Pattern I	Pattern II	Pattern III (For the 1980s)
1. Equity	No local equity required or permitted	Local ownership required or fadeout formula	Equity in parent corporation encouraged or equity in GISC
2. Local content	Low local content requirements; no import licensing	Very high local content requirements, regardless of cost, high import licensing	Local content requirements in areas of worldwide capabilities, or GISC requirements; labor-intensive
3. Profit and royalty remittance controls	Few profit and royalty remittance controls	Very high profits and remittance controls	Planned and equitable profit and royalty remittance patterns as part of firm or GISC
4. Personnel restrictions	No personnel restrictions; foreigners favored	High personnel restrictions, foreigners excluded	Planned personnel exchanges with upgrading of local personnel to worldwide standards or GISC standards
5. Expropriation and nationalization	Little or no expropriation or nationalization	Aim to expropriate and nationalize all large foreign company holdings	Distinguish core industries from worldwide industries in which host has a stake
6. Borrowing restrictions	Foreign firms borrow heavily locally	Foreign firms bring capital in, then "fade out"	Plan reciprocation of local and foreign borrowing activities (local firms borrow in parent country) or in terms of GISC potentialities; labor-intensive
7. Tax discrimination	Tax incentives for foreign firms	Foreigners more heavily taxed	Foreign and domestic firms equally taxed
8. Acquisition	Few or no barriers to acquisitions of any local firms	All acquisitions by foreign firms barred	Acquisitions permitted if worldwide capability planned or a GISC connection included
9. Investment and incentive barriers	Incentives for investment very high; few or no barriers	Investment and incentives are barriers to foreign investment	Incentives for foreign firms which create worldwide centers of excellence with local spinoffs which become parts of GISCs
10. Demand for export	Little or no demand for export	High demand for export regardless of competitiveness	Demand for exports of worldwide specialized produces as part of firm or GISC

THE MIDDLE EAST:
SOURCE OF LDC MULTINATIONALS?

The Middle East offers the prospect that oil-producing nations can (1) affect the world monetary system by shifts in their growing oil revenue; (2) buy with their estimated 100–300 billion dollars of income of the largest U.S. companies, thus reversing the image of poor countries as helpless and exploited; (3) afford the luxury of "century-skipping," as M. Hoveyda, foreign minister of Iran has put it. In short, Decade One should see the rise of the Middle East, or more specifically, OPEC (Organization of Petroleum Export Countries) multinationals!

PROPOSITIONS ABOUT SOCIALIST COUNTRIES IN THE GLOBAL INDUSTRIAL SYSTEM IN DECADE ONE

The expansion of the East-West zone of cooperation appears to be a principal characteristic of Decade One. As Table 8 indicates the de facto appearance of Comecon multinationals as one event, their linkage with Western multinationals (Props. I, II, III) will be more evident.

But there are also here many areas of ambivalence such as (1) limiting the country-by-country approach of Western MNCs, especially if the regional integration process in Comecon is emphasized; also (2) the state-controlled economies' temptation to use products of turnkey plant built by the West "unfair competition" or to take technology, while returning less (see Prop. VI in Table 7).

The R&D links between the Soviet Union and other Western countries should thus be taken seriously if they expand, in that they are irreversible processes.

> 1. For example, what are the Decade One consequences of U.S. General Electric signing a framework cooperation contract with the Soviet State Committee for Science and Technology? This agreement calls for an exchange of technologies in the fields of power generation, including steam and gas turbines and nuclear energy. The agreement provides a framework for the planned purchase of Soviet technology by G.E. and the future sales of licenses for the production of G.E. products in the Soviet Union.
>
> 2. UK's Beecham Group and the Soviet State Committee for Science and Technology agreed on exchange of documentation. The main emphasis will be on joint R&D for antibiotics. In addition, working groups of three to five representatives from each country will be in permanent contact and arrange symposia and conferences. As a first step, the Soviets have turned over new penicillin preparations for clinical tests in the U.K.[5]

On balance, Decade One should see a more organic integration process, just underway, linking East and West—but subject to outbreaks of ideologically instigated distrust (See Table 8, Props. III A, B, IV, and VII).

5. *Business International Eastern European Reports.*

The issue is clearly whether Comecon should take primacy over the centrifugal forces which Western countries induce in Eastern European countries like Rumania, Poland, and Hungary.

The overriding concern will be the perception that increasing reciprocity, bilateralism, cooperation, and interdependence are preferable to direct competition. For example:

> The Hessische Landesbank—Girozentrale and the Polish Foreign Trade Bank [Bank Hondlowy W. Warszawie] have agreed to establish a new bank in Frankfurt, the Multileuropaeische Bank, A.G. [Central European Bank]. The Polish bank will hold a majority of the new capital, estimated at DM 20 million. The new bank which will begin operations as an all-arouna commercial institution next Spring, is expected to concentrate on financing West German-Polish trade and on establishing Polish contacts with German and other European money markets.[6]

This idea should be more evident as Eastern European firms link with the distribution and financial systems of the West and accept that the LDCs are not a suitable arena for political competition. Given the ideological commitment that remains in socialist countries of Eastern Europe, Decade One should be a period of some difficulty within the bloc, particularly as the new leadership in the Soviet Union begins to assert itself.

THE PEOPLE'S REPUBLIC OF CHINA IN THE GLOBAL INDUSTRIAL SYSTEM

Although the rate of entry of the People's Republic of China into the global industrial system will be the slowest in Decade One, covert preparations are being made. First, *the linkage within Hong Kong ought to intensify.* Events involving the PRC which signal trends for Decade One include the following:

> 1. Hutchinson International Ltd. (HIL), Hong Kong's largest public company, recently became the first Western firm in the colony to get involved in retailing products from the People's Republic of China. . . . HIL announced plans to open a new department store this summer that will specialize in selling China-made products. . . . HIL envisions that investment leading to closer ties with the PRC, while Peking hopes to reap some benefits from HIL's marketing expertise. More importantly, the deal reflects Peking's new pragmatic approach to business in that it has chosen Hong Kong's largest conglomerate and trading house as a business partner through which to push its exports.[7]
>
> 2. Japan's Export-Import Bank has announced willingness to finance exports of plant to the People's Republic of China. This decision marks the demise of the policy formulated in the "Yoshida letter" of 1964, which

6. *Business International Eastern European Report,* December 29, 1972, p. 189.
7. *Business Asia,* February 9, 1973, p. 43.

promised the Taiwan Government that no Exim financing would be made available for sales to the PRC. But more importantly, the reversal in Japanese policy may shed some light on the PRC's attitude towards foreign credits. Since its rift with the USSR China has shown no interest in obtaining long term credit from any source, and Peking has stressed that China has no government debt, internal or external. Consequently, PRC acceptance of Exim credits at this time would represent something of an ideological shift, as well as an indication that greater emphasis is being placed on industrialization and economic development.[8]

3. The British Industrial Technology Exhibition to run in Peking from March 26 through April 7, 1973 will help international companies pinpoint the interests and requirements of the People's Republic of China. By identifying the products and fields of technology that appeal to the PRC this exhibition will help manufacturers determine whether or not their own products stand a good chance of being marketed in China. . . . The exhibition is divided into nine major categories: (a) industrial plant, equipment and components, (b) electronic, electrical, radar, radio and television equipment and components, (c) instrumentation and scientific instruments, (d) engineering components, (e) transport equipment and components, (f) engineering and chemical materials, (g) computer plus data processing and office machinery, (h) photographic and visual aids, (i) miscellaneous. . . . Participants will include UK giants like Dunlop, Plessey, Shell, Pfizer through Matheson & Co. Ltd., Kodak, USM (and at least three hundred others). . . .[9]

Second, *Taiwan could become the future industrial zone of the PRC— a safe distance from the mainland, and hence more acceptable politically.* The passing of Chiang Kai-Shek may change perceptions of the future of Taiwan rather drastically.

Finally, we should not omit those countries who actively seek the role of bridge countries by simultaneous association with EEC and Comecon— such as Finland, Austria, and Yugoslavia—despite the limited success in legitimizing the building of a unitary East-West economic community in Decade One (Prop. IV in Table 8).

CONCLUSIONS

Our Decade One view of the MNC in the global industrial system underlines the present paradoxes that surround this potentially significant institution. On the one hand, the MNC is seen as U.S.-owned, very large, private, uncontrollable, and irresponsible during Decade One; on the other, it becomes increasingly obvious that some MNCs will be based in most countries, whether the countries are advanced, developing, or socialist. The class of MNCs will further include micro- and mesomultinationals, public and mixed public-private multinationals, Comecon multinationals, and East-West multinationals.

8. *Business Asia*, January 12, 1973.
9. *Business Asia*, March 16, 1973.

Table 8. PROPOSITIONS ABOUT SOCIALIST COUNTRIES IN THE GLOBAL INDUSTRIAL
SYSTEM IN DECADE ONE

Prop.		Prop. (continued)	
I A	As Decade One passes, in all countries of Eastern Europe investments will increase by Western European, Japanese, and U.S. firms; whether that instrument of investment be cooperation agreement, joint venture, licensing, etc.	IV B	Some countries will become East-West bridge countries, maintaining relationships with EEC and Comecon (e.g., Finland, Austria, Yugoslavia).
I B	The concept of the transideological corporation will be increasingly acceptable in many countries (although the term "transideological" may be unacceptable for political reasons).	V A	As Decade One passes, the development of an East-West financial and service infrastructure will increase.
II A	As Decade One passes, efforts to build Comecon multinationals will persist, even though distrust of Soviet ethnocentrism will be a continued obstacle.	V B	The concept of bilateralism will gain force (in having Western firms have a stake in Eastern economies, and Eastern firms have a stake in Western economies).
II B	Eastern European multinationals will be based in a number of countries, with efforts to integrate into foreign countries.	VI A	As Decade One passes, as Eastern firms attempt to expand in the West, the concept of unfair competition will gain force as regards pricing, use of Western technology to compete in Western economies. Rule-making efforts will be considered seriously.
III A	As Decade One passes, the integration processes in Eastern Europe will change the character of East-West cooperation. There will be stronger tendencies to phase out the polycentric approach, leading to some regional restrictionism.	VI B	Reciprocity in technology transfer will be demanded between Eastern and Western firms and governments.
III B	The quality of interdependence between East and West will improve toward more organic technological integration (bypassing the FTO).	VII A	As Decade One passes, coalitions among advanced countries to deal with LDCs will take precedence, be preferable to East-West coalitions.
IV A	As Decade One passes, efforts will be made to design an East-West Economic Community (EEC-Comecon) with little major successes.	VII B	LDCs will be hooked into transideological GISCs as a way of depoliticizing economic relationships and assuring some measure of independence from external political influence.

Thus Decade One is a time of anticipatory institutional transformation in the sense that nations who require their constituents to carry their own passports have a narrower base than MNCs who can literally hire anybody in the world. This increasing awareness in political leaders will not, however, automatically bring a concurrent multinationalization process in the state, trade unions, or individual citizens.

Indeed in Decade One, the individual confronted with geocentric prospects might very well prefer a world of cultural differentiation and heterogeneity. Perhaps at the heart of the human soul there is the fear, if not Biblical, then existential, of a world of Babel. Retreatism in the face of increasing interdependence seems like a comfortable and safe way to reduce the uncertainties of having to deal with global turbulence. Subnationalism; cultural, religious, and linguistic renewals; historical antecedents, however superficial, may begin to emerge in proportion to the multinational destiny of man's institutions in the global industrial system.

This cultural affirmation is not pathological. It is not even maladaptive because it represents an enriching of individual and national identity with the vicissitudes and nuances of the human condition in history. Indeed it is a prelude to a kind of unlearning wherein persons and institutions faced with abstract rootlessness of a multinational identity try on all the old identities first. Decade One thus is the period in which the MNC is simultaneously feared and admired, because it symbolizes the inner struggle to find safety on one small piece of earth, an earth that is mainly water and non-national space—a planet existing in a universal, interplanetary context that is even smaller.